Counselling in Transcultural Settings

SAGE has been part of the global academic community since 1965, supporting high quality research and learning that transforms society and our understanding of individuals, groups and cultures. SAGE is the independent, innovative, natural home for authors, editors and societies who share our commitment and passion for the social sciences.

Find out more at: **www.sagepublications.com**

Counselling in Transcultural Settings
Priorities for a Restless World

Patricia d'Ardenne

SAGE

Los Angeles | London | New Delhi
Singapore | Washington DC

Los Angeles | London | New Delhi
Singapore | Washington DC

SAGE Publications Ltd
1 Oliver's Yard
55 City Road
London EC1Y 1SP

SAGE Publications Inc.
2455 Teller Road
Thousand Oaks, California 91320

SAGE Publications India Pvt Ltd
B 1/I 1 Mohan Cooperative Industrial Area
Mathura Road
New Delhi 110 044

SAGE Publications Asia-Pacific Pte Ltd
3 Church Street
#10-04 Samsung Hub
Singapore 049483

Editor: Alice Oven
Assistant editor: Kate Wharton
Production editor: Rachel Burrows
Copyeditor: Annalisa Welch
Proofreader: Neil Dowden
Indexer: David Rudeforth
Marketing manager: Tamara Navaratnam
Cover design: Lisa Harper
Typeset by: C&M Digitals (P) Ltd, Chennai, India
Printed by MPG Books Group, Bodmin, Cornwall

© Patricia d'Ardenne 2013

First published 2013

Library of Congress Control Number: 2012936296

British Library Cataloguing in Publication data

A catalogue record for this book is available from the British Library

MIX
Paper from
responsible sources
FSC
www.fsc.org   FSC® C018575

ISBN 978-1-4462-0066-7
ISBN 978-1-4462-0067-4 (pbk)

For our grandchildren Oliver, Jessica and Felix
—morning stars above a restless world—

CONTENTS

ABOUT THE AUTHOR

Patricia d'Ardenne is a clinical and counselling psychologist with 40 years' practice, teaching and research in London and overseas. She began work researching in Nashville, Tennessee, returned as psychology lecturer at the Institute of Psychiatry, and then established an English-language mental health service in Brussels. She returned to East London, and published adapted psychological treatments for the young Bangladeshi community there, as well as those with refugee experience. Her doctoral thesis was on multicultural psychology approaches for diverse communities. Patricia co-founded the Special Interest Group on Race and Culture within the British Psychological Society, where she met Aruna Mahtani, and with her, wrote *Transcultural Counselling in Action*, first and second editions for SAGE (1989 and 1999). In the past decade, Patricia established the Institute of Psychotrauma, an East London Foundation NHS Trust specialist service, where she undertook research on the use of interpreters in trauma-focussed therapies.

Patricia currently chairs a Global Health Link between East London and Uganda – a government-supported partnership for mental health development, where she has been training practitioners since 2006 in psychological therapies in post-conflict settings. Patricia teaches transcultural psychological approaches at Queen Mary College, London. She is an Associate with Interhealth Worldwide, preparing and supporting staff on humanitarian missions overseas, and was recently elected to join the Psychological Health of Travellers Group within the International Society for Travel Medicine.

FOREWORD BY COLIN LAGO

Patricia d'Ardenne is to be congratulated on writing this exciting and extremely informative new book within the field of transcultural counselling. With Aruna Mahtani she co-authored a previous landmark text, *Transcultural Counselling in Action*, which was first published in 1989, subsequently reprinted almost annually throughout the 1990s, before penning a second edition in 1999. This new text reflects and evidences Patricia's long-term commitment to and experience of delivering mental health services to people from a very wide range of diverse communities, both in the UK and overseas. As such, this new book is a goldmine of ideas, resources, references and clinical examples rooted in everyday practice. Few writers in this field can claim such extensive clinical experience.

In previous correspondence with me, Patricia noted: 'I have painted a broad but I hope very practical book.' This is without doubt. She has brought together a unique blend of subject areas (that are not replicated in any other texts I know), with contents dedicated to informing the quality of professional practice in different settings and contexts. She has provided a range of further website references and practice exercises for the discerning reader. This book comprises a solid working text suitable for students of many mental-health-related professions as well for professional colleagues seeking to improve their skills, knowledge and awareness within the transcultural arena.

Upon opening the text I immediately found the list of contents thoroughly engaging. Again, quoting from Patricia's own book abstract:

> Specific chapters examine counselling refugees, using interpreters, screening and supporting aid workers who provide psychosocial interventions, and supporting journalists, military and missionary staff. Other cross cultural domains include healthcare, spirituality and religion, and The User Movement. New directions include working with developing nations, the stressors of globalisation, and the use of telemedicine.

This breadth of coverage is breathtaking in its vision and extensive in its application.

Much of the early literature concerned with the provision of interpersonally sensitive, anti-discriminatory, culturally informed counselling practice was published in the United States, where this professional focus continues to stimulate new ideas, research and publications. Indeed, the practice of multicultural counselling within the USA was claimed to be the 'fourth force' in psychological treatments after the first three forces of psychoanalysis, cognitive-behaviourism and humanistic approaches. This bold but necessary assertion by American theorists and exponents was made on the basis that therapeutic practitioners from all three main bodies of theory would inevitably work with all members of society. The fourth force of multicultural counselling thus highlighted the need for skilled practice right across society. Theoretical knowledge, they argued, though of great value, was insufficient to ensure sensitive, anti-discriminatory, effective therapeutic interventions with all clients. Predominantly, much of this early American literature was devoted to the improvement of counselling services to those within minority groups within the USA.

To some extent, the UK has seen a slightly later emergence of its own dedicated transcultural counselling literature, devoted to the delivery of culturally sensitive psychological practices with the various Black and minority ethnic groups resident in Britain. Inspired and informed by the original, and still emerging literature from the USA, British theorists have begun to develop new terminology relevant to this particular cultural milieu.

A further development within this arena in recent decades has been concern for the wider implications of human diversity and how these additional fields of application both require necessary further considerations on behalf of transcultural therapists and, in equal measure, challenge such practitioners (and their professional bodies, researchers and writers). The contemporary inclusion of the 'big seven' stigmatised identities of race, ethnicity, gender, sexuality, age, ability and religion under the rubric of 'diversity' has had the important consequences of alerting the professional field to the complex life experiences of many of those inhabiting minority group status within society. It has also challenged the creation of new bodies of theory and practice that will prove robust and effective with this wider population.

Historically, within the psychological helping professions, the advice to beginning practitioners was 'therapist, know thyself'. Transcultural counselling, through its awareness of the enormous impact of 'social situatedness' (i.e. where and how one lives, works, grew up, was educated, earns, etc.), has begun to advocate the concept of 'therapist, know thy identity'. The transcultural counselling project is doomed before it starts if practitioners have little conscious awareness of their location within society and how it and they relate to the various members of the other communities with whom they come into contact.

Patricia is so right when she states that 'transcultural counselling is in its infancy, and faces many challenges'. Globalisation, vast material inequalities across countries and communities, the sheer speed of travel compared with the complexity and slowness of adaptation to new cultural surroundings, the impact of violence, ill health, poverty and international politics are all profoundly complex, interrelating phenomena that demand enormous repositories

X

of commitment, knowledge, awareness and skills for the mental health professional seeking to work in this arena. The pursuit of core cultural competences is a necessary yet extremely demanding professional requirement.

This book really takes readers beyond their own cultural framework and indeed beyond their own national borders. It considers many fields of application; it critically pays attention to the words and views of service users (a much neglected yet critical source for understanding and practice development); it evaluates the very important functions and use of interpreters; it requires consideration of ethics; it demands psychological helpers pay great attention to their supervision, ongoing development and self-care; it contains very useful web references for further details; it poses a wide range of counselling issues and situations combined with practice-based exercises; and finally, it contains an extraordinary wealth of reference and resource material.

I believe this book will come to be an absolute 'must have' for all therapists training to be and working within transcultural settings. I believe Patricia has, in this volume, made an extraordinary groundbreaking contribution to transcultural counselling and I dearly hope that in future years consideration will be made to have it published in other languages.

Colin Lago, DLitt, MEd, FBACP, UKRC, BACP Accr. Counsellor and Trainer

FOREWORD BY DINESH BHUGRA

In the rapid shrinking of the world as a result of globalisation, not only has the movement of goods become easier, but the movement of people across national boundaries has become significant. We carry our cultures wherever we go, and while coming into contact with other cultures – either directly or indirectly – we may adjust accordingly, depending upon a number of factors. Globalisation has also contributed to increased urbanisation with internal migrations and changes in family structures. People have always been on the move for a variety of reasons, which have included economic, educational and political. Political and economic discrimination, along with religious persecution, add to the likelihood of moving away from one culture towards another one. The process of migration and subsequent cultural adjustment is fraught with difficulties, and a large number of studies from across the globe have shown that migrants experience higher levels of emotional and psychological distress.

In several countries, counselling is increasingly being seen as acceptable and is indeed becoming available. However, working across cultures brings special challenges. The individual comes into the therapeutic setting with certain expectations and models of explanation, as does the clinician.

Patricia d'Ardenne, in this excellent volume, brings wide experience in writing, research and clinical settings in her overview. She sets the scene admirably by highlighting problems related to discrimination. The system within which health care is provided is undoubtedly influenced by the culture within which the system is delivered, but the accessibility and availability of the system is also determined by the resources provided by the society. Migrants may not be aware of the healthcare system, as well as not see their problems in a 'medical' manner. This is where anti-discriminatory practice, both at the individual and institutional level, becomes critical, and d'Ardenne provides a superb overview. Her practical overview and approach in getting the counsellor to think both of theoretical and practice points is critical in making therapists think of major factors in delivering care. Her approach is pragmatic, easy to follow and extremely helpful to the reader. D'Ardenne deserves our congratulations and thanks in delivering what hopefully will become a classic text.

Dinesh Bhugra CBE, FRCP, FRCPsych, PhD
Professor of Mental Health and Cultural Diversity
Institute of Psychiatry, King's College London
Immediate Past President, Royal College of Psychiatrists

PREFACE

Why then to me this restless world's but hell.

Richard III, *William Shakespeare*

There were several core ideas in creating *Counselling in Transcultural Settings: Priorities for a Restless World*. I wanted readers to have a resource for work beyond their own culture, where counselling and psychotherapy are understood to be as dynamic as the political and social contexts in which distressed people seek help. If the big human stories today are globalisation, terrorism, migration and racism, then counselling practice now needs a proactive response, where present demand and future directions are grasped, tried and updated. The aim of this book is to provide a practical update of counselling for changing worlds, where ethnic, linguistic, religious, economic and environmental differences collide, creating rich settings for contemporary practice. The first half of the text visits these settings for transcultural counselling; the second half addresses how practitioners can care for themselves and the quality of the service they provide. More than that, I hope that the chapters will give readers some inspiration and confidence, encouraging a reconsideration of model or practice, and then seeing if it makes a difference to outcome.

We all have formative experiences, but nothing in my education or professional training in clinical, and later, counselling psychology prepared me for diverse practice. Cross-cultural studies were the domain of anthropology and politics (see Chapter 1). Implicit assumptions in the psychology curriculum were that human traits, development and behaviour could all be universally defined and observed independently of their cultural or linguistic contexts. The generalisability of psychological models was rarely questioned or investigated. The word 'culture' implied the exotic, the alien and, above all, the unknown.

But the real world soon imposed another agenda. An undergraduate project on the authoritarian personality (Adorno et al., 1950) engaged us in comparing two Northern English cities by questionnaire; a mono-cultural, white, working class community disclosed more prejudiced and racist attitudes than another with an established Asian community in its textiles industry.

A Kennedy Research Fellowship took me to work in a state penitentiary in Tennessee in 1970. It was a stark introduction to institutionalised racism in the USA. Even in the aftermath of the American Civil Rights movement, 98 per cent of the 2,000 inmates were young black offenders, some as young as 14, incarcerated for crimes ranging from rape to cattle rustling. My psychology colleagues, the prison officers, the medical and academic staff were, without exception, all white.

I directed a mental heath service for English-language people in Brussels for several years and began to understand the impact on mental well-being when multinationals placed their employees without preparation to live in the capital of the European Union. Those employed certainly had to make a cultural transition; but their spouses at home and children at schools faced the bigger daily challenges of language, values, education and health systems, with its many potential stressors. Our first three children were born outside the UK – making acculturation a personal and fascinating priority. Marriage to a journalist made me aware of the emotional impact of reporting distant events on overseas correspondents and their families.

Further teaching, training and editorial work allowed me to see different models of social and mental healthcare in India, Canada, Australia, Cuba, South Africa, China, France, Italy and Turkey, and compare them with the development of counselling and psychotherapy professions within the UK. This was alongside 30 years' clinical practice in East London – one of the most culturally diverse (and economically deprived) neighbourhoods in the country. Staff were given no additional training for diversity, but we did get a chance to ask patients what they wanted, to adapt our methods to their needs and evaluate the outcome of our work (Crown and d'Ardenne, 1982, 1986; d'Ardenne, 1986).

These experiences increased my conviction that, in essence, all counselling and psychotherapy is about difference and is, in a sense, transcultural. Effective practice, therefore, incorporates the principles of transcultural counselling, although these need to be identified and evaluated.

The British Psychological Society (BPS) Special Interest Group in Race and Culture had members who were the most supportive but candid critics of my naive prejudices about cross-cultural work (Crown and d'Ardenne, 1986; d'Ardenne, 1986). However, out of this grew a friendship that led directly to co-authoring *Transcultural Counselling in Action* with Aruna Mahtani over 20 years ago (d'Ardenne and Mahtani 1989, 1999). This small book was written at a time where there was much less published in the field, and still offers readers a 'how to do it' approach. That text, however, now seems simple – even simplistic – in some of its assumptions and exhortations. We wrote it as a black and white therapist – and worked through the text with clients defined either as 'culturally close' or 'culturally different' from ourselves. From this we derived, quite literally, a black and white grid of equivalent counselling comparisons (d'Ardenne and Mahtani, 1999).

Counselling in Transcultural Settings: Priorities for a Restless World instead considers the many shades of grey in contemporary practice. Our counselling clients, for example, may not see themselves as belonging to the dominant culture, and have transcultural needs, but equally may not classify themselves as black or white. Some clients, when asked, prefer to define their culture through faith or spiritual belief, gender, gender preference, education, political beliefs or health status – to name but some of the identities considered throughout the text. Similarly, counsellors are not culturally neutral; they come from their own historical, cultural, educational, gender-specific and linguistic backgrounds, both individually and shared, both at home and abroad (Ryde, 2009). Good practice in transcultural counselling requires us to understand the impact of our own cultural identities on our practice, and to use supervision and continuing professional development (CPD) to help us with that process. If curious about every aspect of our own world and that of our clients, we can try always to meet them in a shared space.

In the last decade I have trained mental health workers in psychological therapies with a mental health team, as part of a Global Health Partnership between a UK NHS Mental Health Trust and a National Psychiatric Referral Hospital in Uganda. Many identities divide and unite us. Mental health training in East Africa has until now had to focus on the psychiatric sequelae of malaria and malaria-induced epilepsy. Practitioners there now want to learn about psychological and counselling approaches for those who experience mood disorders, relationship difficulties, behavioural problems, substance misuse and – for a country riven by civil conflict – those with post-traumatic disorders. Most of all, our colleagues want to be able to support service users and their families within their own communities and refer individuals to precious regional hospital beds only when local interventions have proven inadequate. There are currently no texts about how to address their needs: rather we are collaborating on objectives, piloting our teaching and training, and evaluating this transcultural work as we go. At the same time we have provided an account of that input and its sustainability to the service users and to our joint funders (d'Ardenne et al., 2009; Dorner, 2008).

These clinicians will no doubt benefit from partnership with the West, but they need to be supported in valuing their own knowledge and skills and finding solutions within modest resources (Baillie et al., 2009; Crisp, 2010). Equally important is how we can learn from those who counsel in harsh economic and physical conditions, with a level of unpredictability and inequality that many of us would find hard to imagine, let alone tolerate (d'Ardenne et al., 2009). Future directions for transcultural counselling research will focus on the resilience of overseas mental health workers and their capacity to adapt counselling models to the cultural needs of their own communities. We shall also be able to use new technologies to share knowledge – their most precious commodity – for preserving mental health and well-being.

Recent personal influences include working with Interhealth Worldwide (www.interhealth.org.uk) who screen and support humanitarian aid workers and others in non-government organisations, and assist distressed people in very different cultural settings overseas (Hargrave et al., 2011a). Screening began historically with physical preparation, for example vaccinations, but now includes the personal resilience of workers exposed to hostile environments. Similarly, the International Society for Travel Medicine (www.ISTM. org) has developed from considering the physical needs of travellers to include mental well-being, and has recently established an international mental health group to address this important topic. Those of us who have joined this group hope to stimulate an interest in any psychological factors affecting the health of all overseas travellers. The Health Information for All 2015 network (www. hifa2015.org) was established to provide free online health information and libraries to colleagues around the world, and has helped me understand the importance of sharing and translating information, as well as the considerable benefits of models of telemedicine, with mobile phones and remote supervision and teaching. Most recently, colleagues and students on the MSc Transcultural Mental Healthcare course at Queen Mary College continue to inform my thinking about the impact of racism and cultural relativity in all counselling relationships.

The first half of this book introduces readers to a selection of transcultural contexts. Such evidence as there is, or established good practice, is described and sourced. Fictionalised case examples will be used to illustrate a model or issue, but are based on real stories. The bias towards African and Asian cases reflects personal experience, but the principles are universal. Summaries, discussion and practice points have been included to guide the busy reader, and further reading or websites are also listed.

Chapter 1 tracks the history of racist and discriminatory practices and beliefs in psychiatry and psychology, and how they still exist today. It considers how transcultural work has grown in response to these, and readers are shown the ethical requirements for current professional practice.

Chapter 2 considers the previously neglected needs of the international worker, moved to hostile environments at short notice, supporting local people. Attention is given to the prevention of secondary traumatisation and culture shock for those who counsel the victims of disaster. Examples described include development workers, humanitarian aid workers,, the armed forces, journalists and missionaries on overseas assignments.

Chapter 3 examines transcultural counselling with those who have refugee experience, including asylum seekers, vulnerable migrants and the victims of human trafficking. Case examples focus on their losses, their resilience and response to trauma, and the complex social and legal processes they face when seeking asylum in the West. Readers are introduced to engagement, narrative approaches and the central role of accessing and processing traumatic memory in counselling.

Chapter 4 reviews the role of interpreters and translators in transcultural counselling and provides practical guidelines through case histories to help them in that process. Attention is given to preparation and debriefing of the interpreter, and the models of interpreting suitable for counsellors, with some research findings about feasibility. Telephone interpreting services and the role of advocates in counselling, with specific examples of how and when to deploy them, are reviewed.

Chapter 5 highlights the importance of faith and spirituality – topics that have not always been a priority with counsellors – and how these can be understood to achieve a better outcome in transcultural settings. The chapter refers both to clients and counsellors as potential believers, as well as those providing pastoral counselling across cultures.

Chapter 6 looks at counselling in healthcare settings, from early life until death and dying, and discusses how an understanding of cross-cultural difference can be used to help patients. It shows how counsellors can improve treatment compliance, requiring collaboration from families and friends, as well as changes in lifestyle.

Chapter 7 considers how transcultural counsellors can collaborate with clients, empowered by the Service Users' Movement. Innovations in the West and in developing countries, including patient experts, users' groups within specific cultures or diagnostic categories, and peer support workers are described. Counsellors are shown how cultural knowledge can increase support to clients in a range of health, social, economic and ethnic contexts.

The second half of the book covers professional priorities for the counsellor in transcultural settings.

Chapter 8 addresses ethics in transcultural counselling, and contextualises them within clinical governance, current law on discrimination and social inclusion. The particular demands of working across cultures with black clients and counsellors who endure racism, the power imbalance between practitioners and supervisors from the dominant culture, and the drivers of policy and research agendas from the West are all critically reviewed.

Chapter 9 incorporates supervision and CPD – and the additional resourcing that counsellors require to ensure the quality of their work and the preservation of their well-being is maintained. The power permutations of a black or white supervisor/counsellor/client are described. Reflective practice and group supervision are proposed as an immediate and effective means of learning across cultures.

Chapter 10 discusses practitioners' responsibility to work from an evidence base, with practical guidelines on how to achieve this with a heavy workload. It looks at a range of sources including reflective practice, individual casework, literature reviews and audits, as well as the more formal requirements of individual and multicentred research, and common methods used.

Chapter 11 presents existing requirements in practice, training and research and how well they have been addressed to date. New directions include telemedicine, globalisation, global health, the environment and the evolving levels of interpersonal violence. A case is made for transcultural models to be integrated into all counselling training, but since this has yet to occur, an appendix of some transcultural courses around the world is included.

There are exclusions. There is nothing on children and young people, nor on counselling in educational settings. Similarly, the counselling needs of those with serious mental and physical disorder has not been covered. No specific reference in case examples has been made to Romany travellers; the word 'traveller' is only used in its more general meaning. But transcultural counselling is developing and specific texts are emerging covering some of these areas (Lago, 2011).

This text should be of use to readers who counsel across cultures, including those who coach and mentor. It does not prescribe specific counselling models, nor does it seek to train readers as cultural experts. Rather, it aims to bring together a range of professional settings and topics that better cover contemporary issues, and to plot a chart for trainees and counsellors where future practice and research might develop.

The world spins on. The helping professions (all counselling professionals), and those who train and supervise them, are considerably better prepared for working with diversity than when I qualified in 1972. But in another 40 years, will there will be the political and professional commitment to transcultural issues that will make counselling globally relevant?

Patricia d'Ardenne, London, 2012

ACKNOWLEDGEMENTS

I am indebted to all these people for their help, but own all errors in content or form:

Professor Kamaldeep Bhui, Dr Ken Carswell, Dr Nasir Warfa and the students at QMUL
Malcom Downing at the BBC
Cerdic Hall and the Butabika Link Committee
Annie Hargrave and Dr Ted Lankaster at Interhealth Worldwide
Dr Sarah Heke and colleagues at the Institute of Psychotrauma
Catherine Kenyon at Action Aid
Richard Mpango, for his insights into psychotherapy in Uganda
Carleen Scott, for her experience as a black trainee in supervision
My friends at Progressio and CAFOD
Jonathan Hinchliffe, for his unfailing and meticulous editorial and research assistance
Alice Oven, Rachel Burrows, Kate Wharton and colleagues at SAGE Publications, for their patience, professionalism and kindness

And lastly, a big thank you to Peter and our growing family for their understanding and unconditional love.

1

ANTI-DISCRIMINATORY PRACTICE: ITS ORIGINS AND DEVELOPMENT IN TRANSCULTURAL COUNSELLING

Science and experience has also shown that no race is inherently superior to others, and this myth has been equally exploded whenever blacks and whites are given equal opportunity for development.

Nelson Mandela, Robben Island, 1978

Summary

Chapter 1 provides an historical account of transcultural counselling in the Western world, with its colonial past, from the study of madness and the exotic, to ideas of difference in recent psychiatry, psychology and counselling practice. Concepts of race, racial differences, culture-bound syndromes and cultural psychology are critically reviewed in the light of modern human rights, ethnic monitoring, personal and institutional racism, social identity theory, and what they tell us about the nature of human prejudice and exclusion. Current counselling theory is revisited and priorities identified for ensuring anti-discriminatory and anti-oppressive practice.

Introduction

This chapter shows how Mandela's conclusion forms the basis of modern anti-discriminatory practice in caring professions. Science, however, has not always served this moral purpose, either by ignoring or perverting the evidence of different peoples' outcomes in care, where there is unequal opportunity, wealth, or racism. Current anti-discriminatory practices in UK settings will be defined, as well as policies that have been introduced for more ethical and effective outcomes. What evidence there is for change in recent decades for all counsellors – both white and black – is described. Historical and political themes are considered for readers working in transcultural settings to understand better the impact of personal beliefs on the counselling process. Case examples are from mental health, but applications are possible in other counselling domains.

Beyond that readers need to read more widely and critically on the issues and debates in Mandela's discourse. The paradox remains that our globalised world – some have called it a 'village' – with easier jet travel, the internet, instant messages and images from mobile phones remains as xenophobic as ever, divided by race, religion, culture, gender and ability (Bhugra and Bhui, 2007; Thomas, 2000). Many aspects of multiculturalism are reflected negatively in the media; for example, 'social problems', 'language barriers', 'failed asylum seekers', 'our overcrowded island', 'undercutting local jobs and houses', and, of course, 'radicalisation', 'extremism' and 'terrorism'. Indeed, current British political leaders think that 'state multiculturalism' has failed, and that separate ethnic identities matter less than being assimilated into a British 'Big Society' (Hasam, 2011). The Prime Minister, David Cameron, said: 'we have tolerated segregated communities behaving in ways that run counter to our values. All this leaves some young Muslims feeling rootless. And the search for something to belong to and believe in can lead them to extremist ideology' (Hasam, 2011).

In addition there is a heavily politicised contemporary debate about how migration, policing, education, public housing, health and related social issues feature in an economic recession where resources are being cut. There are questions raised about why the West 'should bother' giving aid to developing countries. It is a rare event to hear a public figure speak of the benefits to society of multiculturalism (Abbott, 2012); it is just as rare to hear counsellors speak enthusiastically about diversity as providing them with the essential and unique knowledge and skills for a restless world.

Madness and the exotic

Understanding the present requires consideration of the past. Historically, Britain has had a long-standing love affair with anthropology and the alluring pursuit of the foreign and madness – stemming perhaps from its seafaring tradition, its colonialism, its slave economy and its culture of excluding people, sometimes literally, 'all at sea'. *The Ship of Fools* in the fifteenth century was an allegory of one such exclusionary practice, where mad people were sent away from their villages and actually packed into ships and sent 'abroad' (Foucault, 1988).

As late as the nineteenth century, criminals, dissidents, trade unionists – anyone who was different or undesirable – could be deported on a ship to penal colonies, as far away as possible, to Britain's dominions on the other side of the world. Even in the mid-twentieth century, orphans or children in care could be shipped to Australia, for which the British Prime Minister, Gordon Brown, apologised in 2010 (Bowcott, 2010; Barnados, www.barnados.org.uk). In 1948, the first ship, MV *Empire Windrush*, brought black families from the Caribbean *to* the British Isles. These men and women, direct descendants of those enslaved and shipped from Africa by British traders for plantation work in the seventeenth, eighteenth and nineteenth centuries, were actively recruited to run UK transport, postal and health services in the twentieth century (Lago and Thompson, 1996; National Archives, www.nationalarchives.gov.uk). The ship had come home.

The definition of race, ethnicity and culture

The West has had many debates about the meanings of the terms 'race', 'ethnicity' and 'culture'. The first 1790 US census referred to 'free white men', 'free women' and 'slaves' (United States Census Bureau, 1790). The Office of the High Commission for Human Rights (OHCHR) (1949) defines not racism, but *racial discrimination*, as 'any distinction, exclusion, restriction, or presence based on race, colour, descent or natural or ethnic origin, which has the purpose or effect of nullifying or impairing the recognition, enjoyment or exercise, or an equal footing, or human rights and fundamental freedoms in the political, economic, social, cultural or any other field in public life' (www.ohchr.org). By 2010, the American Anthropological Association recommended the term 'race' be eliminated from the census, since 'race has been scientifically proven to not be a real, natural phenomenon'. It recommended that 'ethnicity' or 'ethnic group' was more salient and had fewer racist connotations. At the same time it acknowledged the damage done by 'racial', i.e. racist, terms to the many diverse people within the US population (American Anthropological Association, 1998; United States Census Bureau www.census.gov).

In the UK, racial and ethnic data have been collected only since the 1991 Census – notably after a decade of ethnic tensions and urban conflict. Concern was then expressed about the lack of information on families who had migrated to the UK after World War II, including their access to education, work, health and housing. The Census used a process of self-definition, where ethnicity and culture remain dynamic and complex, and hotly debated (Office for National Statistics (ONS), 2011). Some of these categories may have been fit for purpose but not applicable to health and social care. McKenzie and Crowcroft (1996) recommended that clinicians describe individuals being studied or treated and avoid depending on categorisations. Since ethnicity and culture are confounding variables, it is often not possible to have a specific ethnic hypothesis at the start of research. Rather, they recommended that the Census categories be used, but additional personal historical information be added. The *British Medical Journal* suggested: country of birth; parents' country of birth; first language; special diets; religion practised; years in the UK; and socioeconomic status (McKenzie and Crowcroft, 1996).

Anthropology, psychiatry and the alienists

It is 30 years since a white psychiatrist and an anthropologist published a seminal work on the impact of racism on mental health in the UK (Littlewood and Lipsedge, 1982, 1997). They argued, with plenty of evidence, that the consideration of 'culture' as a variable in an otherwise value-free pursuit of therapeutic objectivity, was unsustainable. They highlighted two disciplines that consider its subject as *aliens*, namely anthropology and psychiatry, where race and madness have been considered as indices of 'otherness'. More importantly, they showed that *alienists* (once the actual word for psychiatrists in France) are active agents who create aliens: alienation itself is thus a social and political process.

The tragedy revealed by their analysis was that black people, especially immigrants to the UK, have been alienated by a dominant white culture that more readily diagnosed madness (psychosis) in black people than white (Bhugra and Bhui, 2007; Burke, 1984; Sashidharan, 2001; Sproston and Nazroo, 2002). Nor has this process been confined to history. Fernando (2002) showed that when identical case histories were given to UK psychiatrists using either English or foreign names, that psychosis was diagnosed more frequently in the latter group than by chance. Practitioners were 'ethnocentric', i.e. locked in the cultural assumptions of their own ethnic histories, and frequently confused the social with the biological.

Specific culture-bound syndromes

In the last century much emphasis was placed on understanding exotic psychiatric disorders. Recurrent, locally specific patterns of atypical behaviour and troubling experiences have now been mapped out and are all examples of *culture-bound syndromes*, which may or may not be attached to international diagnostic categories such as the Diagnostic and Statistical Manual of Mental Disorders (DSM-IV-TR) (American Psychiatric Association, 2000). Here are some of them: *rootwork, amok, brain fag, dhat syndrome, koro, latah, evil eye spell, susto* and *zar*. These are all culturally accepted explanatory mechanisms or idioms of illness that do not match Western models of distress (Bhugra et al., 2007). These syndromes cannot be considered outside their wider social and historical meaning. For example, Kirmayer (2007) cites Dick (1995) with the following example of *Pibloktoq* or 'Arctic Hysteria': 'Inuit women were seen by European explorers under Admiral Peary becoming agitated and stripping off, running out on the ice, needing to be restrained for their inexplicable "hysterical" behaviour' (p. 6). In fact Peary had sent their menfolk off when the ice was dangerously thin, and their protests had not been heard. The women were engaged in Shamanistic prayer to intercede for their safe return. Thus, an abuse of power by the white explorers led to the development of a bogus psychopathology. In an overview of Western culture-bound syndromes, Bhugra et al. (2007: 154) conclude: 'There are significant problems in the use of terms such as culture-bound syndromes, because all psychiatric conditions are culture bound, and the time has come to abandon the concept...Such usage indicates its colonial heritage.'

4

Jahoda (1961) describes how odd or deviant behaviour used to be seen as having travelled from abroad. There was a nineteenth-century discourse about how 'superior' white Europeans could tame and civilise primitive people. Of interest, the colonial psychiatrists who established Western hospitals in the Empire noted *lower* instances of mental disorder, and believed that the simple, i.e. primitive, lifestyle was less stressful and therefore less pathogenic. By contrast the West, with its use of industrialisation, technology and urbanisation, invented 'neurasthenia' and a range of neurotic disorders, presumed to be the product of a more sophisticated and demanding social order (Kirmayer, 2007). Some of the studies they quoted, such as alleging that black brains were smaller, therefore individuals were less intelligent, now seem almost comic in their racist naivety. But race was the centrepiece of the concept that distinguished white people from the rest of the world, and accounted for national differences or inequalities. For example, one bizarre hypothesis was that black people had underdeveloped frontal lobes and were thus more uninhibited in their behaviour. This has left us with the racist legacy that young black men are deemed less likely to benefit from, or be offered, talking therapies. They are also more likely to be detained under the Mental Health Act 1983 than their white counterparts (Fernando, 2002).

Multiple studies since have shown that distressed black patients are more likely to end up in forensic environments, be offered less psychotherapy and be more heavily medicated. Cochrane and Sashidharan (1996) describe the combined effects of racism and prejudice, economic uncertainty, poor housing and harsher working conditions on the reduced psychological well-being of black and minority ethnic (BME) patients of all backgrounds. There have been major developments in transcultural psychiatry in the last two decades of the twentieth century – at the time when the UK was (reportedly) becoming a multicultural society. Three topics have dominated the psychiatric agenda: the use of the Mental Health Act 1983; the rates of schizophrenia among young black men (Cochrane, 1977; Fernando, 1989); and suicide and eating disorders among the Asian communities (Littlewood and Lipsedge, 1996; Fernando, 2002). Even in the twenty-first century, there is evidence that black people of African and Caribbean heritage are six times more likely to be sectioned than white people, and Asian people are four times more likely to commit suicide than white people (Fernando, 2010).

Ethnic cleansing, genocide and the Holocaust

Europe struggles to forget its slave-owning history; but gross human rights abuses persist in our restless world. There is a tradition in psychiatry and psychoanalysis concerning the impact of the Holocaust (the specific mass murder of Jews and other persecuted groups by the German Nazi regime 1941–1945) on its survivors, in studies carried out over the last six decades (Levav et al., 1998). Sigmund Freud (who himself barely escaped the Holocaust) and other psychoanalysts have provided a cogent and unique account of racial identity, hatred, apartheid and genocide, and readers are recommended to visit Goldberg and Solomos (2002) for an excellent overview of this historic link with traditional psychiatry and psychology. There is evidence that Holocaust survivors are more prone to mental ill health, and have reduced biological and psychological resilience, and that their descendants have specific counselling needs (Schlapobersky, 2010). There is related work on the impact of genocidal hatred and reconciliation, mental well-being and health. Examples include training refugee survivors as counsellors in the Balkans (Arcel and Simunkovic, 1998) and psychosocial interventions with survivors of the Killing Fields in Cambodia (www.tpocambodia.org). This agenda continues to resonate with current conflicts where whole populations are oppressed and forced to resettle without adequate support and identity, and which will be revisited in later chapters.

Psychology and psychological therapies

Medicine is not the only discipline with an oppressive history. Psychological doctrine has the dubious reputation of both instigating racist theory, as well as undertaking research on the effects of racism. A good example of this lies in the work of Francis Galton (Forest, 1995), often called the father of modern psychology and psychometrics. Galton aimed to show the intellectual superiority of the white race through anthropometrics such as measuring head size, and was a keen promoter of *eugenics* (controlled breeding to increase the occurrence of desirable heritable characteristics). He was a gifted scientist and made the distinctions and classifications of races a respectable object of empirical enquiry; hitherto it had been a branch of natural philosophy. As recently as 1972, Hans Eysenck, Professor of Psychology at the Institute of Psychiatry, London, caused a furore at the London School of Economics when he gave a lecture on the innate intellectual differences between the races (Eysenck, 1971). To some, this approach appeared little different from Nazi eugenics, and he was banned from the University precinct. There were many who criticised his work not just morally, but scientifically, and who concluded that the demonstration of racial differences in IQ was an invalid concept (Coleman, 1972).

In 1992 the British Psychological Society (BPS) formed a Special Interest Group (SIG) in Race and Culture, which has now become a Faculty (www. bps.org.uk). Many of its members are BME practitioners, who recognise the needs of their own communities, the needs of the profession to be more ethnically representative (Shepherd et al., 2010), and the need to promote racial awareness in current UK training curricula. The faculty lists its purposes as: ensuring that services are accessible to BME communities; improving communication on race and culture; informing the profession of good practice; promoting cultural competencies in individuals, groups and institutions of the needs of BME communities; challenging racism through adherence to policies; promoting strategies that increase the access of BME applicants to the profession; training; research on the needs of BME service users; the dissemination of BME knowledge; support and consultation; responding to policy documents; and liaison with users, voluntary organisations and other community groups (www.bps.org.uk/raceandculture).

In the 1980s and 1990s, many community groups established counselling services (of varying quality), partly because their own communities were not accessing counselling, due to the institutional racism of mainstream services, and partly because they dealt with the social and economic realities of their communities at street level (sometimes quite literally). Transcultural counselling was still a marginal activity, tolerated as having political legitimacy – but not the main topic of interest. One outstanding UK organisation that rose to its brief and provided high-quality services across London, long before it became fashionable, was Nafsyiat, a multicultural therapy centre that still employs therapists from many cultural and linguistic backgrounds. Despite its modest street frontage and budget, it has spearheaded cross-cultural practice, training and research in the UK for over 30 years (Kareem and Littlewood, 1999).

Change has slowly been achieved, as more regulatory bodies have re-examined their curricula and recognised that training was not preparing practitioners for work in a multiracial, multicultural society (McKenzie-Mavinga, 2005, 2009; Patel et al., 2000; Turpin and Coleman, 2010). In Chapter 8, on ethics and governance, we shall be looking in more detail at how major counselling and mental health bodies have developed their own anti-discriminatory codes of practice and how this complies with human rights and the law.

Discussion Points

Has your training dealt with racism in the caring professions?

Can you recall examples of racist or racially stereotypical assumptions in any texts, lectures or seminars?

Practice Point

Use your training/supervision to provide you with space to reflect on these, and find other places to go if this is not possible.

7

Social casework

Social work has spearheaded good anti-racist practice, perhaps because as a discipline it has been closer to the wider social and political realities of oppressed communities. It has also shown a willingness to examine how institutions intended to alleviate suffering actually perpetuate stigma (Bhatti-Sinclair, 2011; Dominelli 1989). There has been consensus at promoting social and cultural integration both in the USA and the European Union throughout the latter half of the twentieth century. Legislation has been introduced to tackle all forms of exclusion of BME communities in employment, health, housing and education. Social work practice has debated the many types of racist language used in the West to define ethnicity, power relationships and how we research racial identities. Social scientists now use a more nuanced approach, using field research, and have demonstrated that individual identities are shaped by many constructions such as gender, political affiliation and education, and not all imposed from above. Social casework has given us a clearer framework for thought, practice and, above all, for training in transcultural counselling (Wilson and Beresford, 2000).

Cultural psychology

Psychology itself has developed the specialist topic of *cultural psychology* (Kazarin and Evans, 1998; Pederson and Ivey, 1994). Here the subject of study is assessing and describing whole populations of ethnic peoples, and how their attitudes, behaviour, intelligence, personality, response to crisis, differ from each other and from the white (i.e. Western) 'norm'. The purpose of these texts appears to have been to sensitise the reader to the existence of these differences, helping the practitioner develop cultural expertise. Much of this work took place in the USA, where different communities were studied – often without reference to the power imbalance between a minority ethnic community and the dominant white culture. As recently as 1985, a leading text in cross-cultural counselling and therapy (Pederson, 1985) incorporated a pan-American and UK scheme for considering therapy, methods, client populations, research and training, without a single reference to institutional or individual racism. Lowenstein (1985), however, referred coyly to 'race relations' or the themes of 'identity', 'self-esteem', 'inter-cultural awareness' and 'inter-racial interaction'.

In their chapter on eating disorders, Federoff and McFarlane (1998) place much emphasis on Western ideals of body shape, and the role of non-white women who might be vulnerable to such ideals, but without reference to power or racism. Similarly, the chapters on anxiety (Al-Issa and Oudji, 1998) and depression (Kaiser et al., 1998) give detailed descriptions of difference in presentation and diagnosis in Afro-Caribbean and Hispanic communities compared with white groups. However, they again make little explicit reference to racism or racist structures that could contribute to this agenda. So we have a branch of psychology properly concerned with cultural differences in approach and outcome to counselling and psychotherapy, but not always rooted in an historical or political framework that could account for such differences.

Discussion Points

How does psychological and psychiatric practice maintain the status quo of the dominant culture?

What do you understand by the term 'white norm'?

Social identity theory

Social psychologists provided the counselling world with some elegant research results with UK schoolboys on intergroup discrimination over 30 years ago. They showed that the mere perception of belonging to two distinct groups was sufficient to trigger intergroup discrimination favouring the 'in-group'. In other words, the awareness of the presence of an 'out-group' is sufficient to provoke intergroup competitive or discriminatory responses (Tajfel, 1981; Tajfel and Turner, 1986). The process, which they called *social identity theory* begins with categorisation, common to us all – to make sense of the world and organise experience, followed by identification and comparison between ourselves and the out-group. At a benign level, think of your politics, lifestyle, geographical roots or football team. Their results superseded those of earlier workers like Katz, Brady and Sherif (cited by Hogg and Abrams, 1999), who had postulated that *competition*, especially for dwindling resources, was a prerequisite for discrimination to occur. The social identity model shows that malign discrimination can occur for much more superficial reasons, such as looking different. It has been used to help understand the Rwandan genocides, the Holocaust and the 'ethnic cleansing' in the Balkan wars, by focussing not on the victims, but on the behaviour of the perpetrators of stereotypy, prejudice and discrimination (Tajfel and Turner, 1986). In summary, this important work laid the way to further studies on the impact of transition on individuals, and racism on whole communities, and also informed politicians about the integration of ethnic communities in the West, as enshrined in the European Convention on Human Rights (Greer, 2006).

Black issues within counselling practice

Many counsellors in mainstream Western societies are white, female and middle class; their clients will almost certainly not be (Ryde, 2009). Being black is a social and political construct – not a biological one. Remember that national Census data in the UK asks residents how they *wish to define themselves* (ONS, 2011). McKenzie-Mavinga (2009) interviewed both black and white colleagues and trainees and identified some uncomfortable issues for counselling practitioners. Major themes emerging were feelings about racism, guilt, history and trust, all needing processing to remove fear of talking about racism and to achieve transformation. All counselling students need training in the experience of racism. McKenzie-Mavinga's research established the need for change, i.e. avoiding the dangerous silence about racism, where either the client will stop attending, or the client will not approach the counselling relationship at all.

The white counsellor

Judy Ryde's model (2009) of being a white helping professional takes the agenda a little further. Although white people may be aware of their responsibility to practise without discrimination, they often fail to recognise their own cultural identity and the impact this has on their practice in a multicultural environment. White practitioners may perceive 'white' as the norm, and remain unaware, or in denial, about how our history of colonisation has benefited white communities, and has an impact on all our identities today. This position is still referred to when services are described as 'colour blind' – a term meant to suggest non-discriminatory, or even multicultural practice, but one where so-called neutrality can all too often refer to white values as normative (d'Ardenne and Mahtani, 1999). In counselling research, for example, the default position for describing participants would be that they were white and English speaking; the implications for practice would be that the results did not apply to anybody outside this cultural norm – a topic returned to in Chapter 10 on the evidence base.

CHAPTER **1**

Ryde (2009) suggests that white practitioners also have to acknowledge their privilege – a process called 'white-awareness'. Further, racism is built into the organisation of all Western societies and, because of this, white counsellors need to develop a 'dialogic and inquiring' attitude to understand something of the experience of black clients and colleagues.

White practitioners need to acknowledge feelings of guilt and shame. They can use a sense of shame for the history of their white ancestors; but they may also have to respond to their sense of guilt in how they continue to be complicit with racism today in their practice.

Finally, Ryde (2009) proposes that change in helping professions comes as part of change in the individual, as well as society at large. The proposed model is applied not to race *per se*, since the limitations of such a concept is recognised, but rather to racism within difference, for example refugees, class, disability, religion, disfigurement and visible difference, different sexual identities and those with multiple identities – disabled, female, poor and elderly. Lago and Smith (2010) observe that the dominant majority rarely defines itself in relation to those in minority groups or stigmatised identities, and they cite an example of how white Americans never define themselves as such – although this might change with a black US President elected in 2008.

Discussion Points

How do we define our identity in counselling, either individually or as a service?

How helpful is the term 'colour blind' in counselling services?

Anti-discriminatory practice

Transcultural counselling has now moved to a broader agenda that accepts the whole of the 'otherness' of our clients – class, ethnicity, gender and many more indices of difference. Lago and Thompson (1989) suggest that *anti-discriminatory* and *anti-oppressive* practice are both ethical and best practice. Anti-discriminatory refers to working within the law, supported by government acts, laws, policies and practices as prescribed by the Race Relations Act: Amended (2000) and enforced by the Commission for Equality and Human Rights (CEHR). Anti-oppressive practice refers to that which is humane. If discrimination is the unequal distribution of power, rights and resources, then oppression – the experience of hardship and injustice – is the product of it.

Lago and Smith (2010) review anti-racism in the seven years between the two editions of their book, and conclude that anti-discriminatory practice is no longer an adjunct to the world of 'real therapy': rather it is *central* to all practice, including training, supervision and research, and that differences between people are

---

11

integral to how everyone obtains a sense of self. As Mike Cooper points out: 'In a world where there is so much hostility, judgement and discrimination towards people...we are unlikely to help them or ourselves without addressing and overcoming issues and challenges in these areas' (Lago and Smith, 2010).

The implications of this position are that, first, it is not enough merely to tolerate difference, although that is often what is enshrined in the laws on non-discrimination – see the specific laws and governance on anti-discrimination in Chapter 8. Therapy is often about helping the client to change. In anti-discriminatory practice, it is therapists who have to change – for example by developing the capacity to find strength in the differences between them and their clients in their working relationships. If counsellors do not incorporate anti-discrimination in their work, there is evidence that they could be harming their clients. For example, clients have asked that counsellors familiarise themselves with the specific challenges their marginalised groups suffer; it should not be for the clients to have to school them (Cooper, 2008).

Case Example

You are the referrals manager of a counselling service that serves a diverse urban population. You receive a referral from a physician to see a young woman from Trinidad who is clearly distressed. The case history is incomplete and you know very little of the circumstances under which she entered the UK. In the letter the doctor says, that 'due to the language barrier, 'it has not been possible to obtain a complete history of this woman's circumstances'.

Practice Point

Identify anti-discriminatory practices that could have prevented this incomplete referral.

Discussion Points

What is the impact of racism on the mental health of your clients?

How might your service address that in its practice?

Multiple identities and exclusions

From cultural sensitivity and cultural competence Lago (2011) takes the agenda towards the big seven dimensions of identity: gender, race, class, sexual orientation, disability, religion and age by which anti-discriminatory and anti-oppressive practice can be implemented and judged. If we ask our clients how they *define themselves*, then they are open to many identities. We could find that our clients define themselves, for example, by their birth order, their economic status, their education, their social networks, their fertility, their creativity, their allegiances, their political affiliation, their occupation, their moral code, their athleticism and so forth. Here are two case examples.

Case Example

You are counselling a young male Christian Ugandan client who has a range of relationship difficulties, including his sexual orientation. He comes from a country that considers homosexuality to be a Western abomination that is anti-Christian and that should be treated as a capital crime. You are concerned about his sexual rights, but he absolutely refuses to discuss this topic.

Practice Points

This client has constructed an identity that leaves him 'a sinner'.

You need to find out more about his country's history and traditions.

Your well-intentioned agenda of human rights may need a fresh focus.

Case Example

A black client from South Africa is referred for counselling and refuses to fill in the ethnic monitoring form that the service has carefully prepared to ensure that it reaches all members of the community. You are his counsellor and explore this. He replies he is first and foremost a Communist, and that this has represented his lifelong struggle against apartheid, which he see as a fascist conspiracy. All other categorisations are irrelevant.

Practice Point

Find out about the history of Communism in South Africa from the client and elsewhere.

13

Case Example

Rita is 62 and is referred with long-standing depression and anxiety. At assessment you discover she has a severe hearing impairment, although she lip reads well. She explains that her disability was not recognised at school and that she left at 14 unable to read or write well. She has been too ashamed to share her lack of literacy and has coped by social avoidance and taking unskilled jobs. She has had several abusive relationships with men, but lives alone. The referral was precipitated by her arrest for shoplifting. She announces at the end of the assessment that she cannot start counselling, but does not explain why.

Discussion Points

What are the likely barriers to Rita's help seeking?

What can you and your service change to help her engage in counselling?

Conclusions

Culture in mental distress has moved from the study of the exotic – to a wider agenda of social inclusion. It has been the discipline of social casework that has spearheaded an anti-racist approach, where the onus lies with the caring professions to look at systemic issues, and how they have prevented BME people from accessing talking therapies (Wilson and Beresford, 2000). The development of anti-racist approaches has expanded to include anti-discriminatory and anti-oppressive practice for all excluded or marginalised people.

Anti-discriminatory practice revisited shows an increasing use of therapy services by BME communities. There are a wider range and increasing number of qualified therapists from different and diverse groups (Patel et al., 2000). Ethnic monitoring has enabled comparisons to be made over time, but there remain others who are excluded. These may be people living in poverty, the homeless, those with disability, morbid obesity, chronic illness, literacy problems and those with learning disabilities (Lago and Smith, 2010; Nadirshaw and Torry, 2004).

There remain problems, for example the lower status of creative arts therapies in some public sectors, and a skew against dynamic models, especially in the public sector where cognitive behavioural therapy (CBT) approaches have gained political preference. There remains potential discrimination of clients who are not competent in English, even though there may be interpreting services. We have yet to address the counselling needs of people who do not speak standard English (d'Ardenne and Mahtani, 1999), and those who, for cultural or linguistic reasons, cannot fill in the many written forms required in transcultural counselling. Good practice requires us to reach out continually, and ask: Who is not here and why not? What can we change to ensure counselling reaches everyone?

14

2

TRANSCULTURAL COUNSELLING FOR INTERNATIONAL WORKERS

Summary

Chapter 2 considers transcultural counselling for people who travel and work in hostile environments, using as examples the distinct needs of development workers, journalists and the armed services exposed to extreme changes of culture, often within very short time frames. It also examines the support needs of staff in non-governmental agencies (NGOs) and humanitarian aid agencies, as well as the populations they serve. This will also include those undertaking development work and training with emerging nations, particularly attending to the prevention of secondary traumatisation for those who counsel the victims of war and natural disaster.

Culture shock and the stress of being overseas

In a restless world we are very familiar with the concept of airlifting personnel around the globe – not just for trade or education, but to assist in economic development, provide defence and assistance, and inform us what is happening in many insecure places.

We expect these people to arrive, work hard, minister to others and return home in good shape. We presume that professional staff, paid or voluntary, are prepared and informed beforehand about what they are likely to face. There is a further presumption that they will be able to do the job as soon as they touch down – never more so than when every hour that passes costs lives.

Social psychology includes psychological reactions to unfamiliar environments, and *culture shock* (Furnham and Bochner, 1986) became a focus for a systematic approach to the adjustment and adaptation of various groups of travellers (see also Bochner, 2003; Ward et al., 2001). These included economic immigrants, political refugees, business people and students, and how best to help them with 'the disabling but enriching effects of cultural disorientation'. A variation on this was the proposed diagnostic category of 'uprooting disorder'

(Zwingmann and Gunn, 1983) – a type of mental collapse occurring with extreme culture shock, and this has been well described in international students as a long-term and serious illness (Barty, 2011). The failure of overseas placements for the US Peace Corps in the 1970s gave impetus for this research. Furnham and Bochner (1986) were able to demonstrate that exposure to other cultures is both stressful and alienating, and their approach was dynamic, interactive, generalisable and replicable. Their solutions were a culture learning/ social skills model of bi-cultural competency before they travel:

- social support systems – travellers need at least one intimate contact in the host country; the traveller has to participate in, not just observe, the host society; positive engagement in intergroup relations.

Cultural stressors are immense, complex and ever-changing. For example, there is now an increasingly insecure environment for humanitarian aid workers in emergency settings. The World Health Organization (WHO) Inter-Agency Standing Committee (IASC) has published guidelines (IASC, 2007) on how to manage mental health and well-being among staff and volunteers. Organisations are requested to ensure the availability of a concrete plan to prepare, protect and promote staff well-being for the specific emergency. A healthy working environment means:

- addressing work-related stressors
- ensuring access to healthcare and psychosocial support for local and international staff
- providing support to staff who have experienced or witnessed extreme events
- making support available after the mission or employment. (IASC, 2007)

There are organisations that now screen staff who are sent on overseas missions. Examples include Interhealth Worldwide (www.interhealth.org) and People in Aid (www.peopleinaid.org) in the UK, the Antares Foundation in the Netherlands (www.antaresfoundation.org) and Aid Interaction (www.aidinteraction.org) in the USA. All provide medical and psychological support to their staff. Counselling alone cannot reduce stress here; rather, it is part of a wider picture where screening, local and overseas support and ethical standards of care for international organisations involved with aid are being developed and evaluated.

Curling and Simmons (2010) surveyed key stressors affecting humanitarian aid workers and staff support strategies for international aid work. Work and workload were the biggest stressors in aid work – more so for women. Those in emergencies were more stressed than their counterparts in the organisational headquarters. The political, social and economic situations in emergency missions were more stressful to international staff than locals, and again affected women more. Workers valued social support in the workplace, access to in-house counsellors and to trained and supported peer helpers, especially in local settings.

People in Aid (Porter and Emmens, 2009) list the following potential sources of stress in insecure environments:

- continuous exposure to a foreign culture and language(s)
- overall lack of security – especially for female workers; a harsh and/or unpredictable climate
- personal and organisational isolation
- malaise, sickness and injury that arise from being in such an environment
- poor transport and logistical infrastructures, with high rates of road traffic accidents
- poor and dirty living conditions
- limited food and drink
- irregular and uncomfortable sleep
- poor or non-existent information technology (IT) communications
- chronic burnout by being on duty 24/7
- emotionally demanding environments, e.g. traumatic grief, the death of children
- human rights abuses
- witnessing atrocities directly, with dying and dead bodies
- witnessing destitution and starvation
- the meaninglessness of suffering; feeling guilty
- being blamed (as a Westerner, for example) for causing suffering
- combat zones.

The impact of trauma on international workers

Figley (1999) demonstrated that clinicians risk post-traumatic stress, but few studies have looked at the other effects of prolonged exposure to human suffering on aid workers. Shah et al. (2007) found a prevalence of secondary traumatic stress in a group of 76 humanitarian aid workers. Humanitarian aid workers were defined as non-clinician employees or volunteers who might be asking details of or providing care to those exposed to severe physical or psychological trauma. In the past, humanitarian aid worker culture has been cavalier and orientated to the needs of others (Diamond, 2002), with staff working six to seven days a week and no chance to process the suffering witnessed. Diamond quotes humanitarian aid workers from India who have little support from peers or employing agencies. The adverse effects included negative changes in professional functioning, diminished self-view, a bleaker world view and a sense of insecurity. Their psychological needs increased with early warning signs of more serious morbidity including anxiety, depression, substance misuse and post-traumatic stress disorder (PTSD).

Although it is clear that staff may be well trained and supported at home, the capacity of individuals to survive and perform well in such adverse circumstances can no longer be assumed. There have been numerous casualties of staff requiring repatriation where their own physical and mental well-being has been compromised. The mistakes are distressing and very expensive, and do nothing for the reputation or goodwill of the agencies involved. Fawcett (2003) cites a study of 215 international humanitarian workers, which found that trauma symptoms were lower for those with high social support; the effect was more marked when this was from outside their organisation. When this support was compromised, front-line workers were significantly more likely to have symptoms of stress and trauma.

Staff care in international NGOs

People in Aid/Interhealth (Porter and Emmens, 2009) have developed a programme of preparation, support, consulting and training of aid workers on other cultures, and from that has evolved a Code of Good Practice. The Code is not legally binding but it provides the organisation with some ideas about a good level of support for humanitarian aid workers.

The principles are as follows:

- there needs to be equitability of resource between local and overseas workers
- support for workers in remote rural areas is a priority; support needs to embrace culturally relevant care of staff
- the role of spirituality and faith in the aid agencies has been a neglected resource.

What support exists at present?

Porter and Emmens (2009) looked at 20 aid organisations; six had little or no support where implicitly, staff would seek their own help if needed. Eleven had moderate support, with people available in the organisation who could be approached, but who might have other organisational responsibilities. Three had a high level of support, and the authors used the United Nations Children's Fund (UNICEF) as a case example of an organisation that provides a high level of care, including an employee assistance programme. It also has confidential, trained counsellors based in the organisation's host country

(Switzerland). In addition, it provides telephone and email support for out-sourced staff – especially pre- and post-assignment.

Interhealth looked at:

- long-standing counsellors; outsourced Western counselling in the field
- in-house at-home psychological support
- in-house field support; referrals to lists of counsellors; psychological 'first aid' from peers online peer support.
- When the authors asked the clients, i.e. the culturally varied staff of the organisation, whether they wanted their counselling at home or overseas, they replied that location was less important than counsellors who were part of the same humanitarian culture, so *sharing the values and practices of the organisation was paramount.*

Practice Points

Counsellors can work in-house, at the headquarters, in the field or online.

Outside counsellors need to understand and share the values of the aid organisation.

Counsellors can train staff on the mission to provide peer support.

Case Example

A national staff member of an aid agency is working in an earthquake area in Turkey close to his own district that was also destroyed. He works because he is destitute. But his colleagues report to their manager that he shouts in his sleep, and becomes irritable with his colleagues. His manager decides to approach an older male colleague from a neighbouring district to talk with him to consider his mental health and support needs, prioritising his grief, unwanted dreams and hyperarousal. She also briefs the team about the impact of traumatic grief on the entire workforce.

Discussion Points

What are the issues for this employee and his resilience?

Could his current difficulties have been prevented?

Practice Points

Local staff and their families may be much more directly affected by disaster than international staff.

An effective manager provides a specific and culturally appropriate intervention to a local employee (Porter and Emmens, 2009).

Resilience briefing

Efforts have been made to develop a process for development workers to identify their strengths and vulnerabilities, and reduce risk to health and well-being while on assignments. *Resilience briefing* (Hargrave, 2011a, 2011b) is aimed at boosting strength and ensuring that staff are better equipped for challenging work. It covers the following five domains:

1 family, friends and colleagues (including the team), and the psychosocial networks for the individual
2 the meaning and motivation to do any assignment
3 adaptability and resourcefulness, managing change, problem-solving and recent changes
4 current health and well-being, including staying resilient to past trauma or adversity
5 nature of the assignment and the degree of preparation for it.

This model is tailor-made for each staff member receiving it, incorporating known risk factors and those that increase resource and resilience, as measured by increased outputs and reduced casualties (Hargrave, 2011a). It takes systemic and individual resources into account and is flexible in its applicability to large and small organisations. This model is currently being evaluated but already provides counsellors working with these staff clear points of focus. The client is the one who has to identify strengths and who is best placed to negotiate additional resource from the employing agency and the communities in which the mission is being carried out. Most importantly, it can act as a screen to prevent the more vulnerable staff (e.g. those recently bereaved) from an occupational hazard likely to place them at further risk of injury, breakdown or potential tragedy.

Case Example

A young English woman works for a humanitarian agency working with the survivors of rape and is about to leave for a mission in the Congo. On routine pre-assignment screening, she discloses that she was herself raped in her teens. She was not believed and nothing was reported to the police. She has not mentioned this to her employers, and she is determined that they should not be informed, as she says that the situation in the Congo is 'completely different'.

Discussion Points

Is she right?

What are the ethical issues for you and her?

What are the risk issues for her if she goes to the Congo?

The counselling needs of the media on overseas assignments

Another group of personnel exposed to extreme stress on overseas missions includes the media, who have cultural needs of their own. Some war correspondents say they are addicted to war zones, such as the adrenaline rush and camaraderie that they experience, and that on returning home they feel empty, without purpose and become depressed (Feinstein, 2006; Marinovich and Silva, 2000). Others suffer post-traumatic difficulties but are reluctant to seek help from statutory authorities because there remains a low-key but macho culture that says: 'don't ask for help', 'it's part of the job' and 'best handled on your own' (Reporters without Boundaries, 2009).

In the UK there has been a growing awareness in news organisations of their responsibilities for their staff on overseas missions. The Dart Centres for Journalism and Trauma (both in the UK – http://dartcenter.org/europe – and the USA – http://dartcenter.org/), are run by journalists, for journalists. They aim to address these cultural deficits and offer a safe place for traumatised staff to obtain confidential counselling and support. Among the issues addressed are how much the reporting of wars and disasters overseas damages journalists. Many media personnel are exposed to distressing stories and images: these include reporters, producers and camera crews who have directly witnessed events, as well as home editors and picture editors processing uncensored news. Hight and Smyth (2001) assert: Reporters, photojournalists, engineers, sound men and field producers often work elbow to elbow with emergency workers. Journalists' symptoms of traumatic stress are remarkably similar to those of police officers and fire-fighters who work in the immediate aftermath of tragedy, yet journalists typically receive little support after they file their stories. While public safety workers are offered debriefings and counselling after a trauma, journalists are merely assigned another story.

The French Press Organisation that supports journalists in war zones and dangerous places, Reporters sans Frontières, has a Safety Charter within its Handbook for Journalists (2005) for its media workers (www.rsf.org/IMG/pdf/guide_gb.pdf):

- a commitment to safety from all editorial staff
- voluntary assignments only – always with an option to come home if desired
- experience and maturity a prerequisite for safety
- preparation and information
- equipment of the highest standard
- insurance provision
- psychological counselling on return from assignment if desired
- legal protection.

Practice Points

Journalists prefer counselling to be voluntary.

Counselling journalists is only part of a larger programme of care for them.

Journalists can do much to protect themselves and tap into their resilience. Schmickle (2007) organised a summer school for journalists that generated the following ideas to protect the mental health of journalists in the field:

- Focus on journalistic goals
- Study risk
- Learn to lean on colleagues and build up your own personal support team
- Contact other journalists in any danger zone for help with logistics and staying safe
- Put affairs in order
- Contact newsroom, home and professional network regularly
- Obtain a full debrief from colleagues in the field
- Cultivate buddies for decision-making and monitoring each other's safety
- Eat and sleep well. Exercise. Take care with alcohol and drugs
- Talk, or keep a diary
- Look out for persistent intrusions or hyperarousal from one or many incidents.

War photographers are more vulnerable because their witness has been silent and traumatic memory less processed (Brewin et al., 1996). When editors send journalists overseas, they can seek to ensure their well-being by having a contact plan, respecting time differences, always having a person at the end of a phone and by understanding the impact of changing plans at the last minute on those on the ground in danger. Schmickle (2007) recommends as good practice that editors organise an airport reception and a full debriefing with emphasis on factual update and shared information. At the same time they can look for signs of stress in their colleagues and de-escalate professional responsibilities, with referral to counselling or mental health services, should it be necessary.

Freelance journalists

There are a significant number of media personnel overseas who are without the support of large employers. The most vulnerable group, it could be argued, are freelance journalists, who are entirely dependent on their own resources. The Rory Peck Trust (www.rorypecktrust.org) is a UK charity set up in the name of a freelance cameraman killed in action in 1995. It promotes good practice on behalf of freelancers working in the news-gathering industry and their right to work safely and in freedom. It also provides information and advice on insurance, training, trauma counselling, safety and other issues to freelancers around the world

Rehabilitation of journalists

Frank Gardner (who is the BBC Security Correspondent) wrote of his rehabilitation experiences at the Royal London Hospital following the murder of his cameraman and terrible injuries that left him with paraplegia, after a terrorist attack in Saudi Arabia (Gardner, 2007). Here he contrasts two very different counselling experiences:

> 'Now tell me,' she began, without looking at me, 'why are you here exactly?''Um... it's all in the notes...''Well, I haven't read those. Was it a car accident?'

> If this woman can't be bothered to find out anything in advance, then I certainly don't feel like baring my soul to her. (p. 376)

> Neil (a Royal Navy psychologist with journalistic experience) put me at my ease immediately, and not just because he had read my medical notes...I talked for hours and he mainly listened. Maybe I was just having withdrawal symptoms from being on air, and Neil was my captive audience. But it felt wonderful to tell the whole story to someone who was a dispassionate listener, someone whose emotions had not been hurt by it all. (p. 377)

Practice Points

Note Gardner's reference to 'withdrawal symptoms' from broadcasting and having the time to tell the whole story in some detail.

His second therapist demonstrated active listening, professional knowledge of the client's circumstances, and an objectivity that reassured and contained.

Schmickle (2007) advocates active listening with a focus on relatives, taking time and space, speaking less and resisting the urge to 'fix' things in those early days home.

Perhaps it needs to be appreciated also that those left behind when journalists are injured suffer too. In a triumph of understatement, Gardner observes: 'The life of a foreign correspondent can be very rewarding, but it is often not a lot of fun for the partner left behind' (2007: 225).

Case Example

Mike is a seasoned reporter with an international news agency, who has just returned from a mission in North Africa where he witnessed combat, killings of civilians and children, and the accidental killing of one of his colleagues. He has been debriefed and returned to work but finds it increasingly hard to sleep and concentrate. He has seen his general practitioner (GP) who has prescribed sleeping tablets but he continues to have bad dreams, and is also irritable with his bosses who are beginning to wonder if they should have sent him back to work.

The needs of the armed forces

There has been a significant change in public attitudes to the needs of the armed forces and veterans in recent years. Men and women in the armed forces are regularly exposed to extreme conditions in combat – including clashes of cultures, religions and ideologies. When de-mobbed, they may then be subject to social exclusion, unemployment, family and marital breakdown, and subsequent homelessness where their social, psychological and health needs may be neglected (Busuttil, 2008).

Those engaged in combat and peace-keeping operations often maintain that they need services from those who wear a similar uniform, according to the US Veterans' Administration mental health service (www.mentalhealth. va.gov) and the UK's Combat Stress (www.combatstress.org). Whether or not this is true – if those exposed to extreme stress believe it to be the case, it will be difficult for a civilian counsellor to achieve credibility. In recent years, the mental health needs of the armed forces have been revealed as neglected, and several UK government-led initiatives have attempted to prioritise these both through public and voluntary sector agencies (Centre for Psychological Services Research, Sheffield University, 2010). These include six veterans' mental health pilot projects across the UK, aimed at increasing knowledge and understanding of veterans' needs by NHS staff. In the USA, the Veterans' Transition Program has provided educational and vocational counselling to service members from 180 days prior to the date of discharge, and up to a year after (www1.va.gov/opa/publications/benefits_book/bene-fits_chap08.asp).

Combat Stress is a veterans' charity that has been working on a nationwide programme across the UK. It is focussed on providing psychological support through 14 community outreach teams, as well as more specialist care at three day centres, with a specific brief for soldiers. The care programme is fourfold, derived from US and Australian models as well as the UK. It consists of initial preparation, stabilisation, disclosure and working through of traumatic material, and finally, rehabilitation.

The pilot evidence (Centre for Psychological Services Research, Sheffield University, 2010) revealed:

- veterans preferred self-referral to being referred
- they sought psychological help from other veterans
- a second choice was psychotherapists with experience of veterans
- mental health work was best provided in multi-agency clinics
- they preferred services and buildings being identified exclusively for veterans
- information sharing with health and other veterans' agencies was essential.

Key to these findings has been the concept of *a culture within* the armed forces and the importance of the counsellor having knowledge of that culture, rather than any specific model of psychosocial support. At the end of the chapter are listed a range of organisations in the UK and US, dedicated to the well-being of service personnel, veterans and their families. These include professional bodies such as Combat Stress, with qualified clinicians who are likely to have military connections. It also includes organisations such as SAFFA which are charities – independent of the military but historically linked to the needs of the armed services. In recent times families and veterans themselves have identified emotional needs and provided informal helplines and websites, such as the Military Families Support Group. The quality of these services has not been compared; what is important is that anyone counselling a member of the armed forces recognises how valuable it is to be able to access those with knowledge of military culture.

It is not possible to say whether these services address all the needs of service personnel traumatised by foreign wars in mental healthcare. Significant features include: their accessibility – telephone and email access on a 24/7 basis; the explicit connection between those making the calls and those answering the phone as both understanding military culture; the inclusion of families of sufferers who are given the same status as the combatants.

In the USA a significant number of personnel returning from mission have PTSD, brain trauma, depression and substance misuse. They cannot or do not seek professional support on return, and neither do their families (www.mentalhealth.va.gov/returningservicevets.asp). There now exists a limited range of online programmes for counsellors, their clients and advocates to address these needs. Emphasis is on behavioural and community interventions with tangible outcomes.

The issue about the culture of the military is an interesting one. Ethnic matching offers no better counselling outcomes than unmatched, but there is evidence that clients of one culture prefer counsellors to match them and engage with them (Farsimadan et al., 2011). Military personnel plead a special case; they relinquish some civil liberties and put themselves at higher risk of death or serious injury than the general population. In return the state promises to help and support them when they most need it – the 'Military Covenant' – and psychological work has to take special account of this (Royal College of General Practitioners, British Legion and Combat Stress, 2011).

Case Example

Jamie from Glasgow served ten years as a lance-corporal on duty in Iraq, Afghanistan and Northern Ireland. He says that when he was in the Army he buried all his health problems because he didn't want to appear weak. But he was aware once he left that he suffered from a short temper, anxiety attacks and insomnia. It has made returning to 'civvy street' difficult. 'My wife is at the end of her tether, but I don't expect you to understand.'

Practice Points

Why might Jamie bury his health problems?

What would your priorities for this veteran and his family now be?

Discussion Point

Can civilian counsellors understand military problems?

Missionary care

There has been increasing recognition of the mental heath needs of missionaries overseas and there are now agencies responsive to their pastoral and psychological care (e.g. in the USA www.missionarycare.com; in the UK www.interhealth.org.uk). Earlier in this chapter, the concept of culture shock was explored and can be well applied to the missionary movement. Whereas culture shock incorporates 'honeymoon, crisis, recovery, and adjustment', *culture stress* is more chronic and affects missionaries on longer placements (Koteskey, 2011). Koteskey observes that early modern missionaries overseas lived in compounds or ghettoes – which gave them some protection. Today, although missionaries retain their spiritual connection, many live physically with their host communities, where they are more likely to be culturally stressed. Koteskey (2011) describes the major factors in cultural stress:

- involvement – missionaries are more personally and spiritually involved in local culture and experience more culture stress than tourists or business people
- values – the greater the gap, the greater the stress
- communication: not just language and grammar, but cognitive approaches, common cultural knowledge and non-verbal signals place additional stress on the outsider

- entry/re-entry: missionaries live in two cultures. They also change their place of residence – never fully acculturating to where they are
- missionaries' children adopt the host culture fast and may aggravate a sense of alienation
- multinational teams may be more effective for the ministry, but may add to cultural stress.

Emphasis is placed on missionaries having specific and long-term strategies, since they are typically placed for longer periods than their business or diplomatic peers. These include recognition of culture stress, acceptance of the host culture, communication with members of one's own culture, regular respite from missionary duties, knowing one's identity and what will never acculturate, physical activity, and befriending a family in the host culture for fun rather than evangelisation.

The needs of missionaries' partners can be addressed through cross-cultural counselling, and e-counselling is possible (e.g. www.missionfield counselling.co.uk). Partners have to leave their own lives and friends, and may not have the same faith base as the missionary. They may have unrealistic expectations of their role, and in Chapter 5 we shall be exploring how faith and spirituality across cultures must be addressed to achieve a good outcome in counselling.

Psychosocial support for people in international crises

Much of the criticism aimed at Western counsellors offering support in humanitarian crises has been that counselling has no demonstrable effect in a disaster (Summerfield, 1995, 2004, 2008). Indeed, some types of counselling, for example individual debriefing, may actually be harmful (Wessely, 2003). There are, however, interventions that pre-empt the need for counselling. *Psychosocial support* has been used by Tribe and Calvert (2005) as 'the dynamic relationship that exists between psychological and social effects, each continually interacting with and influencing the other'. IASC (2007) has developed psychosocial support to mean 'any type of local or outside support that aims to protect or promote psychological well-being and/or prevent mental disorder'. Davidson (2010a) cites seven fundamental principles for this kind of work, aimed to transcend the accusation of a Western model imposed on non-Western communities in crisis: humanity; impartiality; neutrality; independence; voluntary service; unity; and universality.

All of these principles are incorporated within the international agencies offering culturally non-specific interventions, resulting in the model CALMER – an acronym that neatly reminds workers to suppress the adrenalin rush, and which defines the sequence of the response:

- Consider
- Acknowledge
- Listen
- Manage
- Enable
- Resource

The first two of these address diverse communities, including their development, culture, social inequality and their ability to respond to crisis, how trust might be established and rapport facilitated. Davidson argues that this single psychosocial framework is drawn from the ways that counsellors have of conceptualising and responding to the wide needs of individuals and communities. These include listening skills, managing confidentiality and providing information. The model also incorporates community psychology principles with the 'enable and resource' focus on the empowerment of individuals to cope, achieve social change and develop greater resilience in the future (Orford, 2008; White, 2008). Coping is required, but individuals additionally need to work for social change with greater resilience. The CALMER framework has been piloted and is now being developed for different countries and different populations (Davidson, 2010b).

Psychosocial first aid

Psychosocial first aid is a model widely deployed in international emergencies. It is being evaluated overseas as more agencies are being asked to demonstrate their effectiveness, and their ability to provide a relevant and effective service. Psychosocial first aid incorporates the rapid establishment of trust, increasing the critical exchange of information about experienced stress and putting others at their ease, i.e. by lowering anxiety and by showing immediate compassion (Fogarty et al., 1999). For example, after the Twin Towers attack of 9/11, a bereavement charity called CRUSE sent volunteers to New York to assist UK families affected by the disaster. They found that counselling was of no value in the initial aftermath. In fact, the volunteers were at their most effective in the *practical arrangements* for the identification of the dead and the repatriation of bodies and personal belongings (BBC News, 21 September 2001).

Davidson (2010a) cites the Red Cross experience after the Haitian earthquake of 2008, where victims were not asked to re-live trauma. Rather, they were reassured, kept calm, given practical information and help with contacting loved ones. Here again, psychosocial first aid addressed the immediate needs for support, a validation of experience, shared information and, above all, immediate safety issues. The diversity of people's experiences and backgrounds also has to be acknowledged (Patel et al., 2000), as has the role of psychotherapists working more closely with local communities, (Gilbert, 2009a).

Overseas workers have many roles, but at times of disaster, are faced with whole populations under considerable stress, whose capacity to respond will be severely impaired. Aid workers who are not trained counsellors are capable of providing psychological first aid – just as those without medical training are able to save lives through physical first aid. This model has been developed by mental health researchers like Jenkins et al. (2010) for transcultural training in countries affected by natural disasters and wars.

Debriefing

There has been much debate about the value of debriefing for populations in crisis, as the practice originates from the theatre of war (Wessely, 2003). Debriefing generally refers to helping people to describe their response to a particular situation – as it were, unloading their experience. The psychological significance of whether such unloading either eases distress or reduces vulner-ability to post-traumatic problems is disputed. There is no convincing evidence that such interventions reduce the development of psychiatric illness, nor that they prevent the onset of post-traumatic difficulties (Raphael, 2003; Ursano et al., 2003). Debriefing with groups where the focus is on personal experience runs the risk of re-traumatising the participants and is not recommended.

'Operational debriefing', by contrast, refers to an immediate review of an operational response, for example by a team, or an informational exchange among survivors of trauma and rescue workers. Operational debriefing fosters a better understanding of the experience and promotes social cohesion. Further, it can prevent individual isolation, and allows rescuers to see those who are beginning to succumb to mental health problems (Raphael, 2003). Debriefing is best when it is used with homogeneous groups who have shared a similar experience, and where the debriefing focuses on *factual elements* of the disaster such as to debunk myths or mis-attribution of blame or responsibility.

Conclusions

People working overseas are vulnerable to culture shock, which can be miti-gated by preparation and engagement with the host culture and its people. Overseas workers in hostile environments can be psychologically screened for their resilience to stress, and models of resilience are currently being devel-oped and evaluated to reduce the risk of forced repatriation. Psychological and psychosocial work overseas is most complex and dynamic in the after-math of disaster. The effectiveness of psychological work with victims depends on safety, reassurance and information exchange, and the order of interventions is critical. Debriefing is best done for those who have shared a similar experience and should be focussed on factual exchange rather than emotional catharsis.

Aid and development workers in NGOs have their own psychological needs and receive very uneven levels of support, especially when in the field. Aid workers choose many models of support but, critically, prefer counsellors to understand something of the culture and values of the organisation that has sent them overseas.

Armed forces prefer to refer themselves to those who understand military culture, and may not respond to civilian counsellors, however competent. They need help with traumatic experiences and with the unique stressors of returning to civilian life. Journalists are excellent networkers, able to use these abilities to prepare and protect themselves from stress in reporting extreme violence, but photographers and camera persons may have greater mental health vulnerability. Editors have a role in agreed communication and planning, and may be the first to recognise counselling need. Missionaries face very direct cultural stressors and are likely to use dedicated services, including online access. Their spouses and children who may not have the same faith base have different needs and these are now being recognised by counselling communities in the West.

Additional resources

Journalists

Dart Centres for Journalism and Trauma (both in the UK and the USA: 48 Grays Inn Rd, London WC1 8LT, 020 7242 356.

Reporters Sans Frontières: www.rsf.org – Charter for the Safety of Journalists Working in War Zones or Dangerous Areas.

Rory Peck Trust: www.rorypecktrust.org – gives charitable grants to freelance newsgatherers in need, and to the families of those who have been killed, injured or persecuted as a result of their work.

Without Apparent Injury (Sans Blessures Apparents): http://sansblessuresapparentes.blogspot.com – French-speaking agency for war journalists.

Veterans

Civvy Street (part of the Royal British Legion): www.civvystreet.org, helpline 0800 169 4073 – the Royal British Legion offers help with jobs, qualifications and business loans.

Combat Stress: www.combatstress.org.uk, 24-hour helpline 0800 138 1619 – for help with PTSD and mental health generally, offering residential courses and support.

Military Family Support Group: www.mfsg.org.uk/page/index.asp?pageCatID=10 – run by families, providing emotional and practical support to veterans and access to serving soldiers for confidential exchange.

SSAFA: www.ssafa.org.uk – welfare for service personel, veterans and families, independent of military chain of command. Established over 100 years.

Royal British Legion: www.britishlegion.org.uk – a general welfare organisation for all UK service personel in action and life long.

US Veterans' Administration mental health service: www.mentalhealth.va.gov – a useful guide to a wide range of services available to US service members.

Veterans Aid: www.veteransaid.net, helpline 0800 012 6867 – for accommodation and finance.

Norcare: www.norcare.co.uk or call 0191 261 2228 – veterans' centre for homeless ex-service men and women in the north-east of England.

Missionaries

Oscar: www.oscar.org.uk/service/pastoral/counselling.htm – the UK Information Service for World Missions.

Interhealth, London: www.interhealth.org.uk – providing medical and psychological screening and support services.

Bethany Ministries, Hong Kong: www.bethanyministries.com – a member care organisation providing spiritual and counselling care in the Orient.

Link Care: www.linkcare.org – US resporation and personal growth programme for missionaries.

Budapest Care Center, Hungary: www.budapestcare.com – counselling service for Christian workers in Europe, Russia and Central Asia.

3

TRANSCULTURAL COUNSELLING FOR REFUGEES

Who overcomes by force,

Hath overcome but half his foe.

Paradise Lost, *John Milton*

Summary

This chapter defines the transcultural counselling needs of refugees who have migrated and found themselves in various stages of resettlement, or potential repatriation. It examines the antecedents of seeking asylum, together with the further difficulties and barriers refugees face in the West. It draws on evidence and good counselling practice from health and social settings, legal services and specialised refugee agencies working in the UK. A number of counselling models are evaluated, including narrative and non-verbal approaches. The issues of boundaries and safety, and conflicting values about human rights, as well as the needs of women in honour violence, are visited. For simplicity, 'refugee' refers to anyone with refugee experience.

Definitions

In the 1951 United Nations Convention Relating to the Status of Refugees, also known as the Refugee Convention, a *refugee* is defined as a person who:

> owing to a well-founded fear of being persecuted for reasons of race, religion, nationality, membership of a particular social group or political opinion, is outside the country of his nationality, and is unable to, or, owing to such fear, is unwilling to avail himself of the protection of that country or return there because there is a fear of persecution...

> (United Nations, 1951)

There remains debate about how the term should be used in everyday language. For example, the media often confound the terms 'economic migrants' – those migrating to earn money or increase their income – with refugees. Sadly, it is sometimes done in the context of inciting fear about lost jobs or economic opportunities. Indeed, national xenophobic media give the impression that the West (and particularly the UK) is 'flooded' with 'bogus' asylum seekers (Article19, 2003). The facts say otherwise. The 2009 quarterly figures show that there was a fall in the number of asylum applications to 4,765 compared with the same period in 2008 when 6,775 applied, a 30 per cent drop (ONS, 2009; Refugee Council, 2010). In addition, increasingly draconian UK legislation (Immigration, Asylum and Nationality Act, 2006) aims to reduce the numbers of people given asylum status. Those without documents are criminalised, discredited, deprived of access to work, money or permanent housing.

A special category are people who may have been forced to flee their homes for the same reasons as refugees but have not crossed an international border. These people are *internally displaced persons*. By the end of 2009, there were approximately 27 million internally displaced persons worldwide (United Nations Refugee Agency, 2012). Most world conflicts involve disputes between political or ethnic groups rather than between states. Displacement is not to be confused with *dispersal*, which is the process by which the UK Border Agency seeks to move refugees from the capital to around the country.

International law recognises the right of individuals to *seek asylum*, but does not oblige other countries to provide it. Nations at times offer 'temporary protection' when they face a sudden influx of people and their regular asylum systems would be otherwise overwhelmed. In such circumstances people can be speedily admitted to safe countries, but without any guarantee of permanent abode. Refugee protection and assistance organisations generally promote three 'durable solutions' to the fate of refugees:

- *Voluntary repatriation*: refugees are able to return to their home country because their lives and liberty are no longer threatened
- *Local integration*: host governments allow refugees to integrate into the country of first asylum
- *Resettlement in a third country*: repatriation is unsafe and the first asylum country refuses permanent leave to remain.

Most of the world's refugees wait for durable solutions to their predicament. Although many have been granted provisional or temporary asylum in neighbouring countries, they are not able to regularise their status or integrate. Travel and work are highly restricted, and educational and recreational opportunities are often non-existent or severely lacking. These refugees may also be subject to attack, either by local security forces or by cross-border incursions from the country of origin.

Health issues for refugees within the host nation

In the UK all emergency and primary healthcare is accessible to refugees, regardless of their legal status, but this does not extend to secondary or specialist services – especially for so-called 'failed' asylum seekers. Referrals from GPs can be discretionary – even for life-threatening conditions (Burnett and Peel, 2001). Burnett and Rhys-Jones (2006) have provided a comprehensive list of factors that contribute to the vulnerability of refugees to poor physical and mental health. These include the effects of personal and institutional racism, social isolation and dislocation, exclusion from health information or monitoring, cross-cultural communication gaps, stress, injury and poor economic conditions. Webster and Robertson (2007) argue that the mental well-being of refugee communities can be better addressed through community-based services, because problems may not be construed individualistically. Also there are insufficient resources to meet all refugee needs in traditional clinics, and many refugees will not attend centralised mental health services. Even in community consultation, however, there are unheard refugee voices – including women, children and elders.

Practice Points

Safety is the first priority for counselled refugees. Try to make an immediate risk assessment prior to undertaking any formal psychological assessment.

Those who arrive with injuries or who look unwell should be gently questioned. Delay counselling if necessary and seek medical or nursing assistance.

Case Example

Ella is a South African refugee with a history of gang rape, abduction and knifing while working as a political agent for the African National Congress. She is referred for counselling for anxiety but her notes indicate that she also suffers from insulin-dependent diabetes. At assessment, she appears pallid and unwell, and has difficulty in concentrating. She becomes agitated and talks about her medication left at home. You realise she has no insulin with her and ask for the name of her diabetic nurse. Before she leaves counselling, you call the nurse and arrange for an immediate appointment, and for Ella to bring her medicine to the next session. Ella does this and you discuss the impact of diabetes and insulin taking as additional stressors. Her mother and maternal grandmother both died from untreated diabetes. Ella believes that she will die from this untreatable illness, but she agrees to discuss these beliefs with her nurse and doctor. She returns at the next session appearing in better physical health and begins to disclose in more detail the rape and subsequent violence that she endured.

Impact of racism on counselling refugees

Patel and Mahtani (2007) review how refugees have endured human rights violations, including genocide, ethnic cleansing and torture. Refugees come to the UK
to seek a safe place and a new life. The host culture is biased against them, if not
hostile, at individual, organisational and systemic levels, and provision of psychotherapy and counselling to refugees is often avoided by counsellors who say that
the work is too complex, too overwhelming or too stressful. No counsellor or
counselling service sees itself as racist: but it is racist practice that enables services
to exclude refugees. Services often redirect refugee clients to 'specialised' services
including community resources with volunteer counsellors. Another strategy
involves rejecting initial referrals because of no money for interpreting, or
because of the extra time or consideration required for refugee work.

When services are provided, counsellors use Western models that are presumed to be universal (De Silva, 1999; Summerfield, 2004; Van de Veer,
1998), although assessment tools are often not validated on refugee populations. Chapter 10 will consider ethnocentric assumptions made about participants in psychological research, as most counselling outcomes are evaluated on
English speaking, non-refugee participants.

Case Example

*Sara is a woman from Eritrea who has sought asylum in the UK after she
was persecuted for her faith (she is a Jehovah's Witness), and is referred
because of depression. She describes her living conditions in a single
room in a Manchester suburb with poor public transport. She is shunned
by her neighbours and told to 'go home'. She is unable to work but she
volunteers at a local community centre where her language skills allow
her to help other refugees. She is hopeless and had believed that the UK
would be a welcoming and safe place. But her experience of poverty,
isolation and casual racism in the UK are as hard for her as the
violence, threats and losses she endured in the country she fled.*

Discussion Points

How will your service avoid 'casual racism' in working with Sara?

Which of her strengths will you be able to use in counselling her?

Family separation and tracing

Family separation is one of the tragic consequences of armed conflict or natural disaster. Under the 1949 Geneva Convention, the International Federation of Red Cross and Red Crescent Societies (IFRC, www.ifrc.org) are mandated to re-establish contact between close family members who have been separated by armed conflict and political upheaval. The IFRC provides tracing and message services and claims to be neutral, independent, impartial and humanitarian.

In counselling a refugee who has lost family contact, a search is not automatically undertaken. Refugees who request tracing must be prepared for bad news. If there is no news, the client may be in the same factual position as before, but feel more hopeless if an agency with big resources has been unable to locate the family. It may be that there is bad news. The family is in exile, in prison or suffering in some way. Worse, members of the family could have died or been killed in violent struggle. Although it may be better to have some closure on the whereabouts of family members, refugees suffer terribly. They are bereaved or separated from those they loved. They may experience guilt at having survived when others did not. They may experience shame that they did not do more for the family left behind, and begin to doubt the reasoning behind their seeking asylum. Finally, there may be scepticism from their host country about the truth of their family's circumstances. When counselled, some clients make a decision not to trace their families as they are not yet ready to face any of these possible outcomes. No knowledge comes to represent the least of all evils.

Those who hope to be reunited may have to face poor, expensive and sometimes unsafe telephone and postal communication with their loved ones. They receive heartbreaking and unrealistic requests from their family for rescue or escape, urgent pleas for money or air tickets and documents allowing them to be reunited. The refugee feels a need to describe a better world – which it may not be – and becomes a hostage to fortune when the family eventually finds out the truth. Added to all this is the complication that the refugee is indeed trying to make a new life and new relationships in a host country, and is, in a sense, having to turn away from the past. The refugee stands between two worlds, accepted by neither.

Practice Points

Use local communities/refugee organisations to broker direct communication with families. They are sometimes able to arrange a safe house for post that ensures that the family's exact whereabouts remain secret.

Telephone calls to families may be easier with an advocate or a friend present. Emails or texts may be less stressful, and give both parties time to reflect on what is being said – especially when a big decision has to be made.

> Encourage clients to update about their country, however painful. Visit libraries, BBC World Service radio and reliable news websites. Counsellors can share these tasks with their clients. Living in history may be a way in which clients avoiding present reality and this prevents them from processing a traumatic past.

Even when the family is reunited, hopes and aspirations have to be tempered by their current circumstances. Spouses have to make stark adjustments after the initial euphoria. Long separations may have led to new partners and children. Expectations may be mutually unrealistic, leading to significant tensions. The children of refugees may be assimilated immediately into English-language schools but alienated from parents slower to adopt the new culture. Children become unofficial interpreters, translators and advocates for their parents, thus reversing their biosocial roles (see Chapter 4, when we discuss how they feature in interpreting dilemmas).

Case Example

Abia has obtained leave to remain in the UK with her eight-month-old son. She and her husband have been forced to flee their home in Morocco. He ran an illegal website challenging the current government. Both were arrested, tortured and escaped at different times and to different countries. Abia wants to trace her husband in France as he has made no attempt to contact her.

Discussion Points

Why might Abia's husband not have contacted her in the UK?

What are the counselling issues facing this couple if they find each other?

Trafficked people

Vulnerable people are not always refugees. There are many women and children in developing countries, in Eastern Europe and in the old Soviet Bloc, who have been coerced, bribed or lured to the West with false promises of wealth. They end up as prostitutes, sex slaves, domestic servants or machinists in illegal sweatshops. They share as much of the refugee experience as those who have faced state persecution. They need safety, the protection of the law, housing, education, social services and employment opportunities. Counsellors will see them usually when they have just emerged from being trafficked – and at a point of transition. The fear of being found by their pimps, their suppliers, or even their husbands, dominates their emotional landscape, and, again, counsellors must attend to issues of risk both for their client and themselves.

Case Example

Leila, recently settled in the UK from Bosnia, is referred for counselling assessment following a history of arrest and abuse in the Balkans and arrives in the waiting room. Beside her is a large, unsmiling man who immediately stands up and introduces himself in good English as the client's husband. He states that he would like to help you by attending assessment. Your client looks at you appearing fearful but eventually nods and says that she would like him to attend. What is your response, and what are the risks?

Practice Points

Give Leila, your client, time on her own first. Ascertain if she is there of her own free will, and if she feels safe.

Find out if she wants her husband in. Allocate an amount of time to both of them, and give her time on her own again afterwards, noting any changes in Leila.

Trafficked people have entered their host country illegally and will have a story to tell. Counsellors need to understand this and not judge the truthfulness of their legal status.

However, when you meet a credible witness, say so, but reassure the client that you are not part of migration control.

Terror, torture and post-traumatic difficulties for refugees

Not all refugees who have experienced violence develop PTSD (d'Ardenne et al., 2005). A significant proportion of those exposed to life threat develop mood disorders especially depression and anxiety, as well as PTSD. All need additional support and help with using the resilience they may have developed in the past to help them with their new lives in the host country. The Medical Foundation for the Care of Victims of Torture (www.freedomfromtorture.org) and the Helen Bamber Foundation (www.helenbamber.org) are human rights organisations that offer a range of services, including counselling, for those affected by torture. Refugee people who have been tortured, however, may need justice more than therapy.

Post-traumatic difficulties including PTSD and depression are common. One transcultural issue for refugees who have experienced trauma is that distress is expressed through cultural norms. For example, *shame* may be as much a characteristic emotion for a victim of rape as fear or anxiety (Gilbert and Proctor, 2006). The counsellor can update personal knowledge through continuing professional development (CPD, see Chapter 9), users' groups, refugee networks, supervision, the media, personal study and reading.

Refugees who suffer PTSD, including intrusions, hyperarousal and avoidance can benefit from traditional Western exposure therapy (Ehlers and Clark, 2000). This involves revisiting the past in some detail, but with additional reassurance and support. There is evidence (d'Ardenne et al., 2007c) that refugees, with or without an interpreter, both achieve alleviation of PTSD symptoms with this approach, but do not fare as well as non-refugees. Refugees may be isolated from their communities and may not have sufficient emotional support at home. Their fears or re-traumatisation may be from having been questioned about their past so many times by the police, lawyers and migration officials. Young (2009) gives an extensive description of how these barriers can be overcome in four stages:

- Attending to the client's primary needs such as safety, medical treatment and housing, as recommended by the National Institute for Health and Clinical Excellence (NICE, 2005)
- Processing traumatic memories, by revisiting them in some detail, updating them with the counsellor and placing them into a more accurate biographical context
- Challenging unhelpful self-appraisals, such as being powerless or not surviving
- Increasing levels of meaningful and pleasurable activity in the present.

Young (2009) shows that testimony about torture, for example, can be constructed gently over a number of sessions, together with updating of any unhelpful appraisals (e.g. 'I deserved it'). Testimony is audiotaped and the client is asked to listen to all tapes between therapy sessions and to update memories that may be reactivated during exposure.

Narrative exposure therapy

Refugees who have been exposed to multiple and extensive traumatic events as a result of war, civil conflict or organised violence, particularly where they continue to live in insecure environments, may benefit from a slightly different approach. There is now evidence (Mueller, 2009; Robjant and Fazel 2010) that *narrative exposure therapy* (NET) – a short-term intervention developed in refugee camps, is at least as helpful as traditional revisiting and exposure. It involves emotional exposure to the traumatic memories, and the reorganisation of these into a clear chronological story. The traumatic story is thus embedded into autobiographical contexts, and this allows the integration of 'cold' verbal memory with 'hot' memory – inducing sensory, cognitive, emotional, physiological and motor responses related to the trauma (Brewin et al., 1996; Ehlers and Clark 2000). Narrative exposure therapy's transcultural value is that it can be adapted to specific groups such as children, elders and refugees who have shared a similar conflict. It normalises exposure since story telling is a universal human activity, suitable for people of any background or ability. Furthermore, NET counsellors can be recruited and trained from refugee populations in just six weeks (Robjant and Fazel 2010).

Clients construct a lifeline – a road map of key events in chronological order. The lifeline is made of string/wool and laid on the ground, coiled to show there is a future; flowers symbolise positive events and stones symbolise negative events. The client is then asked to look at a whole life in the present day, and to summarise key events – which the counsellor records – as the start of a more coherent and objective narrative. The lifeline can also be drawn or depicted as a living tree. Narratives can take several hours to compose, with a detailed discussion about key events – with more emphasis on the client's behaviour during story telling than on the meaning of them – as would be done in re-living. The counsellor attends to early life events – often overshadowed by trauma – and comes to understand the cultural and political context of the refugee client. Sessions always end on an event symbolised by a flower. Errors are corrected, and additional updates woven in. The client and/or the counsellor reads out the new narrative – the final version being in the past tense, in the client's preferred language.

Counselling those who are not verbal

Some people with refugee experience have been so traumatised that they cannot or will not speak about their past, and may still require alternative help. But they may have expressive, recreational and artistic energies that could be explored in counselling. Creative arts therapies, occupational therapy, sport, music making, poetry writing, writing, drama therapy and play therapy have all been tried with some good outcomes but the studies have been small (Dokter, 1998). Carr et al. (2012), for example, used a pilot study of 16 traumatised refugees who had received music therapy, employing world music, and showed a reduction in PTSD symptoms. Furthermore, a third returned to the talking therapies that they had initially been unable to use.

Practice Points

Establish the exact contexts in which a refugee declines to speak of the past.

Find out which non-talking interventions or activities could engage the client.

Liaise with other therapists and reconsider talking therapy in the future.

Counselling the perpetrators of violence

Refugees from areas of conflict include combatants and also those who are caught up in violence. Some of these will also have perpetrated violence. War brutalises everybody. Fear of reprisals or revenge, shame and guilt may make disclosure of this very difficult. Refugees might see the counsellor as a spy – and in Chapter 4 on interpreting, we shall see how this influences the choice of interpreter for the client.

Practice Point

It is appropriate to enquire routinely and in a non-judgemental way if violence has been perpetrated. The Life Events Scale (Horowitz et al., 1979) for assessing PTSD has an item that specifically refers to violence perpetrated against others.

It is important to make the distinction between intentional violence and harm done to another either by accident, by neglect, under duress or sometimes by mis-attribution.

The rules of confidentiality must be explained to the refugee before counselling begins. Counsellors disclose only to those who have a legal right to know about the client's past. Issues of harm to the self or others, in the present or future, however, involve risk assessment and may require disclosure, for example under the Child Protection Act (Department for Children, Schools and Families, 2010)

Case Example

Luke is an 18-year-old from Sierra Leone who was abducted and forced to watch his family neighbours being killed by local militia when he was 11 years old. He was taken and forced to become a child soldier for four years before rescue, and now lives in the UK, seeking asylum. He has strong aggressive feelings towards all young black men, and threatens to seek revenge for the murder of his family by planning to kill them. He is referred to you for help with his aggression. He discloses that he is a trained killer and has tortured and killed his kinsmen. He has no concept of duress. Instead, he holds himself responsible for all deaths he witnessed, as well as those he carried out.

Discussion

What are the risks around Luke, and how will you prioritise these?

What additional help might you need?

Practice Points

Set your limits from the start and indicate to the client when you have to inform others who have a right to know. Reassure the client about confidentiality.

Avoid using interrogative history taking, especially with those who have already been questioned and tortured. Direct, closed questions may help you to get the

(Continued)

41

facts; but they are not how people tell their story and leave them controlled by your agenda.

Invite your client to put on the table any weapons being carried at the start of the counselling session. Refugees sometimes have these because they feel insecure or vengeful, unaware of UK law concerning offensive weapons and firearms, which you can explain. Help the client generate a sense of safety, security and self-esteem in other ways, such as learning new skills or making new friends.

Disclosure

Another transcultural issue is around disclosure. Refugees may already have had to give detailed accounts of what happened including their trauma history to many officials and come to see disclosure as leaving them vulnerable. An important question in your counselling practice with refugees should be – who else has heard this story, and for what purpose?

Case Example

Gordana is a Kosovan woman who was granted asylum status after she had been persecuted and beaten up by Serbian forces near her village. Her husband had already fled the country, but she found him later in the UK. She settled in London much less easily than her husband who rapidly learnt English. She was referred for depression and during the history she disclosed that she was repeatedly raped by the militia. She has never disclosed this to anyone, and she begs you not to mention it to her husband, whom you had planned to see during her assessment.

Discussion Points

Why might this client have disclosed to you?

What is your priority for her now, and how can you help her?

Practice Points

Read documents accompanying any referral carefully, because refugee stories are shared with many people who may all have a legal right to know.

Stories will have been tailored to the varying legal and cultural needs of the situation.

Discuss with your supervisor/manager.

Refugees can be kept several years awaiting a decision about their asylum applications in the UK (Harvey, 2000). During that time they cannot enjoy citizenship or have the right to work or take up permanent abode. Some will have been kept in detention centres where they may have experienced further abuse and exploitation. Those who are resident are required to report to the local police station, itself traumatic for those who have been violated by state terror, where all uniforms look the same. At the tribunal, the process is adversarial, meaning that the court will be sceptical and wait to be convinced about the truth of the refugee's story. Inconsistencies, omissions or exaggerations may be seen as proof of lying. In fact there is evidence (Herlihy, 2002) that inconsistent recall does not imply that asylum seekers are fabricating their accounts. Refugees with high levels of PTSD are more likely to give inconsistent accounts if they have a long wait between interviews and are more inconsistent with experiences they judge to be peripheral.

Tribunals are conducted through an interpreter. If the application fails the consequences may include deportation to a country where the refugee believes he or she will again be abused, arrested, tortured or even face the threat of death. In brief, far from being treated like the victim of human rights violations, it is the refugee who becomes the accused.

Discussion Point

How much should counsellors from the dominant culture seek to know about the asylum-seeking process and its possible impact on the counselling process?

Practice Points

Counsellors can write to the Home Office and request that the frequency of reporting to the police be reduced (not eliminated) to reduce the stress on the client.

Any reports for the client that could be used in a refugee's appeal should always make it clear that incomplete or inconsistent stories *are common* in trauma, and do not indicate that the person is lying.

Clients who are credible to the counsellor should be told so and this recorded in reports submitted to a migration tribunal.

If new evidence that is not in the original application for asylum is uncovered, for example that rape accompanied the alleged torture, it helps the client if a psychological explanation be provided that is culturally sensitive. In Gordana's case it might be that the client was too ashamed to disclose to the authorities, or that she feared reprisals because of dishonour.

Counsellors need to communicate what is scientifically known about inconsistencies in stories to their clients' legal representatives.

There are sadly a small number of suicides each year for clients facing repatriation. The counsellor may face threats such as 'I will kill myself if I am sent home', or 'I would rather die by my own hand than face torture again'. There is little evidence that migration tribunals view threats of suicide as a way of persuading them to grant asylum; rather they view such statements as coercive, and may still refuse leave to remain.

Practice Points

The counsellor can encourage the client to reflect on and state more positively what life in the new country offers. For example, a client who has made progress in assimilation, learning written and spoken English and developing new friends or skills, should have this emphasised in any reports from legal representatives.

If a client is unsuccessful at the tribunal, read the judgment carefully with the client.

Discuss the decision with the client's lawyers, if appropriate, and seek any additional evidence that might be useful for appeal.

Encourage the client to stay engaged, calm focussed and hopeful.

Differing values between counsellors and refugee clients

Refugees come from states where human rights are often abused, and may themselves hold the very values they are trying to flee. Counsellors cannot make assumptions that someone who is escaping violence or injustice shares their values. Victims of torture may seek revenge and have murderous intent towards those they hold responsible, or people they think might be responsible. Men whose wives have been raped as an act of war may see them as dishonoured and therefore deserving of being divorced. Worse, their wives may believe that too, and the subject becomes a dangerous taboo. Those who have learnt not to trust the state may perceive all public employees as untrustworthy (Crown and d'Ardenne 1982, 1986; Van de Veer, 1999). These views are complex, autobiographical, culturally and historically positioned ideas that cannot be shifted by a brief cognitive intervention. They require engagement, trust, and patience no different from any other form of counselling (d'Ardenne and Mahtani, 1999; d'Ardenne et al., 2005).

Practice Points

Counsellors use all their professional resources, especially supervision, to reflect their own value base.

The counselling relationship establishes common values. Counselling practice may not be valued, but education, practical help and access to healthcare or social benefits could represent a starting point for collaboration.

Refugees' ideas about accuracy and chronology vary (d'Ardenne et al., 2005). An adult educated in the West who does not know his date of birth is unusual. However, it is more common in nomadic communities where time is understood and valued differently. Diary keeping, appointments and regular attendance for counselling may be difficult for those who have never had to attend to them before. Refugees have to deal with many professional agencies and appointments from the start of their asylum application. It may be difficult for the refugee to understand the bureaucracy, or how to prioritise meetings, for example clinical visits, housing meetings, police registration or attendance at court.

Practice Points

Transcultural counsellors can organise sessions with flexibility over time keeping, such as end-of-day appointments, times when public travel is cheaper, sessions within a school day.

Drop-in sessions may be easier for those whose lives are more chaotic.

In a recent group music therapy trial for traumatised refugees, non-attendance was recorded for the following reasons: police reporting; threat of eviction by the housing department; being offered a place in college; lack of child care; no money for the bus fare to come to therapy; and admission to hospital (Carr et al., 2012). These responses indicated many stressors facing these clients who nevertheless achieved exceptionally high attendance levels and reduced trauma symptoms.

The needs of women

There is exploitation and violence against women universally (Women for Refugee Women, www.refugeewomen.com). Asylum Aid (2011) published a report where women were asked why they had not gone to their local police station after they had been raped or been taken at widowhood by the brother-in-law as part of a tribal tradition. They replied that their stories were trivialised or not believed, and that they experienced extreme shame. There has been more difficulty in group counselling for the female victims of rape than for other problems. Gilbert and Proctor (2006) and Lee (2009) proposed compassionate mind training to provide more opportunities for dealing with women's' individual shame. Rape groups are problematic for individual rape survivors for fear of disclosure and retribution from their community.

Case Example

A Kurdish couple are referred for counselling following their exile and arrival in the UK. During history taking, the counsellor interviews them separately and each discloses that they know of the rape of the wife when their village was attacked by Turkish soldiers. Each is unwilling to share the disclosure because in their culture the shame would lead to marital breakdown and divorce.

Discussion Point

In what way is this different from when the husband does not know about his wife's rape?

What would the implications of divorce be for this woman?

In the UK, there has been criticism (Walter, 2011) of the role of detention centres and the complicity of a wider society that denies benefits and forces women onto the streets. 'It wasn't what happened to me at home that broke my spirit; it was what happened to me here' (Walter, 2011).

Case Example

Baba is from Northern Kenya – an activist and journalist who endured abduction, imprisonment, rape and severe beatings. She seeks asylum in the UK and is detained at a centre where a male member of staff offers to help her in exchange for sex. She initially refuses but is told that she may be deported if she does not yield. She continues in this abusive relationship, but finds that her confidence, and sense of self has been more damaged by this than anything she endured in Africa. She begins to take drugs and slips into prostitution – her hopes of a new life washed away. She is referred for counselling after a drug overdose.

Discussion Points

How is sexual violence used as a tool of sexual and political persecution?

What happens to women who resist?

46

'Honour' violence

The concept of 'sexual honour' implies that the reputation and social standing of an individual, a family or a community is based on the behaviour and morality of its female members – an idea that resided in Western cultures well into the twentieth century. The origins of sexual honour, according to anthropology researchers, came from early man wanting to ensure that the children raised were carrying their father's genes; where men who controlled their women, therefore, came to be seen as leaders. Women every day, as a result of this tradition, are threatened with physical violence, rape, death, mutilation, abduction, drugging, false imprisonment, withdrawal from education and forced marriage by their own families (Iranian and Kurdish Women's Rights Organisation, 2012). Although UK law now bans forced marriages (Forced Marriage (Civil Protection) Act, 2007), there remain many abuses. Estimates in the UK for 2010 were 17,000 (Centre for Social Cohesion, 2010) although this is hard to verify, and the problem is underreported. In 2010, this one organisation took 1,500 distress calls. Crimes of honour violence are not always isolated practices: rather they may be part of a self-sustaining social system. Women's rights organisations have recently reported that police and other professionals do not know enough about protecting women from their own families, who have allegedly 'shamed' them, often by having a relationship with the 'wrong' sort of man (*Guardian*, 21 May 2012). Police and social workers now receive much more training about honour but the topic is politically controversial. In a recent telephone poll of trauma services in Bangladesh one organisation dealt exclusively with the victims of acid attacks – a traditional weapon used against women who had violated their families' ethical code. The Bangladeshi authorities condemn such attacks, and provide support for these women – and have recently trialled an educational programme to prevent such attitudes developing in the first place (Pathan and d'Ardenne, 2010).

Welcoming refugees within a counselling service

Engagement is the first responsibility of a counsellor to the refugee client and there is much that the service can do. Webster and Robertson (2007) found that service users complained of poor access to services, poor communication and the cultural inappropriateness of the service, which they perceived as a barrier to help seeking.

In the next chapter you will be introduced to appointment letters in differ-ent languages and the kind of explanation of your service that refugees require. Services for diverse communities need to provide a safe, welcoming and culturally appropriate milieu. Good practice includes signage in the most common community languages, images and photographs depicting people from BME communities, information and booklets about services in community languages, a separate waiting area for interpreters, appropriate toys and writ-ing materials for children in attendance, separate toilets for men and women and, above all, privacy and quiet for consultation (d'Ardenne and Mahtani, 1999; d'Ardenne et al., 2005). World maps may help refugees to feel wel-come, as will plants or flowers, and ornaments and paintings from around the world. Counsellors can use Google Maps to locate and print out images of remote places where refugees have lived or been persecuted, and which can be a really useful tool to encourage trust, and validate a shared understanding of the refugee experience.

Conclusion

This chapter has shown that the needs of refugees can be addressed by coun-sellors who are mindful of the many stressors faced by such clients in their own country, during migration and in seeking refuge in another culture. It has focussed on the additional alienation, isolation, exploitation and neglect that shames many of our statutory and voluntary agencies. People counselling refu-gees in these services could achieve better outcomes with distressed refugees if they actively sought to understand the refugees' individual experiences, the wider political and social contexts of their asylum seeking, and ways of dismantling the barriers to seeking the counselling help.

Additional resources

Asylum Aid: www.asylumaid.org.uk – 'provides high quality legal representation to people seeking asylum in the UK'.

Iranian and Kurdish Women's Rights Organisation: ikwro.org.uk – help with 'honour' violence in Farsi/Dari, Arabic, Kurdish and Turkish.

Crown Prosecution Service: www.cps.gov.uk – legal website explaining the rights of women suffering crimes of honour and forced marriage under UK law.

Refugee Action: www.refugee-action.org.uk

Refugee Council: www.refugeecouncil.org.uk

Refugee Therapy: www.refugeetherapy.org.uk – providing psychotherapy and associated treatments for refugees and asylum seekers with less than ten years in the UK; training refugees in psychotherapy and counselling, advocacy and administration.

Poppy Project in London: www.eaves4women.co.uk/POPPY_Project/POPPY_Project.php – provides accommodation and support to women who have been trafficked into any form of exploitation.

Unseen (UK): www.unseenuk.org – campaigns against the sex-trafficking industry.

Women for Refugee Women: www.refugeewomen.com – works to ensure justice for refugee women and their children in the UK.

Women's Aid: www.womensaid.org.uk – domestic violence helpline for women and children from diverse backgrounds.

PsyRAS: www.psyras.org.uk – forum for psychologists working with refugees and asylum seekers.

4

USING INTERPRETERS IN TRANSCULTURAL COUNSELLING

First say to yourself what you would be; and then speak.

Epictetus, first century AD

Summary

This chapter focusses on working with clients who need language support, and discusses how to use interpreters. It defines terms, considers inequality in communication, describes the best use of both professional and informal interpreters, as well as telephone interpreting services and advocacy, and their different roles and advantages. An extended case example shows how to engage and assess the language support needs of the client, brief the interpreter before counselling, conduct an interpreted session, and, finally, how to debrief and assess communication. Systemic issues within counselling services are described to ensure that interpreting and translating result in a good outcome.

Introduction

In a restless world, clients increasingly move across national borders and reside in places where they have no or little local language. Our clients have a right to be understood, as enshrined in the European Convention for the Protection of Human Rights (Council of Europe, 1950). Healthcare, including counselling practice, now places both legal and ethical requirements on practitioners to ensure that services be inclusive and accessible to all. Effective work with interpreters, therefore, is a necessary competence for transcultural counsellors. In the UK, training bodies are moving towards including interpreted work as part of their curriculum, such as the British Association for Counselling and Psychotherapy (BACP), the Royal College of Psychiatrists, the British Association of Social Workers and the BPS. In its Guidelines for Psychologists, the BPS recommends that 'working effectively with interpreters should be a skill every psychologist possesses, to ensure equal opportunities are upheld, and extended to diverse communities' (Tribe and Thompson, 2008). There is also evidence that engagement, accurate diagnosis, risk evaluation, treatment and rehabilitation in cross-cultural settings all critically depend on accurate cultural and linguistic exchange (Bhui, 2002).

Interpreted counselling is now on the main agenda but can only take place within overall transcultural sensitivity (d'Ardenne and Mahtani, 1999; d'Ardenne et al., 2005; Tribe and Morrissey, 2004) that recognises difference in perception, priority, the meaning of emotion and the distortions where there is no linguistic equivalence.

Definitions

Face-to-face interpreting refers to any verbal translation, with the interpreter, client and counsellor sitting in a triangle. The interpreter is accountable to the practitioner for two-way verbal communication and non-verbal and cultural communication from the client. Interpreting is provided in short sequential, 'chunks' of speech, rather than simultaneously, and is the most commonly used model (Patel, 2003).

Diplomatic interpreting requires the interpreter to sit closely behind the client, whispering into the ear, while looking directly at the therapist, in the same direction as the client. The client speaks only to the counsellor, and does not turn round. The counsellor holds eye contact simultaneously with the client and interpreter without having to turn her head. This model preserves immediacy and intimacy between counsellor and client (d'Ardenne et al., 2007b).

Telephone interpreting involves the therapist sitting opposite the client, each holding a telephone handset and speaking remotely to the interpreter, who is unknown to them both. It is useful for counselling in brief or emergency situations, when a face-to-face interpreter is unavailable. It guarantees anonymity when a client does not want a third party in the room (e.g. with very small cultural communities) and is useful for initial contacts to establish language support need or to make future face-to-face appointments.

Simultaneous translation/interpreting involves an interpreter converting one language into another only while the speaker is still talking. It is used in international settings and is non-interactive.

Sequential interpreting entails converting two-way but only after a speaker has completed a phrase and paused. It is interactive and slower, and is ideal for one-to-one interviewing.

Advocacy involves a community worker, usually from the same culture as the client, supporting and advising the client and explaining cultural differences and nuances to the counsellor. An advocate may or may not interpret, and may be employed by the counselling service or the local community, but is not usually accountable to the clinician.

Bilingual or multilingual advocates combine the functions of literal interpreting and giving the client a voice, and are recruited from specific communities. They work with clients in their preferred language and communicate with the rest of the service in the dominant language.

Translation often refers to any written work from one language to another, and is characterised by its denotative accuracy.

Back translation is when material is translated again back into the original, to check that the meaning has been maintained from the language of origin. It is usually done by a second translator.

Inequality in communication

In Western settings, the language of the dominant culture holds power over those for whom, at best, it is learnt as a means of integration. But it is never a language between equals. Racism occurs at individual and organisational levels, and may still involve neo-colonial attitudes towards immigrants and those of immigrant heritage. In mental health settings, patients are already in a power imbalance, and face those who care for them in a distressed state, endeavouring to communicate in a language that is not their own. In the words of Bhui:

> Language offers one set of rules that give meaning and form to experience. Clearly the dominant language presents as a force for the propagation of views held by the linguistically dominant group. And so the minorities, where language preferences differ, are silenced and immediately located in a position of non-thought and mind paralysis, until they master the linguistic skills of the dominant group. (2002: 47)

Informal interpreters

Well-intentioned but untrained interpreters tend to summarise what they hear, respond on behalf of the patient and gloss over nuances in language. For example, Tribe and Thompson (2008) provide evidence that untrained nurses used as interpreters can actually lead to incorrect diagnoses, as well as under-referral to counselling services. Sometimes patients request a relative to interpret, who may also be inappropriate as this practice breaks the boundaries of patient confidentiality. Furthermore, interpreting a traumatic history for a relative or friend places an emotional and linguistic burden on that person, for whom the therapist cannot be held responsible (Drennan and Swartz, 1999; Mahtani, 2003; Raval, 1996; Raval and Smith, 2003). Mailloux (2004) and Shackman (1984) argue that responsibility for well-interpreted counselling lies with the clinician who needs to ensure the linguistic competence of an objective interpreter. Trained, professional interpreters in the public sector are ideal, since counselling and psychotherapy demand a high level of fluency and accuracy.

Practice Points

Opt for professional interpreters, even those without counselling or mental health experience. Linguistic accuracy and fluency in both languages trump any knowledge of counselling process.

You can ascertain whether interpreters are professionally qualified through accessing one of the following UK accrediting bodies: Institute of Linguists; National Register of Public Service Interpreting; National Community Interpreting Project and Institute of Translation and Interpreting.

Budget for interpreting. Counselling services need to factor in additional time, effort and money.

Trauma

A common type of client with significant language support needs is the asylum seeker who has been traumatised by conflict, is seeking a better life, but is disabled by the symptoms of post-traumatic stress. In the UK, NICE (2005) recommends the use of interpreters and states that 'language should not be an obstacle to the provision of effective trauma-focussed psychological interventions' (2005: paragraph 2.3.7.3.4). Regrettably, it has yet to detail how this should be done. Some of the counselling cases here will be based on established protocols for interpreting that were designed and published to address this gap (d'Ardenne et al., 2007b). They were devised at a time when some asserted that counselling was a Western therapy that could never be successfully interpreted because its ideas were too culturally entrenched (Summerfield, 2004). These concerns have not been tested and there is no evidence that interpreted interventions are less effective than non-interpreted ones. In the world of psychological trauma, interpreter-mediated CBT works as well for refugees as non-interpreted therapy (d'Ardenne et al., 2007c). Therefore it may be reasonable for readers to gain confidence in this practice, by trying it.

The case below outlines the many aspects of interpretation, including engagement, reliving and working with alternative realities. The entire therapeutic process is not described; rather, the different stages of each intervention where interpreting issues are salient and the prevention and resolution of common difficulties with interpreting are included. Where dialogue is directly between the therapist and client, it can be assumed that interpretation has been literal.

Assessing language need at referral

Amina is a forty-five-year-old Algerian woman who fled her country because she was opposed to the regime, arrested and repeatedly raped for her beliefs. She escaped to the UK and currently lives alone in a hostel, working illegally as a cleaner, and is now seeking asylum. She is highly educated, non-religious, and speaks Arabic, French and some English, according to her referrers. A female friend always escorts her and interprets for her. Her doctor sends her to the local community mental health team after she complains of hearing the voices of her attackers continuing to humiliate her. The referrer's letter also describes depression and extreme shame about the rape. She is sent an opt-in letter in French, which asks about her language needs, and the preferred gender of her interpreter. She specifies that she would ideally like an Arabic-speaking female interpreter.

Practice Points

It is more ethical to ask the client's need directly (Patel, 2003), rather than rely on the referrer's evaluation. Her choice of gender may be critical as she may experience more shame in the presence of a male interpreter or counsellor.

Amina was not explicitly asked in the opt-in letter whether she was willing to work with an Algerian interpreter. Unlimited choice cannot be offered, but sensitivity to ethnic division can avoid potential tensions in counselling.

Friends may be very supportive and escort patients to the clinic, and may attend counselling sessions at the request of the client. However, they cannot, and should not, interpret.

Preparation time with interpreters

Chris, the clinician, books a female interpreter and sends her information on the service, traumatic reactions, and a list of specialist terms. She enquires about the interpreter's background; she is Egyptian and Muslim and has interpreted for many clients from Algeria. They arrange to meet half an hour before the assessment, when Chris briefs her on Amina's background, current situation and presenting difficulties. The interpreter arrives promptly, a young black woman in Western dress with her hair covered with a hijab. Chris has some concerns about religious differences between the interpreter and her client. She also asks her if she has experienced violence herself (she has not) and assesses her English to be of a high standard. Finally, she checks her availability for assessment and intervention sessions over the next three months, and returns to the waiting room while Chris checks her notes and the consulting room.

Chris:	In therapy we shall be revisiting the worst parts of Amina's experiences many times. I need to know that you can interpret calmly and objectively.
Interpreter:	I have heard many terrible stories of killings and rape, and I know I must not interrupt or express any opinions about what has happened.
Chris:	Yes, good. Do you think Amina might worry about your being Muslim?
Interpreter:	Yes, it has sometimes happened before, and I do understand why. I cannot change who I am. But I don't argue because I know people feel very strongly about these matters...

Practice Points

If the interpreter had disclosed personal victimisation, Chris would have sought another interpreter to protect her mental well-being. Chris would act before seeing Amina, and explain that the interpreter was unavailable. Exposing traumatised interpreters to clients' torture compromises treatment and is unethical for all parties.

She allocates enough briefing time and is ready to cancel the session if required.

She also books in ten minutes before future counselling sessions for briefing.

Engagement and assessment

Amina and her friend arrive early and sit in the waiting room opposite the interpreter, who initiates a conversation, eager to put the client at ease. Chris finds all three women in discussion. She introduces the interpreter to Amina and explains that her friend can wait for her. Amina asks if her friend can come in as well; Chris proposes that she joins them at a later stage, but in the presence of the interpreter. Amina agrees to this. Chris then leads client and interpreter to the counselling room. She has set up the chairs so that the interpreter is sitting slightly behind Amina, speaking into her ear while maintaining eye contact with Chris. Amina faces Chris at all times, who then begins to outline how sessions will progress, including confidentiality, length and content. Early on, Chris observes that Amina makes poor eye contact with her, instead looking down or casting glances behind her at the interpreter.

Chris:	Thank you for coming to talk. I was wondering if you find it hard to speak to me with the interpreter behind you...
Interpreter [Arb]:	Chris is wondering whether it might be difficult speaking to both of us, and she says thank you for coming.
Amina [eyes cast down]:	Hmmm.
Chris:	I realise it's difficult and you may be wondering if you can trust us with your story...
Interpreter [Arb]:	She's wondering whether you can trust us with your story.

Amina:	Hmm. [*Pause*] Yes I don't know who to trust. There are so many Algerians in London. I don't even know about anybody else...
Interpreter [Eng] [*shifting uncomfortably*]:	She doesn't know who to trust as there are many Algerians in London and she thinks they are cruel and powerful. She's not sure about other nationalities. But we're not all the same I am Egyptian and I feel the same as she does.

[*Amina turns back and stares at the interpreter.*]

Chris:	Amina, I need to speak directly with the interpreter so please excuse us a moment...
Interpreter [Arb]:	She wants to speak to me on my own.
Chris [*looking at interpreter*]:	Thank you for helping today. Please remember to speak in the first person, and interpret exactly and only what you hear...not, 'she says' but 'I say'. Please do not add anything about yourself. OK?
Interpreter [Eng]:	Of course!
Chris:	Amina, thank you for being patient. We have agreed how to interpret your words more accurately. People have treated you badly, so I can see how difficult it is to know whom you can trust. [*pauses*]
Interpreter [Arb]:	[*Interprets word for word.*]
Amina:	[*Looking at Chris*] Thank you for explaining what is happening. I want to learn to trust people.

Practice Points

Chris could have given a fuller briefing to the interpreter on confidentiality and self-disclosure, in the consulting room, the waiting room and outside.

The premise of counselling is that clients work on their own beliefs, not those of the interpreter.

If there is space, consider placing the interpreter in another waiting area, or keep the interpreter in the consulting room, to prevent direct interaction with the client.

It is the therapist who should be introducing the interpreter to the client.

Effective transcultural counselling occurs when client and therapist feel they have communicated directly to each other. Part of this requires the use of the same tense and person, yet interpreters may commonly slip into the third person (Bot, 2005). This can confuse the conversation (Bot and Wadensjo, 2004) and detract from the therapeutic alliance. Chris addresses both difficulties by halting the interpreting process to guide the interpreter briefly. She informs the client of what is happening and then returns to interpreted work as quickly as possible, disclosing what has been discussed.

Initial debriefing

Chris: How do you think it went today?

Interpreter: I felt so sorry for her.

Chris: I guess it's hard to stand back – but that is what I am asking you to do.

Interpreter: But she was becoming too upset to talk about what happened. She just wants to forget!

Chris: I think you were upset and, once you expressed your feelings, it was impossible for me to explore her trauma any further today. Please remember that she cannot forget. We are doing trauma-focussed work here. I realise this is difficult, but it is very important that you do not add your feelings when the client is here. But I am always happy to talk about how you feel once she has left the room.

Interpreter: I will try but it is very hard – especially when I am right here. Today – I felt ashamed at what was done to her.

Chris: Please try and look at me as much as possible during the session – and we can talk later – OK?

Interpreter: Yes, yes, I will try.

Chris might have anticipated Amina's anxiety about meeting Algerians, and discusses how much the interpreter should have disclosed at introduction. She quickly evaluates communication in the first session and shares with the interpreter feedback from Amina, given when she escorted her out of the consulting room. In the debriefing, Chris does not directly challenge the interpreter; rather, she acknowledges that the work is painful, and explains that talking about the past does not mean re-traumatising the client. Chris uses debriefing time to focus on the interpreter's understanding about detachment. Professional interpreters add nothing, change nothing and omit nothing. She repeats the invitation to debrief about these matters.

Interventions

Reliving (Ehlers and Clark, 2000) and compassionate mind training (Lee, 2005) are two interventions for interpreted therapy with post-traumatic problems. How far can they be used with interpretation to achieve an effective outcome? In the assessment sessions and ongoing therapy, it emerges that Amina's worst moments (what is known as an emotional 'hot spot') focus around a mock execution she endured. Chris has devoted therapeutic space to discussing the rationale for revisiting and reliving this trauma in some detail (Harvey et al., 2003), and the client agrees.

In order to prepare, Chris, the interpreter and Amina practice reliving a neutral scene of the client's choice: a walk she recently went on with her friend. Chris emphasises to the interpreter again the importance of interpreting as precisely as possible, including her use of the present tense. She also explains and models how reliving involves interpreting only one or two phrases at a time. Lastly, she speaks in a softer tone, and directs the interpreter to do the same. After spending a session on this practice, the triad move to relive the mock execution.

Amina: [eyes glazed]: They were blindfolding me...

Interpreter [Eng] [quietly]: [Interprets literally.]

Chris [quietly]: Remember to speak as if it is happening now. 'They are blindfolding me.' What do their hands feel like?

Interpreter [Arb]: [Interprets literally.]

Amina: Rough, cold. I can feel them pulling it so tight that my head hurts...And now they are taunting me, teasing me, telling me I am going to die now, and that I deserve it. I am so stupid to fight them. One of them has a really sneering voice. I feel so angry with them. How dare they? They are not men, they are like animals...

[Chris looks at the interpreter, catching her eye and nodding for her to gently interrupt Amina by interpreting.]

Chris [quietly]: Where can you feel your anger towards them?

Interpreter [Arb]: Can you feel the anger in your body?

Amina: My stomach feels like it's in a tight knot, I feel like I'm going to faint...

Interpreter [Eng]: [Interprets quickly and literally.]

Practice Points

The practising of a neutral scene before reliving a trauma helps to reveal and resolve any misunderstandings about the reliving process, for both the client and the interpreter.

The length of interpreted speech needs to decrease during reliving, to maintain *temporal proximity* between client and therapist. At one point, Chris is concerned that this proximity is being lost as Amina goes deeper into reliving her feelings. There is a fine balance here between allowing this reprocessing, while gently interrupting, so that the therapist can connect with the client's experience.

Interpreting during reliving demands discernment from the interpreter and therapist in knowing when to speak. After Chris indicates the need for shorter interpreted 'chunks', the interpreter develops the habit of interrupting and interpreting words quickly so that longer narrative phrases do not occur.

Interpreted reliving involves much more discussion. Clients may also have difficulty imagining being in a different time. Subtle differences, such as speaking quickly and quietly, may help.

The interpreter slightly changes the question about feeling angry to ensure that the metaphor is entirely transparent.

In trauma-focussed therapy, reliving sessions are sometimes recorded for the client to listen to between sessions to help reprocessing of the traumatic memory. Chris has not taped the sessions as Amina's prison interrogations were tape-recorded, and she does not consent. Instead, Chris adapts Narrative Exposure Therapy (NET) (Schauer et al., 2004) for use with an interpreter. She jots down what Amina says during reliving, writing it up afterwards while retaining the present tense and all detail, and she gives this to the interpreter to translate. This version is given to Amina in the following session, to read every day that week. It transpires that the interpreter's written Arabic is not as fluent as her spoken, which impacts on how vivid the account feels to Amina.

Amina can fully describe her trauma, as well as her feelings about herself, including guilt and shame, and the negative self-appraisals and low mood that arise from them. Chris decides that *compassionate mind training* using a perfect nurturer (Lee, 2005) in the presence of the interpreter might be helpful. Neither Amina nor the interpreter has experience of creating imagined people to help Amina reframe her critical thoughts with more compassion. Chris therefore explains the rationale of the nurturer to Amina and the interpreter several times.

Chris: Imagine your perfect nurturer, and when you feel comforted, ask her to change, 'I got what I deserved'.
Interpreter [Arb]: [Interprets literally.]
Amina: Please strengthen me and help me see how special I am. I know you love me. Stay here with me, and accept that it wasn't my fault I was raped.

However, not all of Chris' approaches work as well. In a later session, she re-evaluates Amina's intrusive symptoms with the following question:

Chris: Which memories still haunt you from the arrest?
Interpreter [Arb]: What ghosts visit you from the arrest?
Amina: I see no ghosts! Why do you think I'm mad?

Practice Points

Both reliving and compassionate mind training require clients and interpreters to work in an alternative reality. It is harder in some languages to speak of the world as how it might or could be. Chris uses the interpreter as a linguistic consultant checking what is possible.

This case involves written and oral communication, and it is therefore essential to clarify at the start that the interpreter is competent in both forms.

Chris shares with the interpreter the frequent use of figures of speech. She consults about metaphors and conditional tenses (Bjorn 2005; Fox, 2001; Miller et al., 2005). In the above example she uses a metaphor 'haunt' which gets interpreted literally and is misunderstood.

Chris watches the interpreter carefully to ensure that she does not 'rescue' Amina. She stops interpreting immediately if this occurs.

Endings

At the start of the fifteenth session, Chris receives an answer-phone message (in English) from Amina to say that she has been resettled 20 miles away, and that she cannot continue therapy. Chris arranges a three-way conversation with two telephones and a double jack, and with the interpreter calls Amina. Chris wants to hear Amina speak and assess her mood, as she continues to hold responsibility for the interpreting process (Bot and Wadensjo, 2004). It becomes clear that this therapy ending is unscheduled. Amina and the interpreter become tearful, and start to say goodbye directly to each other on the phone before Chris has a chance to speak. Chris allows this conversation to take place, and then interjects with a request for factual information to enable Amina to get healthcare at her new address. The interpreter is able to regain her composure. Chris persuades Amina to return to her clinic for follow-up once she has settled, and makes sure that the interpreter and Amina are both available.

Practice Points

It may be useful for the interpreter to talk about her feelings with other interpreters working in this area, for example through a peer supervision group. If possible these should be initiated and facilitated by the interpreting or the counselling service.

Chris uses her interpreter to make immediate telephone contact with unscheduled breaks in treatment.

Chris seeks to retain continuity with her interpreter by ensuring her availability for the client's follow-up well in advance.

Audit and supervision of interpreted counselling

Much of what has been described takes place at an individual level, but it would be impossible to provide effective interpreted counselling without consideration of the service and systemic issues. At the very least, clinicians should be able to provide individual interpreters with feedback about their performance after each session. Feedback can also be sent to the interpreting service after each booking, but should also be kept by the counselling service to monitor quality. Interpreting that is well below standard should be reported immediately by counsellors to the interpreting service, and followed up to clarify what caused the dissatisfaction.

Counselling services and interpreting

Many clinical services provide training, supervision and support for their interpreters (Tribe, 1997). Others argue that this is not always practical or affordable when these staff are employed elsewhere. Other models include *quality circles* (held less often but regularly), where interpreters are able to voice their concerns with counselling staff and generate solutions (e.g. regarding waiting room etiquette and privacy). Services can also fund and support the training of clinicians in interpreting as part of their professional development (www. eastlondon.nhs.uk).

Counselling services should keep overall records of who is employed and which languages are used most often, and to what effect. Case-note protocols should indicate that a session is interpreted, with the name of the interpreter and the language used. Such monitoring ensures that more is known about how services are responding to need, and can be matched to provision of other services within the same referral area.

The counselling service is able to establish boundaries around privacy and confidentiality, and relieve the counsellor of direct requests to use relatives and friends as interpreters.

The service can send interpreters booklets about the service especially as psychological work with trauma is counter-intuitive, for example revisiting the memories one most wants to forget. *Understanding Your Reactions to Trauma* is an excellent text because it is written in clear English, and it is the same text used for clients, ensuring that all parties share the same working model (Herbert, 2002).

Finally the service should send its protocols to the interpreting service, and examples of these have been described in more detail elsewhere (d'Ardenne et al., 2007b). Most of all, the service is able to create an ethos that interpreted counselling is an important constituent of its service, and it can enable referrers and service users alike to become aware of this.

Conclusions

In this chapter we have aimed to go beyond what NICE (2005) recommends for the interpreted treatment of trauma-related difficulties. Language does not have to be a barrier but clinicians need a sound knowledge of interpreting principles, coupled with clinical skill in adapting them to suit individual need. In trauma-focussed counselling, for example, specific adaptations included in the above example were:

- temporal proximity within the triad
- reliving past trauma through the first person in the present tense; checking suitable metaphors in the creation of alternative perspectives; translation of clients' written materials; updating interpreted narratives as meanings change.

Interpreting could be tried and modified for use with other therapeutic approaches even within trauma, such as systemic work and group approaches, including creative art therapies. All of these would benefit from interpreting protocols designed for the particular approach. However, interpreted therapy will involve some common principles (d'Ardenne et al., 2007b):

- The counsellor holds responsibility for the quality of the interpreted therapy
- The counsellor has responsibility for interpreters' well-being through briefing, debriefing and feedback
- Individual interpreters, especially those with a refugee background, need not only language skill but emotional resilience and awareness of their own vulnerabilities
- Education of interpreters in the psychological model used assists the process
- Allocation of up to twice as much time is essential.

The additional cost, time, complexity and skills required for interpreted psychotherapy and counselling allow clients their human and legal rights to access effective talking therapy and the benefits that these bring. We have some evidence that shows that patients who need interpreting, but do not make full use of this service, are actually more disadvantaged than those who accept them (d'Ardenne et al., 2007c). Counselling demands a high level of competence in a shared language. Clinicians need to inform their clients of the benefits of interpreted therapy to make the best choice. There remain potential clients, including those whose English is not standard and those with sensory impairment, where an advocate may be more appropriate..

There are also benefits of interpreting for the practitioner and the service (Miller et al., 2005). Counsellors have access to cultural experts in the room who can provide invaluable background information about clients and their social, economic and political circumstances. Some have described the utility of a third party bearing witness to the client's story (Miller et al., 2005). Pauses in verbal communication (in sequential interpreting) allow for attention to non-verbal signs, time for reflection and written recording. Although therapy can seem slow, there are no empty moments in interpreted therapy. Nothing, however, will work as well as good preparation, briefing and debriefing, which must be structured and costed to existing services to ensure good-quality interpreting (d'Ardenne et al., 2007b).

Some of the common difficulties in using an interpreter in counselling have been raised, but not all issues have been covered and readers are recommended to seek further guidance (e.g. d'Ardenne et al., 2007b; Raval, 1996; Tribe and Morrissey, 2004). There is a wider literature of cross-cultural papers defining good practice and ethical imperatives, not necessarily supported by any evidence. This chapter represents a first step in achieving these aims for interpreted trauma work. Good practice, however, will invariably develop as more clinicians undertake interpreted therapy and test the contents and limits of current guidance.

5

RELIGION AND SPIRITUALITY
IN TRANSCULTURAL COUNSELLING

Let no one persuade you to cure the head until he has first given you his soul to be cured, for this is the great error of the day, that physicians first separate the soul from the body.

The Dialogues of Plato

Summary

This chapter considers the ongoing relevance of religion and spirituality as an important aspect of cultural identity. It refers to both clients and counsellors as potential believers, as well as those specifically providing pastoral counselling across cultures. All sections suggest main resources or good practice examples in major religious beliefs and describe seemingly contradictory values within and across cultures. Issues for personal reflection and supervision are identified. Of note, assessment of religious beliefs is important for providing relevant services across cultures, and avoids stereotyping, mis-labelling and inappropriate interventions.

Introduction: distinguishing religious affiliation from spirituality

There is a current trend to refer to religious affiliation and spirituality in the same phrase, but they are different, and the counsellor needs a practical model.

Religion is the way people organise their ways of relating to what they hold to be sacred and transcendent (Hawes and Eagger, 2011). Koenig et al. (2001) suggest that the distinction between religion and spirituality lies in religion referring to an explicit attachment to a named faith. Grayling (2009) asserts that a religion has to have not just a belief in the supernatural or transcendent; there also has to be a practice in response to it with differing traditions and doctrines. Christianity, Judaism and Islam emphasise a personal commitment to and relationship with God, comparable with that of a king or lord. As the world has grown more self-aware, religion now resides within the wider family of spirituality.

Spirituality arises from something internal: a personal quest for understanding and meaning around the big questions of life and death (Koenig, 2001). A person may be spiritual but not religious. It is possible to have a sense of one's place in the universe and how to relate to it, without reference to a higher power. Spirituality involves a broader range of experiences, where individuals place their belief in a power apart from their own existence. Spirituality includes organised or conventional religions, as well as those who have intuitions about the meaning of life, but who may be baffled by traditional theology and dogma (Gregory, 1989).

Self-definitions

The British Social Attitudes Survey has shown that the proportion of people who define themselves as Christian has been declining in its many denominations in the UK for the last 30 years (66 per cent to 43 per cent); non-Christian religions have slowly begun to increase (2 per cent to 5 per cent); 62 per cent never attend a religious service, yet 52 per cent agree that 'Britain is deeply divided along religious lines' (McAndrew, 2009).

In the UK, the Mental health Foundation (Faulkner and Layzell, 2000) surveyed mental health service users; over half interviewed said they had a spiritual belief that was important to them. When asked to describe the role that spiritual and religious beliefs had in their lives, their responses included: the importance of guidance; a sense of purpose; comfort; the permission of expression of pain; the development of inner love and compassion for others.

Hawes and Eagger (2011) note that as the UK becomes increasingly diverse, many users will move across cultural boundaries and move between faiths, or from belief to unbelief, and then back to belief when a crisis occurs. They conclude that spirituality and religion are dimensions of culture, and need to be addressed as part of transcultural practice.

A taboo topic

With the decline of formal religions in the West, modern psychological theory has given individuals charge of their own destiny through (so-called) rational means (Coyle and Lochner, 2011; Dawkins, 2006; Grayling, 2009). Dawkins, in particular, questions why intelligent human beings persist in holding beliefs incompatible with empirical evidence. Freud saw religious behaviour as neurotic; but more modern psychoanalysts have challenged this, and applied psychodynamic ideas to religion and spirituality in more integrated and positive ways (Coyle and Lochner, 2011).

It is not so long ago that religion was something of a taboo subject with practitioners too. Those who studied psychology at secular universities were expected to keep any opinions about religion to themselves, and personal faith was not discussed in professional settings. Similarly, clients' faith, their spirituality and their religious affiliations were not routinely explored by counsellors. There was an unspoken anxiety that such questions would be perceived as too intrusive, only explored if clients themselves raised the topic. Needleman and Persaud (1995) concluded that clinicians were not competent to deal with 'theological' issues and that these were best left to experts. Whatever the barrier, the client may or may not have been religious; but the status of counsellors, unless they were pastors or chaplains, was always presumed to be secular, dispassionate and sceptical.

Foskett (2003) carried out qualitative research on the experience of Somerset's mental health service users. The spiritual insights of mental health patients were routinely pathologised, ignored, condemned and, in some cases, attempts were made to remove or alter these beliefs. He concluded that in such circumstances, spirituality may not be the proper business of psychiatrists. There appears to be a professional reluctance and lack of psychiatric training that fails to integrate spiritual care for mental health service users. The situation has been compounded by the distress of users being unable to ask for what they want, or to defend the spiritual 'self', which may be greater than their experience of mental disorder. It may be that counsellors who have no knowledge of religious matters could pathologise behaviour not understood within its religious context.

Psychologists have also distanced themselves from religion. Collicutt (2011) identified the following barriers, listed by trainees, to the study of religious behaviour and thinking:

- credibility from other mental health colleagues
- religion not central to human life
- trustworthiness – practitioners may be driven by their own religious biases
- diversity – too much unknown about non-Christian traditions
- students of religion often in theology departments and separated from psychology and counselling traditions
- psychology careers do not advance as a result of interest in religion
- methodological and conceptual underdevelopment of religious studies.

Discussion Points

Do these issues relate to your training, supervisory, research or clinical practice agenda?

How might they change for transcultural counsellors in the future?

Case Example

Chantelle, of Dominican heritage, works for her local Catholic church in London. She has a history of childhood sexual abuse from one of her uncles, which she has not disclosed to anyone since moving to the UK two years ago. One of the local churchgoers makes inappropriate sexual advances to her that she resists. She then responds by becoming very quiet and reading her Bible for most of the next day. She informs her parishioners that she has had the devil chase her and that only prayers will make her pure again. When other church members try to help her, she becomes more agitated, and eventually discloses her history and the incident to her priest. She also asks for the 'devil' to be cast out of her. The parish priest is concerned and thinks that her mental health is beginning to collapse. He wants her to be referred for counselling.

Discussion Points

Can the counsellor establish what is normative religious behaviour within this community or faith tradition?

Practice Points

Establish Chantelle's trust to allow a full history and disclosure.

Use Chantelle's religious resources in your formulation and psychological intervention.

In the above case, there may remain significant differences between Chantelle's personal interpretation of religion and its meaning within her faith community. The counsellor needs to access the client's interpretation and draw on personal resource. For example, Chantelle may be able to use prayer as a form of grounding and church attendance as a source of social contact. The *Guide to the Major Religious and Cultural Observance in the United Kingdom* (Home Office, 1998) warns readers that the observance of cultural norms and adherence to religious beliefs is a very personal matter and generalised assumptions about a religion can be misleading.

Spirituality in the wider world

There has been a great sea change, perhaps precipitated but not caused by developments in the Muslim world. In Northern Europe formal religious activity may be in decline. However, Watts (2011) reminds us that elsewhere in the world, religion is immensely important, and that practitioners who work transculturally ignore religion at their peril. And it is not just about Islam and the

West. Religion is universally of huge cultural importance and merits academic study. Estimates at present are that in the world there are 2.1 billion Christians, 1.6 billion Muslims, 900 million Hindus, 376 million Buddhists, 23 million Sikhs and 14 million Jews (*New Statesman*, 18 April 2011). Watts (2011) argues that we also need to study atheism, spirituality and non-religion since they all incorporate ideas about truth and transformation for individuals, as well as their wider communities. Estimates are of at least a billion Humanists world-wide – secular people who seek to promote well-being and propose that God is a human creation from a pre-scientific age.

Equally, clergy may not be fully trained in modern psychological and counselling theories, although exchanges are better in the USA, which has a longer and stronger tradition of religious faith and practice, and religion and mental health training. There has been a significant literature in pastoral counselling, and more recently CBT and religion, demonstrating the importance of incorporating religious belief into assessment and intervention. Koenig (2007) provides a brief overview of this field. William James, a secular founder of American psychology, had a fascination with religion from his agnostic standpoint, and dealt with such questions that counsellors might still find useful to consider today (Miller 2003):

- Why not study spirituality?
- Can we measure religious belief?
- Is it proper to do it?
- Is it a priority for counsellors and psychotherapists?

The impact of religious prejudice on well-being

The United Nations Declaration of Human Rights (Article 18, 2005) states:

> Everyone has the right to freedom of thought, conscience, and religion; this right includes freedom to change his religion or belief, and freedom, either alone, or in a community with others and in public or private, to manifest his religion or belief in teaching, practice, worship and observance.

The United Nations recommended that the WHO definition of health should be modified to recognise that religious and spiritual practices are inher-ent to individual and collective health and well-being. It notes that 'because prayer and religious and spiritual practices around the world are so commonly a response to illness, that mental health researchers have a responsibility to investigate it' (United Nations, 2005).

Spirituality is now referred to in a wide range of health policies around patient care, dignity, community and personalisation (*Our Health, Our Care, Our Say* (Department of Health, 2006); *Putting People First* (Department of Health, 2007); *No Health without Mental Health* (Department of Health, 2011)). Curiously, neither the BPS nor the BACP specifically refer to the impact of religious prejudice and persecution on well-being. There is, however, a British Association for Christians in Psychology – that aims to integrate religious and psychological beliefs (www.bacip.org.uk). The Royal College of Psychiatrists has a special interest group in psychiatry and spirituality (www.rcpsych.ac.uk). The American Psychological Association (APA, 2007) has adopted a policy on religion, religion-based or religion-derived prejudice. Specifically, prejudice based on or derived from religion has been used to justify human rights violations against those holding different religious beliefs, those who profess no religious beliefs and other individuals and groups, depending on perceived theological justification or imperative. The paradoxical feature of religious prejudice is that religion can be both the target and the victim. The right of a person to practise religion or faith does not and cannot entail a right to harm others or to undermine the public good.

Functional and dysfunctional religion

Loewenthal and Lewis (2011) provide evidence that those who believe in a punishing, vengeful or indifferent God tend to have a poorer mental health outcome than those who believe in a benign, supportive deity. Those who derive social support from their religion also do better within their faith from a mental health standpoint – such as individuals with depression (Loewenthal, 2007). But other suppositions about religious stress have not been confirmed. For example, psychotherapists and counsellors have often posited that religion fosters guilt, which in turn raises levels of anxiety, depression and obsessive–compulsive disorder (OCD). But measures of guilt in Christian, Jewish and Muslim traditions are not good predictors of psychopathology – as there are many confounding factors. Greenberg and Witztum (2001) conclude that religion offers a cultural arena for the expression of a disorder, but does not of itself cause or foster that disorder. Similarly, Tek and Ulug (2001) looked at Turkish Muslim people with OCD and found no relationship between religiosity and OCD symptoms. Once more, religion was the cultural expression of the disorder, not its cause (Loewenthal and Lewis, 2011).

And what of spirits, voices and visions? Again, many world religions encourage such experiences and beliefs. Angels, demons, or jinns occur in all of them and there is widespread belief in benign and malign spirits, but no evidence that they either cause or foster psychosis. Dein and Littlewood (2007) describe their questionnaire results with 40 members of an English Pentecostal church. Twenty-five reported an answering voice from God, with 15 hearing Him aloud. The latter groups were interviewed in more detail to understand the phenomenon and context in which the voices were elicited. They concluded that the voice of God is not of itself pathological and described its utility to the participants in situations of doubt or difficulty. So, what is the difference between a religious and a psychotic experience? In psychosis, it has been claimed, that the voices and demons are more unpleasant, more unwanted and more uncontrollable. Peters et al. (1999) and Davies et al. (2001) have all found that psychotic phenomena are more unpleasant, and more persistent than anything that might be described as a religious experience.

Case Example

Waseem is a devout Muslim living in East London. His family has noticed that he spends increasing amounts of time in the night at his prayers. Also, he will not go to bed until he has performed a range of rituals in his family's kitchen, which he believes has become contaminated by outsiders. If he does not perform the rituals, a bad spirit will enter the home. His family is very worried and asks Waseem to speak to the mullah. The mullah reassures him that his beliefs are praiseworthy but not warranted. Once he engages him, he suggests that he might benefit from further professional help with those he knows and trusts. He refers him to a local psychotherapy service, who liaise with both the authorities at the mosque and a local Muslim community organisation for new ideas and resources.

Practice Points

The mullah does not confront or challenge Waseem. Rather he is respectful, affirms his position in faith, but at the same time suggests that his response has been too fervent.

The mullah maintains good contacts with local mental health services and recognises how and when to make referrals.

The service is secular and mainstream. It seeks new learning about Islam and other religious traditions within its catchment area.

Discussion Points

How does a counselling service develop good local cultural knowledge?

What other resources might be of help to Waseem?

The study of religion in psychology and counselling

Barrett and Burdett (2011) provide a model of the cognitive science of religion that combines methods and theory from cognitive, developmental and evolutionary psychology. It tackles four big areas of research on how human psychology informs and constrains religious expression; these include teleological reasoning about the natural world, children's acquisition of concepts of god, minimal counter-intuitiveness theory, and religion and pro-sociality. They have yet to identify whether their model is applicable within or across cultures. Differences in populations studied may have been due to study design rather than actual cultural differences. Universal religious thinking may be present and can be addressed in transcultural counselling practices (Barrett and Burdett, 2011).

Religion and health

Mueller et al. (2001) reviewed the association between religious involvement and spirituality and physical health, mental health, health-related quality of life and other health outcomes. They also reviewed articles about clinicians' assessments and their support of the spiritual needs of patients. Results showed that religious involvement and spirituality are associated with better health outcomes, including greater longevity, coping skills and health-related quality of life (even during terminal illness) as well as less anxiety, depression and suicide (Culliford, 2007; Long, 1997; Merchant, 2006).

The role of religion and spirituality in transcultural counselling

Counselling employs models about personal choice and responsibility, which is encouraged in some religious traditions, but not all. This has been problematic where individuals attribute their distress to malign spiritual forces, but there is evidence that this attribution presents itself in and across many cultures (Bhugra and Bhui, 2007).

Many of the world religions teach that life is determined or ordained, and that individuals must submit themselves to the will of God, or the gods (Coyle and Lochner, 2011). Cultural and religious beliefs are very resilient to environmental stresses and change, and provide their adherents with an historical context in which to place their personal experience of loss, uncertainty and lack of meaning in their lives. This process can buffer individuals from stress. It is also true that religious beliefs can be part of the problem, and create additional stressors, for example where religion is used coercively, or incites guilt or hatred of others.

The events of 11 September 2001 in the USA were followed by a wave of Islamophobia in the West. The subsequent 'War on Terror' and conflicts in Iraq and Afghanistan radicalised young Muslims, with the effect of creating division. But it would be dangerous to reduce these divides simplistically to Islam in the East and Christianity in the West. Political, cultural, economic and neo-colonial factors all contributed to that split. For example, in many African states, Christian and Islamic communities share values that they perceive the West as having lost. Traditional faith communities understand the modern world as afflicted by alcoholism, substance misuse, sexual promiscuity, marital breakdown, teenage pregnancies, violent crime, social inequality and tolerance of what they see as sexual deviance.

In cross-cultural settings, religions and their distinguishing names remain identified causes of major conflicts – such as Israelis (called Jews or Zionists) versus Palestinians (called Islamists); Unionists (called Protestants) versus Nationalists (called Catholics) in Northern Ireland; and Sunni versus Shia Muslims in Iraq and Iran. In these examples people's political and cultural allegiance is labelled *by their faith*. Additionally, terms such as 'infidel', 'heathen' or 'gentiles' are used by those within a religious identity to define the out-group, with additional personal, cultural and political meaning.

Greenwood et al. (2000) showed that the term 'Asian' was problematic, as it failed to distinguish religion and culture, which were often very different. In their study they found that inappropriate and alienating services occurred because cultural assessment had overlooked religion.

But the tide is changing, and religion is less of a taboo subject. Just as there is now a trend to capture ethnicity in census data so there is an increased interest in faith communities with their cultural, educational, economic and health requirements (including counselling). The 2011 UK Census (ONS, 2011) asked about respondents' faith and faith practice. This was included following the Opinions Survey that has been used since 2007 to test new migration questions that included within ethnicity new language, national identity and religion questions. Most of the 1,200 respondents were happy to answer these and able to do so accurately (ONS, 2011: 3.3.4). In addition, specific stakeholder meetings included the British Sikh Federation, the Board of Deputies of British Jews, the British Humanist Association, Stonewall (www.stonewall.org.uk) (a leading UK gay rights campaign), and the Cornish and Kashmiri communities (ONS, 2011: 3.2.3). Critics of the questions observed that 'no religion' was merely one option, instead of it being the default position for most of the current UK population (*Guardian*, 25 March 2011). This may be true, but for the majority who put down a religion (72 per cent) most saw it as part of their cultural and social tradition – even if what they actually believed was subject to doubt (ONS, 2011).

Religious factors in help seeking

Transcultural counsellors deal with the social and psychological impact of referrals from religious communities, especially in mental health settings. One of these factors relates to those who have lost faith and been identified as suffering from *religious trauma syndrome* (Winell, 2011). Those severing connections with a faith and faith community, especially one that is restrictive or mind-controlling experience psychological trauma. Where individuals break out from a religion, they may experience relief from repressive codes of conduct and are able to make better sense of the world with less guilt and confusion. But set against that is the loss of social support, a coherent world view, meaning and direction, spiritual satisfaction and structured activity.

Another religious factor affecting help seeking is that of *stigma* (Loewenthal et al., 2007). Typically, close-knit religious groups may see such a referral to counselling services not only as shameful for the individual and his family, but also as a failure of the faith community to deal with its own distress.

Case Example

Yaakov is a 24-year-old man from the Hasidic Jewish Community of East London, referred to your community mental health service for counselling following panic attacks when he goes out into the local streets. He does not attend the first two appointments; he arrives the third time, escorted by his wife who speaks Yiddish to him in the waiting room. He sits with his head bent low; she is tearful and appears ashamed of her husband and the referral to your services.

Practice Points

Assess the patient alone and then with his wife present, observing how his presentation changes.

Identify their understanding of mental disorder within the context of Jewish faith. Identify resources that might help you with this young couple, for example local rabbi, Jewish community welfare groups.

Assessment

There are a number of protocols for how to ask about spirituality, including the HOPE Questionnaire (Dein, 2010), which covers the following domains:

Hope sources, comfort, strength, peace love and connection
Organised religion
Personalised spirituality and practices
Effects on healthcare and end of life issues.

Hawes and Eagger (2011) and Gilbert (2011) have listed specialist assessment tools used by chaplains, which are more formulaic and comprehensive. For counsellors, standard principles of good practice require the creation of a therapeutic space where client and therapist can feel comfortable in raising and exploring religious and spiritual issues. Pargament (2007) recommends basic exploratory questions:

- Do you see yourself as a religious or spiritual person?
- If so, in what way?
- Has your problem affected you religiously or spiritually?
- If so, in what way?

Mayers et al. (2007) suggest that patience is required because religious clients believe they will be judged negatively by their therapist. The therapist needs to be mindful of this when engaging clients in a transcultural setting.

Religious conflict

Mystical and psychotic experiences may be blurred in the mind of the client, but the counsellor may approach these in a number of ways (Clarke, 2001). Options include the following:

- approaching the religious experiences within its cultural meaning
- liaising with a relevant religious practitioner – priest, rabbi or imam for their perspective
- reframing the problem within religious beliefs where the practitioner has personal knowledge
- discussion with supervisor
- the use of self-help literature.

There are negative impacts of religion in the counselling relationship (Hawes and Eagger, 2011). Religion can promote an overdependence on rules, overlooking personal autonomy. In addition, beliefs that God is punishing or neglectful can be damaging (Pargament, 2007), whilst those trying to escape risk religious trauma syndrome, already described (Winell, 2011). Users who are religious may delay seeking mental health support, or refuse medical or psychological care because they believe that their faith should sustain them. Religious cults, themselves the object of specialist mental health interest, can promote excessive dependence on key individuals and alienate new recruits from family and society (Hawes and Khan, 2011).

In the UK public sector counsellors are often very restrained by the number of sessions offered. But religious and spiritual conflict can still be identified for further action after counselling is completed. Counsellors can ask about faith conflict, and its impact on their clients' problems as seen here.

Case Example

Robert was brought up in Nigeria as a devout Methodist. Since coming to the UK he has lived with a woman who is not his wife. He was referred to a counselling service because of his alcohol addiction, and during assessment he discloses that he no longer feels able to stay within his faith community because of his circumstances, but he asks you if you will pray with him. You are a counsellor who happens to be a practising Christian. You recognise the support that his church has provided him in the past, and want him to find resources that will help him achieve sobriety.

Training and Supervision

Coyle and Lochner (2011) refer to the need for counsellors and psychologists to receive training and supervision in religion, spirituality and therapeutic practice. Trainers and supervisors need knowledge and sympathy about the religious and spiritual needs of the clients. Today, any counsellor asks routinely about spirituality, and will benefit in supervision from a reflection of how faith is expressed and understood across cultures. Counsellors themselves do not have to have faith to do this; but as with any other cultural dimension, they can work out their personal position with their supervisor and trainers. In this process, counsellors can identify misconceptions, prejudices, ignorance and areas of conflict about any of these topics and address them in CPD (see Chapter 9), as well as with the client in session. Training topics could include: the culturisation of religion; the religious meaning of impurity; the role of fasting and abstinence in religion; the concept of personal responsibility, sinfulness and guilt; religious attitudes towards heterosexuality, homosexuality, the roles of the sexes and reproductive rights; and religious understanding of distress and mental and physical health.

Case Example

You are a counsellor who works in a busy sexual health clinic, seeing a distraught 19-year-old Argentinian woman for pre-termination counselling, following an unplanned pregnancy. She says she has not disclosed this pregnancy to anybody else. She describes herself as a 'bad Roman Catholic'. She expresses guilt about her planned termination and also the view that the foetus is viable. She says, however, that she is desperate to proceed with the termination and that a pregnancy would ruin her career and marriage prospects. She then discloses that she will have to go to confession afterwards to tell her priest about what she sees as her unlawful action, so that she can be forgiven for what her faith tells her is killing an unborn child. She says she will then be reconciled to God. She brings no partner and does not intend to disclose who he is.

Distressed people of faith will not necessarily seek help from professionals. Bangladeshi mothers were more likely to seek help and support from religious leaders than health professionals (Hanley 2007). Here is a case from East London.

Case Example

You are working with a Bangladeshi mother in a maternity unit who is about to give birth to her eighth child, and who has requested a sterilisation after the birth. She indicates that her husband does not know about this request and that it be kept confidential. She says he would be very angry with her because such a procedure is contrary to their Islamic faith. Your client's gynaecologist (himself Muslim) believes there are good medical and social reasons for carrying out this procedure but is unhappy that the patient's decision has not been shared with her husband.

Pastoral care

Spiritual and pastoral care leaders and chaplains have well-adapted psychological models when working with distressed believers (Gilbert, 2011; Hawes and Eagger, 2011). They also argue that spiritual care is the responsibility of all who work in the caring professions, and can be incorporated into existing models of care or as a stand-alone service. They argue that chaplains can be part of a multidisciplinary team addressing the whole needs of the client.

Spiritual/religious assessment enables the identification of the needs of diverse communities. Cultural beliefs influence coping style and attitudes to care. Service users perceive treatments as authoritarian and disrespectful when their perceptions are not taken into account (Bhui and Bhugra, 2003). Clients want and seek to be understood within their spiritual framework. Malik (2000) and Cinnirella and Loewenthal (1999) have all undertaken qualitative assessments of users' religious beliefs and mental illness, and identified how prayer helps them to cope with depressive and psychotic experiences, as well as how community stigma results in individuals seeking private coping strategies. Their participants covered a wide range of BME backgrounds, including Judaism.

Conclusions

The request for a spiritual aspect to assessment, therapy and care has been strongly made by service users and their carers, as part of a larger movement focussing on empowerment, resilience, cultural identity and recovery. It is only in recent years, however, that counselling has undertaken to explore it routinely within the counselling relationship (Lago and Smith, 2010). Loewenthal (2007) observes that specific spiritual beliefs and practices are not uniform in any culture. Gender, age, education and life experience are just as likely to shape religious beliefs as being brought up in a specific religious tradition, and some of the case examples have demonstrated this. In addition, with some exceptions, the advantages of religion outweigh the disadvantages, although it has not yet been shown how these may be harnessed for long-term mental health and well-being. However, when the counsellor is unfamiliar with religious traditions and practices then there may be unreliable and socially stigmatising psychiatric and psychological diagnoses, and poor clinical decision-making. Religious coping behaviour has so far been judged to be psychologically beneficial, but it needs to be differentiated from signs of psychological distress. Longitudinal and epidemiological studies that are informed by cross-cultural knowledge would help in the understanding of this (Loewenthal and Cinnirella, 2003). But the implications for counsellors are clear: update your knowledge about the religious practices and beliefs of the communities you serve; ensure religion and spirituality are integrated into the transcultural assessment of need and resource; and examine your own beliefs and attitudes about religion through supervision and CPD.

6

TRANSCULTURAL COUNSELLING

IN HEALTHCARE

Summary

This chapter addresses how and where the practitioner counsels diverse patients to the benefit of their health outcome. Readers can update their transcultural knowledge, and how this combines with counselling activities, in a range of health settings, from cradle to grave. The counsellor is shown how to make key alliances with families and cultural communities to manage symptoms and lifestyle, promote well-being and adherence to health treatments.

Introduction

When I first worked in East London in 1977, I heard the following true story.

Case Example

An unaccompanied Somali mother, who spoke no English, was seen in accident and emergency when her four children had been seriously injured in a house fire. The medical staff needed to communicate with her urgently to obtain permission for life-saving surgery on one child. Sadly, the team also needed to inform her that the other three children had died. There were no relatives and no interpreter available, nor was any member of staff Somali speaking. Hospital staff felt obliged to find a waiter in a local restaurant who agreed to act as an informal interpreter, breaking the bad news of this tragedy. Soon after this incident, that same hospital installed extensive signage in community languages. It also appointed advocates from the many local communities to support and defend the rights of those entering the UK health system, including those from Somalia.

Discussion Points

Who was responsible for this scenario?

How could it have been prevented?

Being unhealthy places a person nearer to social exclusion, and being socially excluded leads to further health disadvantages, which any healthcare system must address within the United Nations Declaration for Human Rights, Article 25 (OHCHR, 1949). Patients from BME communities have specific healthcare and communication needs that are not always met within the dominant culture, and that can aggravate poor health and place patients at risk. In a restless world, counsellors have a specific role to ensure healthcare staff and service users recognise this circular problem and engage all their resources to break it. Healthcare includes health education and health promotion, which themselves may be a more culturally acceptable point of access to transcultural healthcare as the following case demonstrates.

Case Example

You are a counsellor working in an NHS substance misuse team for young people from many ethnic backgrounds in South Birmingham. After service audit, you notice that a certain community never refers to your service, but you are convinced it has needs. You visit a local youth club, which confirms your views, but the leaders there suggest that it would be better to try to prevent substance misuse problems occurring. They propose that you access their young people in school settings as a first step to addressing their potential difficulties.

Discussion Point

Why might certain communities not use statutory substance misuse services?

Practice Points

Discuss the response of the community with your line manager.

Work out the stakeholders at the local schools and how you might approach them.

Seek a culturally acceptable and effective intervention in school by partnering with the local community.

Evaluate the intervention and share it with the community organisation.

Sexual healthcare

Across cultures, there are very different beliefs about sex and sexual heath, sexual behaviour, sexual orientation and sexually transmitted diseases (Bhugra and de Silva, 2007). Health advisors and counsellors working with diverse populations need to understand what these beliefs are and, most importantly, how that affects health compliance and the prevention of communicable disease. The role of counselling here is not to change belief systems, but rather to use an understanding of a specific cultural belief to generate a solution with the patient, family or community that meets health needs and does not place the patient at further risk.

Case Example

You are a health adviser in a sexual health clinic and your patient Marie, has been given a diagnosis of HIV. Marie has a husband and you would like to speak to both of the couple about safe sex. Marie is adamant that he will not come into clinic. She says that he accepts her diagnosis, but believes he cannot be infected by her, because a 'real' man in their culture (Congolese) cannot contract HIV from a woman. Your are appalled and frustrated by the situation, and try harder to persuade her to bring in her husband. You show Marie pamphlets describing HIV transmission, and she reluctantly agrees to read them at home, and leaves the session. You worry, however, that she may never return.

Practice Points

Your priority is to keep this patient engaged with your service.

Keep your views about medical evidence distinct from your patient's cultural beliefs.

Avoid confrontation and seek shared solutions within their cultural framework.

Discuss immediately with your supervisor.

D'Ardenne and Mahtani (1999) argue that the values and beliefs of the counsellor may prove to be a barrier to health gain, where the counsellor from the dominant culture needs to:

- accept, acknowledge and understand the client's culture
- examine the effects of any prejudice on the counselling relationship
- consider how Western models of disease undermine the working alliance and outcome of treatment (p. 46).

Examples of differences between two cultures that would need be addressed in the above case include:

- the relative importance of traditional values
- the differing obligations the counsellor and client have towards Marie's husband
- the use of scientific versus intuitive understanding
- the differing roles of women. (d'Ardenne and Mahtani, 1999)

It is beyond the scope of this text to explain all cultural attitudes towards human sexuality, but others have tried to do this. How sexual attitudes are determined by ethnicity, age and gender has been quite literally mapped out by a senior policy advisor to the WHO (McKay, 2000). The maps cover sexuality, including homosexuality, choosing your partner, reproduction, infertility, sexual health, the business of sex – pornography, prostitution, sexual tourism and trafficking, sex crimes and sexual rites – including circumcision and female genital mutilation. The facts are all correctly sourced and enable the reader to have a starting position before seeing the client. Although there is no substitute for asking about individual history and sexual history, factual information from such an atlas might serve as a point of discussion with the client on a sensitive topic. Introducing some generic material can also provide an opportunity for your clients to tell you more about how their attitudes or practices have evolved. Individuals in transcultural counselling are in a dynamic situation, where beliefs are changing and colliding with others. Global or national descriptions can only be the start of the journey.

Pregnancy, childbirth and obstetric care

Pregnancy and childbirth is a huge transition for most women – even more so when this is done in another country with different values and understandings about the process. It is evident that those counselling families through genetic and fertility advice, contraception, antenatal care, childbirth and postnatal care are likely to be obtain better trust, understanding and treatment compliance by taking an anti-racist, culturally sensitive and patient-focussed approach. Families from BME communities have high birth rates in the West. There is evidence, however, that there are cultural, racial and language barriers to BMI mothers accessing services. The National Institute for Health and Clinical Excellence (2011) recommends that the first antenatal appointment should be at eight to ten weeks into the pregnancy. In repeated studies (Avon NHS Trust, 2008; Confidential Enquiry into Maternal and Child Health (CEMACH) 2007; Downe et al., 2009) BME women, recent immigrant women, single women and those belonging to disadvantaged backgrounds were more likely to:

- recognise their pregnancy late
- book antenatal care late
- be less satisfied with the quality of care
- incur higher obstetric risk.

Services where there are small numbers of BME mothers are in danger of being complacent or overlooking the problem altogether. In areas where there are significant numbers of a minority ethnic community – the use of *health advocates* has been a tried and tested means of engaging women to approach healthcare in the first place. But using advocates can never substitute for a pro-active transcultural approach to health counselling.

Mothers from BME communities have specifically requested:

- translation and interpreting services
- better clinical administration
- more midwives from diverse communities
- direct booking access to a community midwife or multilingual midwifery registration centre.

Maternity services have also recommended:

- assertive follow-up for non-attenders
- active outreach through community bases
- escorting BME mothers to other hospital appointments
- offering drop-in antenatal clinics
- involving fathers in routine antenatal care
- use of bi-lingual maternity support services. (CEMACH, 2007)

Refugee mothers have additional needs where a sanctuary outreach midwifery service improves access to care, obtains a named midwife for each mother throughout pregnancy and supports the whole family by signposting them to other refugee services. Postnatal refugee mothers also have specific health and mental health needs. A significant proportion have PTSD. In a recent audit (d'Ardenne, 2009) on a mother and baby unit in East London, traumatised refugee mothers cited intrusive thoughts, anger and poor concentration, irritability and sleeplessness.

Clinicians noted their concerns about traumatised refugee mothers:

- emotional numbing
- substance misuse
- poorer bonding with the baby
- reduced social contact and activity
- dissociation and accompanying risk, e.g. forgetting the baby in the street.

New refugees mothers with PTSD did not have a decreased pain threshold, but the severity of their PTSD symptoms was associated with the number and duration of intrusive procedures. What appears to have helped their psychological needs included:

- engagement, trust, safety and confidentiality
- education and stress reduction, e.g. relaxation or grounding exercises
- risk assessment including identification of risk antecedents
- sharing with parents all evaluations and use of interpreters/advocates
- acquisition of safety behaviour(s), e.g. seeking help and not lifting baby
- use of community resources and networks, e.g. self-help, playgroups and English classes
- involving the whole family in a shared trauma history.

Sick children

It has been estimated that 10 per cent of children in Western populations suffer from some kind of chronic health condition – affecting the poorest, the most socially excluded and those from BME communities (Newacheck and Taylor, 1992). This figure is rising for certain conditions, such as asthma and obesity, making unique demands on parents and professional staff required to listen, support and assist in management. Parents cope with acute and long-term health issues, behavioural and developmental difficulties, congenital abnormalities, life-threatening disease, injury and the death of a child. Counsellors can help families map out their explanations of illness, for example 'it may be an accident of nature', 'it is our fault', 'it is the price of our sins'. From these they can find a shared understanding of management and disclosure.

Attitudes towards and beliefs about sick children are interpreted in part by the family's model of sickness, which has social as well as medical meaning. For example, the meaning of a sick child may be that it represents a punishment for the parents, or it is the will of God, or that it is a curse, or a stigma or a sign of genetic weakness. It is worth bearing in mind that in the West, it has been only in the twentieth century that parents could regularly expect to be outlived by all their children, a situation that still remains to be achieved in much of the developing world (d'Ardenne and Morrod, 2003).

Case Example

You are a nurse practitioner working with a family, caring for a five-year-old girl who suffers asthmatic attacks. Her mother, Arundhati, is very anxious and believes that the asthma is a sign of weakness that runs in the family. On questioning, she reveals that several other members of her husband's family in India have also had this diagnosis. You are concerned, not just because you do not share this belief, but because it might undermine Arundhati's capacity and motivation to manage her daughter's attacks. Her beliefs appear to make her even more anxious and when she reaches crisis, she is unable to comply with any health advice you and your team have to offer.

Mental healthcare

Chapter 1 looked at the impact of racism on our understanding of mental distress among different ethnic and cultural groups in the West. Within mental healthcare settings, we see higher rates of black people, especially young men, who are detained within secure psychiatric settings, or who are detained under the various mental health acts (Fernando and Keating, 2009). Healthcare practice now requires ethnic monitoring (Department of Health, 2005), which has at least allowed us to see if UK public services provide for all members of the community in an equitable way. Ethnic monitoring of staff also allows the public to see that health staff are representative of all communities, particularly so in mental healthcare. This is an area where alienation and exclusion directly impact upon the quality of life of patients and their carers (Bhui, 2002). All white mental health teams can take big steps to change their practice and the quality of services they provide to diverse communities (d'Ardenne and Mahtani, 1999).

Chronic illness

There are certain long-term illnesses that have a higher incidence in some ethnic communities. For example, *thalassemia* and *sickle cell disease* are inherited blood diseases that affect 3 per cent of the world's population, but especially people originally from the Mediterranean, Middle East, North Africa and Asia (WHO, 2012). It is their social and cultural meaning, therefore, that has to be understood by anyone offering prenatal or genetic counselling to couples who may be carriers of these diseases, and who, although themselves asymptomatic, may face a lifetime of caring for a child with the illness.

Long-term illness requires a much greater understanding of processes and systems, which are themselves culturally embedded. Counselling for people suffering long-term illnesses or impairment and their carers and families has now been recognised as a useful way to help those people live with their own disability and that of others. Seigal (1997) draws our attention to the needs of counsellors to examine their own attitudes to disability and illness, and considers some working principles.

The use of language should reflect the fact that patients with illness are firstly people. Only a generation ago, people were defined by what they suffered from. Consider how terms such as diabetic, epileptic, asthmatic, bronchitic, haemophiliac were, and regrettably still are, used as nouns to refer to people suffering from these conditions. Worse, the names of illnesses are still used as terms of abuse, e.g. 'spastic', 'mong' or 'leper'. Thus, people become reduced merely to their illnesses, and no more so than in the realm of mental health. In the *Daily Mail* (24 March 2009), we see a photo of a young black man with the headline, 'Schizophrenic who killed Jonathan Zito set to be moved from high security prison'. The victim of the killing has a name; the sick person has only a diagnostic label, a visual racial identity and the emphasis on his being a threat to others.

Discussion Points

Are there equivalent abuses in other languages and cultures?

What is the impact of labelling on clinicians, families and sufferers of chronic illness?

Practice Point

The next time you hear or read about epileptics or psychotics, challenge the labels.

Illness as a collective experience

Illness affects whole families and social networks, not just the individual. In non-Western cultures, individuals may be defined more by who they are in their community, and an illness may thus be more shared, with greater meaning for all. Here is an example.

Case Example

A large and voluble Bangladeshi family enter a psychosexual clinic waiting room one day, accompanying a nervous young couple being assessed for their infertility. This couple had been married for three years and not produced a child. This was not only of great concern to their parents, siblings and uncles; it had in a profound sense become everybody's 'illness' too, and a source of shame in their community. Rather than dismiss the family as being too intrusive, the clinic staff invited everybody into the consulting room, and listened to their anxieties, engaging them in the process. The family was asked not to remonstrate with the couple as this was adding to their anxiety, and aggravating the husband's premature ejaculation - the primary source of their infertility. This was done by also ensuring that all the family contributed to giving the couple space, time and privacy. The couple was then able to undertake an adapted form of Masters and Johnson Therapy (d'Ardenne, 1986) at home, with a good outcome.

Practice Points

Even sex and pregnancy are not entirely private matters. Respect the anxieties of the couple's relatives.

Use the concerns of the extended family to positive effect by engagement and sharing of information.

The *meaning* of the illness or disability is as important as the illness itself. 'Why me?' 'Am I cursed?' 'Am I being punished?'. Illness and in particular disability are both biological and social constructions. For example, if I lose my hand, I am impaired. If I cannot write, I am disabled by that impairment. If I am taught to use my other hand, or a computer, I become less disabled. The cultural meaning of illness may include stigma, for example the British Royal Family 'losing' Prince John from epilepsy in 1920. In some parts of the world, such as Uganda, epilepsy may be seen as a sign of witchcraft – where it is called 'ensimbu'.

Practice Points

Clarify the emotional, cultural and practical needs of the patient with long-term illness and the family by active listening.

Remember that disease information and management, such as diet, exercise and lifestyle changes, may require the patient and his family or community to work in a health alliance – and that they are capable of sabotaging health gains.

Locate and then encourage the patient and family to use self-help groups – especially where there is a cultural or anti-racist focus. Support groups for specific diseases usually have websites; ethnic communities may also offer help with disability through advocacy, interpretation, health information or regular group support. Visit them and find out about their work if you habitually refer to them.

Ageing, health and racism

The populations of the West are ageing; those of developing nations remain proportionally younger (*The Economist*, 2010). Ageing correlates negatively with health, but it correlates more highly still if you are male, black, poor and living alone. There is statistical evidence (from the Census in 2001 and 2011, ONS, 2001, 2011) that black people have higher mortality rates at lower ages than their white counterparts, even if gender (women still live longer in the West) and class (middle classes still live longer) are taken into consideration. All of these biological and social factors interact and are always changing. There is a cross-over effect whereby more black people die earlier of the same diseases than their white counterparts, although epidemiologists have not been able to explain why a hardy core of black people of advanced old age have survived in significant numbers. Poverty in old age is stressful; it erodes personal resources and distracts individuals from attending to symptoms and developing strategies for encroaching sickness and death. This picture is compounded by loss of occupational role, social isolation, loss of mobility, bereavement, anxiety and depression (ONS, 2009). People aged 65 and over account for just under half of all NHS hospital and community health services use and expenditure (ONS, 2009).

The counsellor in health and social settings remains mindful of risk and the prevalence of the many issues regarding health preservation for people already disadvantaged through alienation and racism. Furthermore, even though services for later life may be staffed by a diverse community, they may not be specifically geared to the cultural or ethnic needs of patients (Department of Health, 2005). Readers might like to visit *The King's Fund* database for a useful selection of smaller studies in this field that have not been widely published: http://kingsfund.koha-ptfs.eu

Case Example

Kathy, 75, from a rural community in Ireland, was being counselled by her nurse for help with her symptoms of epilepsy and becoming more and more hopeless. Eventually she announced it would be no use returning to counselling because her illness was a punishment from God for having 'abandoned' her first child as she had given up an illegitimate baby for adoption. The nurse responded by giving Kathy biological evidence that several of her ancestors had the same illness that pre-dated the adoption. Kathy responded by insisting that the whole family were cursed and there was nothing to be achieved by talking.

Practice Points

The clinician would be able to engage Kathy more if she listened to her grief about having abandoned her child.

The clinician's model of epilepsy prevents her from hearing Kathy's view of her illness within her life story.

If Kathy gives up on counselling, her health risks may increase.

Death and bereavement and culture

Counsellors now work in accident and emergency departments to support the recently bereaved, as medical and nursing staff may not be adequately resourced for this kind of work. Counselling services for dying and bereaved children are now better established (Rees, 2001), but the cultural and spiritual needs of adults are still neglected. Hospital chaplains of different denominations are expected to address the spiritual needs of adults, sometimes after violent deaths, with unknown cultural implications. Laungani (2005) provides a comprehensive account of world religions but, even here, there is information that could not possibly be remembered by counsellors in practice.

Practice Points

You can learn generic approaches to death by reading, updates and by asking the communities that you serve.

Updates have to be done as part of your professional practice (see Chapter 9). Do not wait for emergencies. Be prepared.

Readers who are contemplating a career in health services should study differences in attitudes to sickness, dying and grieving (Waller, 2002). Whole texts have been written on differing cultural interpretations of death and dying for health professionals, many of them analysed through world religions.

Murray Parkes et al. (1997) argue that although the West has made immense scientific and technological advances in healthcare, it remains uncertain about grief and mourning. Much can be learnt from the rituals and beliefs of traditional cultures. They have to be seen within their psychological and historical contexts, and importantly for transcultural counsellors, how these customs have changed since contact with the West. Rosenblatt (1997) makes the point that in exile, many smaller cultures are forced to abandon rituals, have lost contact with elders who understood the etiquette of dying and forgotten funeral rites, with the subsequent loss of meaning and additional stress for the bereaved. The multiplicity of beliefs and rituals around the dying and the dead meet the emotional needs of adherents, and have a symbolic truth that extends beyond reason. Murray Parkes et al. (1997) neatly summarises it:

- Western secularism is essentially rational and distrustful of strong emotions. Industrialised cultures try to ignore death but may engender more problematic grief
- When death occurs, contemporary culture has no schemas to make sense of it.

Practice Points

Counsellors and other carers would work better in transcultural settings if they brief themselves on culturally different beliefs about dying, for example Murray Parkes et al. (1997); Rees (2001).

Counsellors can help the bereaved to find meaning in dying.

Rituals allow the grieving to signal the passage of time and move to a new life.

Cultures vary significantly in the amount of emotion it is appropriate to express.

Conclusions

Counselling in healthcare has known benefits to the client. Illness is a social and cultural construct as much as an objective medical phenomenon. It is subject to diverse and dynamic influences that require counsellors to update and check cultural knowledge from a variety of sources. The most reliable of these are likely to be clients themselves, although this chapter has highlighted a few resources and websites that would be a useful addition to professional learning.

Health gains are greatest when the patient forms an alliance with their immediate families and communities. This is particularly the case with long-term healthcare where changes in behaviour, attitude and lifestyle have to compete with long-cherished cultural beliefs, such as eating or work patterns. Treatment compliance can be assisted or undermined by those who live with the patient, who also have to be considered as service users in healthcare. In referring on, counsellors need to review the competence of the new agency in understanding the cultural meaning of the illness and what a new referral means to the patient and family.

7

THE VOICE OF USERS IN
TRANSCULTURAL COUNSELLING

Then they came for me and there was no one left to speak out for me.

Martin Noemüller

Summary

This chapter covers the development of clients as service users in transcultural counselling. Client satisfaction and self-help are described as steps to empowerment. It then shows how users have become people participants, patient experts, peer support workers and mental health champions, all with unique cultural knowledge and skill, who can work with the counsellor to alleviate distress. Users now work within the wider User Movement to inform policy, assist research and change care systems locally, nationally and internationally.

Introduction

The nature of all counselling is that of a relationship based on respect and active listening, with implicit assumptions made by the counsellor that the voice of the client has been heard, which is not always the case, as we have seen, in transcultural settings. Counselling services have for many years attempted to hear the voice of their users by carrying out regular confidential *client satisfaction* surveys (Chang, 2005), with questions carefully balanced between the counsellor and the service, as well as between the quality of the counselling relationship and the reduction of symptoms or distress. The results of such questionnaires are offered as proof of the desirability and effectiveness of counselling, with interesting results. The only other source of client information has been through investigating the communities that refer clients.

Client satisfaction

Mallen et al. (2005) looked at cross-cultural counselling satisfaction for clients in an online survey. They found that clients from minority groups and expatriates prefer online to face-to-face counselling. They reported feeling more at ease in their own homes and were less intimidated than with the counsellor seen in the office. The authors do not address why minority clients should feel intimidated in the first place. Neither did they refer to the outcome of the different counselling interventions.

Ewing (1974) looked at the satisfaction of black and white clients with black and white counsellors and found that although black clients preferred black counsellors, there was no relationship between ethnic matching and clients' overall satisfaction with the counselling outcome.

These results show at least that there is a distinction to be made between process and outcome, and that users of services always make that distinction, when thinking about satisfaction. However, reported high levels of satisfaction may be the result of users having low expectations of mental healthcare (Katsakou et al., 2010). Another reason may be that users do not feel empowered to express criticism or dissatisfaction with those on whom their well-being so heavily depends. There is no evidence that counsellors disfavour those who complain; but from the position of the user it may be hard 'to bite the hand that feeds you'. This power imbalance is further aggravated by institutionalised racism, where BME clients may perceive white counsellors as being increasingly powerful (Lago and Smith, 2010). Furthermore, the clients do not themselves design the questions. Counselling services would be better placed in seeking to understand their clients and collaborating with them to design such surveys on shared issues.

Practice Points

You and your service can place an explicit and positive value on user involvement.

Your service can advertise with local BME users' groups.

You and your service can invite these groups to design and carry out satisfaction surveys independently of your service.

Satisfaction with the service, the counselling experience and changes that occur as a result of counselling all need to be distinguished.

Self-help and empowerment

In counselling, the power imbalance between clinician and client does not guarantee full collaboration or mutual respect. In psychological therapies, *self-help* literature abounds (important examples include: Greenberger and Padesky, 1995; Rowe, 2003). Self-help literature often precedes counselling, but can be used very effectively for clients who are in the habit of reading and learning. Clients are expected to do homework between counselling sessions and to become as well informed as possible about the issues that confront them. Black and minority ethnic clients too have many opportunities to search online, or through their local libraries to access self-help texts. These texts inform and inspire, and clients find it very palatable to read at home in their own time.

Practice Points

You can ask your clients if they have read anything that inspires them or with which they identify.

You can develop a library for yourself and loan these to your clients on the basis of what you both agree is currently needed or enjoyed.

Self-help can come in many forms – including novels, TV shows, films, theatre, videos, music, art and websites. All of these allow the client (and the counsellor) to explore other worlds and cultures, and help them to make meaning of their day-to-day experiences.

Examples

- Many young black women find the poetry and personal struggles of Maya Angelou provides them with confidence in the face of great tribulation (Angelou, 1995). One client has memorised her poetry; another keeps print-offs on her fridge, which she says gives her hope when she feels depressed
- A young Nigerian who was traumatised as a child in the Biafran War of Independence was unable to face looking into her personal memories. But she was willing to read a novel recommended by the counsellor – *Half of a Yellow Sun* (Adichie, 2007) – that described the war in some detail, within a fictional context. This self-help activity enabled the client to distance herself from the events while still visiting the bigger picture. As the counsellor had read and recommended the text they have a shared experience while enabling each to consider a war that took place over 40 years ago in a very different cultural setting
- An Arabic-speaking client was being seen for depression and it became clear he was unaware of what was currently happening in his home country of Mali. He was recommended to tune into the BBC World Service (www.bbc.co.uk/world-service) and Al Jazeera (www.aljazeera.com/) to update himself. Self-help gave him access to information that he could listen to in his own time, and in Arabic, and make records to bring back to the counselling session. From this exercise he could 'unfreeze' his memories and input newer information, as well as face the losses he had endured as a refugee.

User participation

In the chapter on healthcare, those suffering specific illnesses such as thalassemia and sickle cell disease, prevalent in BME communities, have developed users' forums and recognised the empowerment that comes from such membership. These forums also share culturally specific information, and target the isolation, barriers and prejudices that sufferers experience. For example, many UK and US mental health services in the public sector have *people participation programmes*. These are aimed at giving users, including carers, an opportunity to contribute to the services on which they depend. Service users are also now involved in making systems work better for them. For example, people participants for mental health services in the East London Mental Health (www.eastlondon.nhs.uk) are invited to:

- assist with the recruitment and selection of staff
- train staff in understanding the users' perspective; contribute to audit and research – especially by interviewing other users; make use of language skills to help with non-English-speaking service users – perfect for users with community skills; actively contribute to the planning and development of culturally appropriate services; provide an insider's role in the development of mental health policies.

Case Example

Ashti is a Kurdish woman referred to a large counselling service in West London following the break-up of a violent marriage that left her traumatised and without self-confidence to return to her job as a waitress. Towards the end of her counselling, she was invited to be a service users' representative where she was able to provide the service with useful cultural and interpreting advice for their Turkish and Kurdish clients. Eventually she undertook basic mental health training and was able to obtain employment as a mental health users' advocate for a neighbouring borough. The experience of being a participant patient gave her the confidence and motivation to seek employment for the first time since her marriage break-up, and she began to achieve full separation and independence from her troubled family.

Discussion Point

What general benefits would BME clients have to gain from user involvement?

Practice Points

Establish who takes responsibility in your service for engaging with users' groups.

Identify how your transcultural service would benefit from user expertise.

Patient experts

An interesting way of empowering ongoing users is to encourage them to become *their own experts*. The expert patients programme (EPP), originally piloted by the

NHS in 2002–2004, was based on the Chronic Disease Self-Management Programme (CDSMP) (www.expertpatients.co.uk). Since then EPP has been successfully piloted and rolled out in primary care across England. In 2005, the UK Government pledged to increase investment in EPP followed by a Department of Health paper: *Our Health, Our Care, Our Say: A New Direction for Community Services* (2006). In April 2007, EPP established its own company with the principle of individual self-management and self-care as a recognised public health measure, deliverable in a cost-effective and sustained way. So far over 80,000 people have attended an EPP course and 1,700 people have been trained as tutors. New products, approaches and research findings have shown positive outcomes for people living with long-term conditions who attend a self management course.

Expert patients benefit in the following ways:

- By identifying and developing self-knowledge they use less medical and nursing time
- They describe increased self-confidence, better communication and overall improved quality of life
- They develop increased mindfulness and from that work out new strategies for managing symptoms like pain or reduced mobility
- Their evaluation and sharing of information motivates them to continue looking for published research on their condition and interventions to improve it (e.g. through library/internet searches), which they are then able to discuss with professionals
- Patients diagnosed with chronic physical illnesses can acquire extensive information about their condition, apply specialist knowledge, share it with other sufferers, outreach and support new sufferers, and engage professionals more proactively and collaboratively.

Discussion Points

Could any of these principles be applied to transcultural settings?

Could any of these principles address mental health issues, including stigma?

The User Movement

Clients are now beginning to identify themselves as a group that has grown in recent years into a movement to find action and purpose. Since the 1980s (Rethink Mental Illness – www.rethink.org; Comic Relief – www.comicrelief.com) there has been a cultural shift towards consumer power in mental health, which has gained prominence in ways that could not have been previously imagined. Since the last century there have been groups of patients and professionals, critical of mental health services (Wallcraft and Bryant, 2003). By the 1980s, local groups of patients met for mutual support and information exchange. Thus, user involvement was formed with national and international connections, and began to use the media. The US survivor movement (Chamberlin, 1988) involved consciousness raising and support with publications and newsletters. At about this time the over-representation of black people in UK mental health services, and the failures of the systems to support them, became a specific concern to both service providers and users. Since then four significant user networks have been formed for mental health:

- UK Advocacy Network – 300 outlets giving information and supporting users and carers (www.u-kan.co.uk)
- Survivors Speak Out (SSO) for users and professionals (www.survivorsspeak-out. ning.com)
- National Voices Network (NVN) 500 members – previously within the National Schizophrenia Fellowship (www.nationalvoices.org.uk)
- Hearing Voices Network: ten groups nationwide developing ways of coping with hearing voices and raising awareness in others (www.hearing-voices.org).

The Sainsbury Centre (Wallcraft and Bryant, 2003) recently researched the User Movement within mental health by a postal survey of 318 UK users groups and found the following:

- Users are an identifiable movement, rather than a selection of users' groups, sharing common values and objectives
- The movement provides support, help with recovery, relapse prevention and active participation in service planning and development
- The User Movement shares information on benefits and discrimination
- Women are well represented but have significant and specific needs
- BME clients are *not well represented*. Some networks are reaching out positively and are organising user-led activities
- There is no national forum, and there is little financial resource or political will (currently in 2012) to make the User Movement more permanent or powerful.

The authors (Wallcraft and Bryant, 2003) conclude that statutory services, including professional counselling, need to invest in local user groups. They argue that a national User Movement needs developing as a matter of urgency. Black and minority ethnic clients need focus and support either for their own groups or for a higher profile within the movement, and national good practice guidelines are required for all service users.

Case Example

In the UK the Afiya Trust (www.afiya-trust.org) has directly challenged the Government's omission to highlight the over-representation of BME communities, more likely to be detained in the mental health system, and still without access to talking therapies. It produces research and disseminates information to service providers and liaises with government to ensure that BME users' issues remain on the national agenda. Most importantly, it incorporates the views of service users and carers as well as service providers in its 'work to reduce inequalities in health and social care provision for people from racialised communities' (Afiya Trust, 2012).

Other developments of the User Movement include: National Survivor User Network (NSUN: www.nsun.org.uk); Race on the Agenda (ROTA: www.rota.org.uk); as well as government initiatives that are now faltering – such as No Health without Mental Health: A Cross-Governmental Health Outcomes Strategy (Department of Health, 2008, 2011); New Horizons: A Shared Vision for Mental Health (Department of Health, 2009); and Count Me In (www.countmeinonline.co.uk). Count Me In is the only UK census that includes all in-patients in mental health and learning disability services, and focuses on improving access to care – from a race equality and social justice perspective.

Practice Points

Find out if your organisation has user involvement guidelines.

Failing that, find local agencies that have user guidelines.

Locate local users' groups – especially those with a BME focus.

Visit these groups and evaluate their impact.

Develop a reciprocal referral pathway with users' organisations.

Across the world

In recent years, there has been a surge of user and self-help movements in many parts of the developing world, where access to professional services has been much more limited. The advent of mobile and smart phones and the internet has made peer support and communication across continents easier to organise. More importantly, the human rights agenda has given fresh impetus to clients believing that they need to know and do more for themselves. Fernando (2010) has described how the User Movement has empowered those in Sri Lanka to tackle the many inequalities that affect those who are detained against their will, as well as those who have no access to services. Users' groups, victim support groups and survivors' websites have all enabled those who use services to meet other users and to form a range of alliances, including the provision of support and counselling services.

In South Africa, the South African Depression and Anxiety Group (SADAG – www.sadag.org) has tackled the stigma of mental distress through education, advocacy and awareness training, and has established working alliances with mental health services. They do this by referring to professionals and requesting professionals to send clients back for ongoing support, crisis intervention and counselling. One invaluable service they provide is a free medication reminder SMS service for patients diagnosed with mental illness requiring medication.

At a global level, the International Alliance of Patients' Organisations (IAPO – www.patientsorganizations.org) is working to raise the profile of the patient voice, in partnership with all stakeholders. 'The teeth that are together are the ones that are able to bite the meat. It is essential that we work together as patient advocates and healthcare stakeholders in Africa to strengthen the patient voice and achieve patient-centred healthcare' (IAPO, 2011). They are ambitious – being the only patient-centred organisation for users and carers in 50 countries, representing 365 million people worldwide. They now collaborate extensively with the European Patients Forum (EPF, 2012) and WHO. Travis et al. (2004) have even suggested that the fifteenth grand challenge for global public health – something more powerful than any drug or technology – is access to health information for all (especially users) throughout the world.

Case Example

In a recent study of severely depressed asylum seekers undertaking group therapy in London, the participants began to form close bonds within the group – exchanging mobiles, travelling together, helping with babysitting, and beginning to share each others' stories outside the therapy room. Because the trial had not fully anticipated this as an outcome, there was initial concern about confidentiality and even exploitation from some within the group. The clinicians' and researchers' fears were unfounded. At follow-up, relationships had been maintained and developed into supportive friendships that exist in the present.

Practice Point

In designing research protocols, the power of the client to form alliances with others should be anticipated and understood. These alliances are not competing with professional input.

Counselling requires a holistic perspective that does not separate clients from a culture of *user resilience* and empowerment – processes that need to be better researched and understood (see Chapter 10).

Case Example

The Heartsounds Project part of the work within the East London Global Health Partnership enables users, or champions, of mental health to learn from each others' experience and share cultural and practical links between East London and Uganda (Heartsounds, 2012). People with personal experience of difficulty have been transformed from victimhood to championship through the support and engagement of this fast-growing User Movement. Heartsounds has empowered those who are triply disadvantaged – by poor mental health, stigma from within their communities, and limited services and wealth in a developing country. It has recognised that all mental health service users have a right to be heard. It has undertaken a range of initiatives that included an exchange between UK and Uganda users to understand better how patients are treated and supported. Other initiatives have included running a café within hospital grounds, hosting workshops on rehabilitation, engaging the local press in its work and story telling. When asked what would improve the situation for service users in Uganda, Heartsounds' director, Joseph Atukunda, replied: 'Psychosocial support should be taken seriously to supplement the medical approach, otherwise the service users are caught in the vicious circle of relapses' (Atukunda, 2011).

Practice Points

The value of work and economic activity features strongly in this user initiative and is key to relapse prevention and mental well-being.

If you have been a service user yourself, consider joining the movement and encourage your clients and colleagues to do so.

If you are aware that there are none locally – speak to the relevant stakeholders about how to start one.

Specific advantages of the User Movement for transcultural counselling

Many potential service users cannot access care because of institutionalised racism. Those seeking help from their communities may find users' groups their first and only access to support. The fact that there is still not enough BME representation in counselling services or in users' groups does not mean that the User Movement is inappropriate; rather that the hurdles to empowerment are greater and need to be understood and negotiated – ideally within a client's own community. Users who have experienced racism are able to share these experiences and learn from each other in terms of coping and fighting back.

In developing countries, users' groups may be the only ongoing counselling or mental health resource because economic and logistical difficulties limit services. Pathan and d'Ardenne (2010) carried out a telephone survey of trauma services across Bangladesh to locate the mental health services available for a country of 30 million people. They found that there was virtually nothing outside large urban areas, and that rural communities had to resource themselves once a service user went home.

In Gulu, Northern Uganda, the local mental health services (Ovuga et al., 1999) train village elders to rehabilitate traumatised children in a post-conflict society. There is evidence that service users and their immediate carers and communities are more empowered, experience reduced stigma and subsequent violence, and make more health gains when they work together for the common good. Unity and solidarity are empowering.

Peer support

Those who have been service users can help others through *peer support* where they use personal knowledge and experience. A report from the King's Fund (Naylor and Bell, 2010) shows that peer support can reduce hospitalisation, demands for other services, improving physical health and improving workforce productivity. The report highlights peer support as being particularly appropriate for specific populations – such as the homeless and minority groups. It argues that BME clients are over-represented in hospital populations and that it would be better for their communities to provide peer support than to allow them to drift into long-term institutionalisation. Naylor and Bell (2010) quote a peer support project where ex-users act as volunteer mentors and friends to those just being discharged from hospital, which is currently being evaluated. The Scottish Development Centre for Mental Health (2006) has published a literature-scoping exercise that looks at the evidence base for peer specialist services in mental health. It found that there were considerable benefits to both parties, and highlights that peers have greater perceived empathy, respect, and trustworthiness – particularly for marginalised and hard to access groups, including BME communities.

Stories of recovery provide encouragement and assistance to others, as well as a powerful role model. Peers take responsibility for their own recovery and encourage individuals to define their problems, think about the choices that are open to them – which may involve professional counselling – and support them in trying different recovery strategies. A culture of health and ability is promoted rather than illness and disability, with ultimately reduced symptoms and numbers of admissions to hospital. Peers also report increased well-being, self-esteem, levels of hope, and openings for employment and educational opportunities themselves.

Case Example

Estere was referred for assessment and treatment for depression and PTSD following witnessing the self-immolation of her sister in Turkey. Estere had been studying for a degree in London, but had given up her studies as a result of her mental health difficulties. As part of her rehabilitation, she was invited by her counsellor to become a peer support worker, where her empathy, language skills and knowledge of mental health were quickly recognised as being of great value to the needs of the Turkish-speaking diaspora of North London. She befriended many and herself grew in confidence. She is now working as a Turkish-speaking health advocate for a local counselling service and has re-registered for her degree.

The benefits to counsellors and counselling services in training peers include: increasing cultural knowledge, engaging hard to reach groups, reducing workloads for the counsellor, and meeting clients' needs for social support, companionship and recreation. Trained peer support workers for any counselling agency working across cultures can increase the number of people served, improve cost effectiveness and provide flexibility in terms of timing and types of counselling service on offer. The quality of transcultural counselling can be significantly improved in this way and ensure that the voice of the user is more easily heard. The role of the counsellor in training, supporting and supervising the peer workers requires just as many skills. Whether or not they are being used more efficiently and appropriately has yet to be evaluated, and research is still needed on this promising model across cultures.

Conclusion

During assessment, the transcultural counsellor can explore routinely the history of the client with regard to other users, as well as the User Movement. Even empowered BME clients may still have undisclosed issues that would make counselling more difficult, such as perceptions of institutionalised racism within the counselling service. The counsellor can refer the client to a users' group for additional and ongoing support either during counselling or when the counselling sessions – often limited by public expenditure – are finished. Clients can become experts or patient participants. They can undertake their own study, carry out experiments and build a knowledge base about their difficulties, resilience and resources. In all of these processes – the voice of the service users can be amplified and accelerate the function and outcome of face-to-face counselling. In the words of the users themselves:

> There can be no mental health without our expertise. We are the knowers and yet we remain the untapped resource in mental healthcare. We are the experts. We want to be listened to and to fully participate in our life decisions. We must be the masters of our life journeys.

> (Pan African Network of People with
> Psychosocial Difficulties, 2011)

8

ETHICS AND GOVERNANCE
IN TRANSCULTURAL COUNSELLING

Summary

This chapter works through current ethical issues of transcultural counselling, derived from the concepts of law and international human rights. It describes ethical principles and governance common to many counselling bodies, and compares them to ethical values in diverse practice. It shows how ethics improves quality of supervision, client care, client trust, counselling research, including capacity to consent in counselling, and refers to the dangers of dual relationships.

Introduction

So far readers have been introduced to the development of transcultural counselling and some of the newer contexts for its application in a restless world. The following chapters look at key professional priorities for the individual practitioner in counselling structures and wider service systems. Although explored separately, these chapters are intimately liked, and their consideration is aimed to provide good client outcomes, improve the counsellor's well-being and maintain the good name of professional standards in counselling.

The BACP has a simple mission, to 'Enable access to *ethical and effective* psychological therapy by setting and monitoring of standards' (BACP, 2010a). Ethical codes in counselling across Europe refer to the responsibility of the individual practitioner to be transparent, honest and autonomous. They refer to competency of work, and to continuing to develop those skills throughout a lifetime of practice (see Chapter 9). Counsellors are required to adhere to national laws, professional codes and guidelines, and current understanding of human rights. Ethics concerns the welfare of the client – especially avoiding exploitation or dependency, as well as professional relationships, communication with the public and research (Tantam and van Deurzen, 2005).

Lago and Smith (2010) include counselling as an anti-discriminatory and anti-oppressive activity, where counsellors from the dominant culture (or gender, race or class) should seek to dismantle the systems and structures that create barriers to effective and ethical practice (Chapter 1). Indeed, *all* counselling can be considered an ethical activity, placed within its legal, professional, historical and cultural conventions (d'Ardenne and Mahtani, 1999). The implication of this is that ethical choices are changing and reflect our own cultural development, histories and shared endeavours. The story of psychology and psychiatry in the West has provided plenty of examples of 'Man's inhumanity to Man' (Chapter 1). It is worthwhile reading older texts about common practice in the West to get a picture of just how rapidly change in ethical practice has occurred.

Here are some examples from my own 40-year career in clinical and counselling psychology:

- Homosexuality in the UK (Sexual Offences Act, 1967) was a criminal activity, punishable by a life sentence. It was only removed from the American Psychiatric Association diagnostic list in 1973. Even then, clinical psychologists (including myself) were trained to treat homosexuality as a sexual disability or deviation by aversive behaviour therapy. This involved electric shocks being paired with a homoerotic image. The client would be 'cured' when he (it was always a he) no longer derived any pleasure from the image – the principle of all classical conditioning (Maguire and Vallance, 1964)
- My first USA research job was for Mental Retardation – a journal that kept its title until 2007, when it was re-named Intellectual Disability, because the editors finally realised that 'mental retardation did not communicate dignity or respect, and in fact, frequently resulted in the devaluation of such persons' (Schalock et al., 2007)
- Depressed patients were given electroconvulsive therapy without general anaesthesia in our training placements. We were told this was acceptable as they would have no memory of the electroconvulsive therapy
- We administered psychometrics to patients with suspected dementia using a method of repeated questioning until performance broke down – sometimes distressingly so – using the Kendrick Battery of Differential Diagnosis (Kendrick et al., 1979)
- Until the 1980s it was common practice to 'demonstrate' patients to psychiatric and psychological students. A patient would be informed (not asked) that his case was to be discussed in front of a room full of students. His 'condition' would be described to the audience in his presence and he would passively answer questions. The consultant would then invite students to put questions, often of an intimate nature, to the patient in an attempt to elicit symptoms. These would then be discussed at a more leisurely pace once the patient had been wheeled out (sometimes quite literally). Family, advocates, interpreters and friends were absent. The patient was alone – the object of our intense scrutiny.

In a single career the rights of the individual client, the psychotherapist and all potential users, have been transformed (Lago and Smith, 2010), although the above examples serve as a reminder of how recently this has occurred. For example, rather than condemn the homophobia that is now endemic in many parts of the world (Dehghan, 2011), it might be more productive to reflect on the rapid evolution, and selectivity, of Western ethical standards.

Human rights

The UK and most other countries are signatories to the 1949 United Nations Declaration of Human Rights (OHCHR, 1949) that enshrines many current ethical beliefs and practices, codified in European and UK law (although most states have caveats). These rights include reference to healthcare, to family life, to work, freedom to practise religion, to democratic freedoms and to education. Counsellors are not routinely shown this in their training – but a simplified version of this makes for interesting reading for all those working across cultures (Human Rights Education Associates, 2012).

In transcultural counselling you will see many clients who have endured or witnessed human rights abuses – both in their culture of origin – and regret-tably, on their journey seeking a better life. You will also meet clients who are habituated or indifferent to these abuses. There are even those who may not be aware of which rights have been abused, for example individuals who have lost their education or continuing family life. There is a probability that you will meet those who are not only the victims of abuse, but also perpetrators. How and when these disclosures occur will depend on your ability to recog-nise subtle clues, as well as your openness to the possibility that it occurs, especially in war (Chapter 3). War brutalises us all.

Case Example

You are counselling a young man who has been referred for post-traumatic stress after he witnessed atrocities in Chechnya. He saw his best friend murdered by Chechen rebels after they had both tried to join Russian troops near their border. Six years on, he has not recovered, even after considerable help, and his mood has been ever more depressed. He agrees to undertake trauma-focussed work, and you note some inconsistencies when he repeatedly revisits his story. He becomes increasingly agitated. You do not press him. He starts to disclose that he himself was forced to kill his friend and was told that if he did not he would die a slow and painful death. He expresses profound guilt and self-loathing and says that he should have chosen death, as it would have been more honourable.

But human rights are abused more casually nearer home. Many clients have had their rights disregarded by migration services, the police and members of the public. Regrettably some counselling services, albeit inadvertently, deprive people of access to healthcare (Articles 25 and 22 Declaration of Human Rights, OHCHR, 1949). This they do through institutional racism, such as no ethnic monitoring, no interpreting, no translations and no diversity training. They do it through poor governance, such as no case notes, poor supervision and training, through ignorance of cultural and racism barriers, and by subsequent neglect (Chapter 1). Counselling services within multiracial communities can address ethics in their practices from a human rights perspective and make an explicit commitment to uphold them, as can individual practitioners (Mahtani, 2003; Patel, 1999). Counsellors who are members of professional bodies with ethical codes are well placed to make these values explicit in their correspondence, their promotional literature, their curriculum vitae (CV) and through their exchanges with service users, referrers and members of the public.

Ethical values and principles

Personal ethics extend beyond the consulting room, and include your associated activities, communication with colleagues, supervision, training, research, and your private and social life. Various bodies that govern counselling (American Counseling Association, 2002; BACP, 2010b; BPS, 2004; British Association for Behavioural & Cognitive Psychotherapies (BABCP), 2010) have ethical codes or frameworks where reference is made to *any* activity that brings the organisation into disrepute. Embodied in these regulations is the concept of the ethical person in ethical practice. 'Good standards of practice and care require professional competence, good relationships with clients and colleagues, and commitment to and observance of professional ethics' (BABCP, 2010).

Case Example

You employ a counsellor in an organisation that supports refugees, and which has an inclusive ethical code. In his private life he becomes involved in a political organisation that has recently developed an extreme antimigration policy. He mentions this to you during an informal conversation after work. You are taken aback and insist that his work is compromised, as is that of the counselling service. He does not see it this way, and insists his personal life is separate and has no bearing on his professional practice.

Discussion Points

Is there a conflict of interest?

If so, how might it be ethically resolved?

Ethical governance

The UK has a variety of regulatory bodies for psychological therapies, for health professionals, for psychologists and for counsellors – and each one of them publishes ethical guidelines for practitioners in the field, to inform the public of minimal standards of practice.

The BACP lists the following values of counselling and therapy in its *Ethical Framework* (2010b):

> alleviating personal distress and suffering
> respecting human rights and dignity
> ensuring the integrity of the practitioner–client relationship
> enhancing professional knowledge and application
> fostering a sense of self
> increasing personal effectiveness
> enhancing the quality of relationships

appreciating the variety of human experience
striving for fair and adequate services.

Practice Point

Place these values within a cross-cultural context.

Discussion Point

How hard do we work at these once we are outside our own comfort zone?

The BACP (2010b) also refers to ethical principles: fidelity; autonomy; beneficence; non-maleficence (not harming others); justice; resilience; self-respect; empathy; integrity; and respect. It lists personal qualities as: humility; competence; fairness; wisdom; courage; and sincerity.

Discussion Point

Which of these moral qualities have specific implications for transcultural practice?

Are there any missing?

Ethics in diverse practice

Transcultural counselling, whether done individually or as part of a team service, exists in the public, private and voluntary sectors, in general or specialised services, in this country and overseas, in face-to-face, telephone or online care. Ethical values, principles and personal qualities in counselling have to be flexible enough to fit into all these expanding contexts. The BACP (2010b: 6), for example, in its section on keeping client trust, suggests, 'keeping trust requires: attentiveness to the quality of listening and respect offered to clients; culturally appropriate ways of communicating that are courteous and clear'.

Practice Points

Identify in your practice an example of a culturally appropriate way of communicating.

How was it developed, and how do you know it is appropriate?

Ethics and quality of care

Clinical governance refers to the regulation of clinical/counselling practice (see Chapter 10), and has practical ethical implications for transcultural work.

- **Competent services with trained, supported and accountable practitioners.** In transcultural counselling you have an ethical requirement to ensure you and your colleagues have adequate training to address the needs of the community(ies) you serve. This is not uniquely achieved through a course in transcultural psychology or counselling; it could be collaborating with a neighbourhood community organisation or learning to speak a new language
- **Knowing the limitations of the service and sources of additional help.** All clinicians are ethically bound to recognise their limits promptly, and to seek other sources of help. In transcultural counselling, this may require more help from representatives of your clients' community, your supervisor, or someone else with more experience. It may be that you are able to access help by referring cases on. Ethical issues extend beyond individual cases. For example, if your BME clients are not regularly attending therapy, you could approach a users' group, or a community-based service to help you
- **Communicating to users their rights and responsibilities.**

In cross-cultural terms, this has implications for the quality of all your written and oral communications. Language is critical and is the means of both empowering and dis-empowering users (Lago and Smith, 2010). The concepts of time-keeping, evaluation, consultation, choice, privacy and confidentiality, for example, are not universal. It may take some additional, culturally appropriate explanation for those whose own boundaries have been violated, who have never been offered choice, who have not lived according to strict time, or for whom privacy and secrecy may be synonymous.

- **An awareness of dual relationships.** Dual relationships can take many forms. They can be blatant, such as where the counsellor becomes sexually involved with the client; or they can be more subtle, such as where the counsellor befriends a client or offers the client paid employment (Shillito-Clarke, 2010). These differences always favour the counsellor and aggravate the existing power imbalance between counsellors from the dominant culture and BME clients
- **Accurate and legal record keeping.** Your duty of care to clients extends to the records you prepare for them, which inform other professionals now and in the future about the client's history and intervention. In transcultural terms, ethnic monitoring is the very least requirement, which complies with the law, and informs others about how inclusive your service is. Records should also carry the language support needs of your client together with the names and origins of any advocates or interpreters used during assessment and intervention. Any translated materials need to be included, and wherever possible, when and by whom they were translated (Chapter 4)
- **Obtaining accurate information about the client.** A good example of this is how often the names of our clients are mis-communicated, especially when they do

not comply with the standard Western format of given name followed by family name. This is critical in ensuring that clients do not get lost or duplicated in alphabetical systems. Many clients know their names have not been accurately recorded but do not feel empowered to correct them with staff taking their details. They may have names that are difficult to spell or pronounce. Anglicisation and subsequent inaccuracies occur. Sometimes names get lost altogether as they do not correspond with names written in previous correspondence, thus disadvantaging the client further. Other inaccuracies occur during history taking when so-called 'language barriers' are used as an excuse for incomplete or inconsistent narratives. In transcultural practice, additional time is given to enable clients to tell their stories in a coherent and chronological order

- **Services reviewed regularly.** Services are always able to adapt to their communities. You can monitor and address the cultural needs of your clients. Regular updates could include audits (Chapter 10), meetings with users' groups, interpreters, advocates and referrers, perhaps on an annual basis.

Ethics of maintaining competent practice

Supervision is integral to competent counselling and must be formal, scheduled and recorded. Anything less than that endangers good practice and is unethical. We have already seen how transcultural counselling is affected by individual and organisational racism (Patel, 2004). Supervision, therefore is not an optional extra to be cancelled or re-scheduled at short notice. Your clients are owed your commitment to supervision and it is as much your responsibility as your supervisor's to ensure it is of the highest quality. The ethics of supervision entail your preparation, commitment and integration of this process into all your counselling casework. The supervisor has an ethical responsibility to convene at regular intervals and to record outcome (Chapter 9). Some counsellors make it clear to their clients that time is spent discussing their cases with their supervisors. It is also ethical to communicate with referrers and other stakeholders in your service, that supervision is part of the contracted clinical time, which may entail additional time or cost.

Monitoring, evaluation and appraisal are all ways you know your work is meeting the requirements of the post. You and your manager require a formal appraisal at least annually to ensure you are meeting targets set, as well as establishing which training or resources are required. Service audits are another way of ensuring that professional standards are monitored for example regular case-note audits allow everyone to see the quality of written work; audits of attendance may reveal patterns indicating variability in counselling quality.

A critical part of maintaining competence is through professional update, which may extend beyond the immediate requirements of the job. It is an ethical requirement for practitioners to ensure that they have read professional and house journals, attended conference, networked with special interest groups and promoted good in-house practice with training, teaching and promotional activities in transcultural care. Transcultural counsellors can also maintain competence through shadowing colleagues with more experience; collaborating with service developments aimed at improving cross-cultural practice, such as running a group for refugees; joining an interest group concerned with ethical practice in multicultural communities.

The legal requirements of your counselling practice must be considered, The UK Health Professions Council (HPC, 2011), which registers all psychologists and counsellors in health settings, lists ethical guidelines where you can find the following:

'You must not allow your views about a service user's sex, age, colour, race, disability, sexuality, social or economic status, lifestyle, culture, religion or beliefs affect the way you treat them or the professional advice you give.'

The HPC ethical principle is formulated in practical terms, and meets the letter of the law on discrimination by advocating impartiality – what used to be called 'colour blindness' (d'Ardenne and Mahtani, 1999). 'Views' in this context can refer to beliefs about another culture based on false or prejudicial ideas. The guidelines are for all health professions and do not capture the more proactive model of transcultural counselling (Chapter 1). However, it is easier to demonstrate when a clinician has shown discrimination, rather than lacks a particular quality or commitment.

The Code of Conduct of the British Psychological Society (BPS, 2011, 5.4) refers to personal conduct where clinicians must 'not allow their professional responsibilities or standards of practice to be diminished by considerations of religion, sex, race, age, nationality, party politics, social standing, class, self-interest or other extraneous factors'. We can reasonably assume here that the equally negative terminology provides a very low threshold for psychotherapists' discretion.

In contrast to this, the BACP (2010b) lists many more positive values including respecting human rights and dignity, appreciating the variety of human experience and culture, and striving for fair and adequate provision of counselling and psychotherapy services. Similarly, the BABCP in its guidelines on Conduct Performance and Ethics (2010, item 8.0) refers to communication with cross-cultural implications:

> You must communicate properly and effectively with service users and other practitioners.
>
> You must take all reasonable steps to make sure that you can communicate properly and effectively with service users. You must communicate appropriately, cooperate, and share your knowledge and expertise with other practitioners, for the benefit of service users.

Lago and Thompson (1989), Ryde (2009) and McKenzie-Mavinga (2009) have all argued that white counsellors, especially, have an ethical imperative to do much more about themselves than this to fulfil anti-discriminatory requirements.

The ethics and governance of maintaining client trust

Ethical practice extends beyond the rules of not actually harming or discriminating against others who are culturally different. Listening and *respect* for others – especially those from other cultures, seems like an obvious point of departure in the ethical requirement to show respect, but lack of respect comes in many forms.

Case Example

A local mental health team refers a patient for counselling assessment, following the breakdown of her marital relationship through domestic violence. In the referral letter she is described as 'this very nice lady who speaks only Indian'. Of note, the team has little information about her, and no record of any assessment of her language or communication or cultural needs. The counselling team agrees to accept the referral because they believe that the referrer is well intentioned, but they are aware that she will be returned to the referrer after any psychological work has been undertaken.

Discussion Points

What does the term 'very nice lady' suggest to you? How might you have responded if she had been judged 'not very nice'?

What have the referrers made of her cultural and communication needs?

Were the team right to accept this referral, and what should they communicate back?

Practice points

Establish the exact communication needs and preferences of your client – by asking her, her family or advocate – and make these explicit to the referrer as soon as possible and in the patient records.

Identify language(s) spoken and fluency and literacy with any changes and support needs.

Another practical example came from a letter from a senior colleague: 'due to the language barrier, it was not possible to obtain a family history from this client'. Again, the writer's well-intentioned words reveal a perception that it is the patient's language that is the barrier. This represented a sufficient reason for not taking a history, although it did not prevent a referral being made to a specialist service. There is an ethical requirement to provide full healthcare services to all members of the community (Care Quality Commission, 2012). In this example, the clinician was clearly not able or willing to provide it, thus undermining client trust from the start.

Communication with non-English speakers is not just about interpreting and translating materials. Much documentation in counselling and psychotherapy contains jargon or elaborate phrasing that is hard for anyone to understand or translate. Plain English is good for everyone and more inclusive (www.plainenglish.co.uk).

Practice Points

Check your service documents for jargon 'creep'. Give them to a lay person for feedback.

Use plain English for your routine letters, making complaints and compliments forms, client advice and clinical protocols (see Chapter 4).

Privacy, dignity and safety in the counselling environment are crucial to maintaining trust. Look around your consulting rooms. Are they clean, comfortable, sufficiently spacious and well insulated for sound? Allow the client to choose where to sit and ensure that the space between chairs and any tables are comfortable. What can be seen from the street? Might it be more appropriate to have blinds or curtains? Are your reception staff smiling and kind? Do you have any signs in other languages? In Chapter 3, some practical recommendations were made for ensuring that refugee clients feel *welcome* in the counselling environment and not alienated. All counselling services should have protocols for risk and ensure that staff are fully aware and compliant. For example, out-of-hours counselling sessions should be serviced by reception staff, or at least by colleagues working nearby. Unqualified staff should never see clients without a supervisor available. In brief, if either the counsellor or the client feels uncomfortable, there is no basis for an ethical counselling session.

Practice points

Visit other counselling centres, schools, libraries and community groups that serve diverse communities for new ideas and feedback.

Audit previous and current clients about what makes them more trustful of your service.

Not everyone from other cultures adheres to the strict therapeutic hour, and in transcultural settings it may be more ethical to offer clients flexibility or possibly a walk-in clinic (Chapter 3). Do not book clients on their holy days or special feast days. Clients who arrive in the waiting room with small children or older relatives, (or pets) may have limited support and organisational resources (e.g. babysitting). See them anyway and engage them for the future. School-age children, however, brought as junior interpreters, should be gently encouraged to return to class. Regular attendance needs the establishment of a rhythm and pattern that suits you and the client. Ask at the start for consent to prompt before appointments (e.g. through texting or calling) to help with the many demands on time. In all these respects, you can engage your client ethically if you show a willingness and flexibility to accommodate them.

Capacity to consent, confidentiality and the law

Consent to counselling, disclosures of confidential information and entering a contractual understanding all have cultural and, increasingly in the West, legal underpinnings. Clients who have had secrets betrayed may have no concept of professional boundaries, and it may be necessary to explore the meanings of these before consent can actually be given. Clients who have been punished and interrogated by the state may find questioning about their past, or agreeing to sign documents consenting to therapy, reminiscent of their ordeals (Chapter 3).

The ethical obligation here is to allocate extra time and effort with clients to explain confidentiality and consent to the counselling contract. The client also needs to understand mutual rights and obligations of the contract as well as what is meant by those who 'have a right to know'. In Chapter 3 the needs of those who have perpetrated violence were discussed. Bond (2005) outlines how counsellors need to work legally. The Terrorism Act, 2000, the Drug Trafficking Act, 1994, the Children's Act, 1989, the Data Protection Act, 1998 and the Human Rights Act, 1998 all place specific obligations on the counsellor concerning confidentiality. Clients need to be informed prior to consent about who can access documents, case notes and supervision notes. Confidentiality also refers to the clients' access to their own records in health settings and what may be withheld under the Access to Health Records Act 1990. The situation is changing with new legislation (Jenkins, 2005). The distinction between confidentiality and secrecy is sometimes quite subtle. Trust can be generated if the counsellor repeatedly communicates clarity in these matters, and the services of advocates can sometimes be of great value here.

Ethics in counselling research

Clients who have consented to taking part in research need to understand that they have a right to withdraw without penalty or prejudice to their current or future treatments (Patel and Mahtani, 2007; Shillito-Clarke, 2010). This is a particularly sensitive area where the power relationship is already skewed towards the practitioner from the dominant culture (Chapter 1). It must also be made explicit to participants that they may not be the direct beneficiaries of the research and consent explicitly on that basis. Local research ethics committees are highly sensitive to cross-cultural issues and to the vulnerability of people being counselled. They will seek absolute clarity in what you are undertaking, but just as importantly, how you communicate your proposals to participants and potential service users. Ethical practice refers not just to whether the research proposals are rigorous or understandable, but whether or not they are appropriate to that culture. Moreover, if the researcher has not already done so, the committee will seek advice from those communities about how research is to be approached, by whom and in what format. The committee always holds the power to veto any research proposal that fails these considerations. Local ethics committees have the responsibility of protecting the public, but also the good name of research and the counselling profession.

Case Example

You are interested in evaluating the impact of multiple pregnancies on young Bengali women in East London. You are particularly interested in accessing the women without the presence of their husbands, and propose that participants be recruited from local GP lists. You are aware that some women will not disclose their family planning choices, or would need consent from their husbands, but this is not made explicit when you write your research proposal and submit it to the ethics committee. The committee considers your proposal and asks you how you plan to ensure that the husbands of participants would not know about your approaches. It also asks you if you have made clear that participants will be seen alone. You have not made this clear and your research proposal is refused ethical clearance.

Practice Points

Communicate with the local ethics committee and read the guidelines very carefully before designing a research proposal.

Locate key stakeholders in the community you are studying.

Identify previous successful applications in this field.

Dual relationships

All ethical guidelines in counselling organisations refer to the issues of dual relationships in counselling as an exploitation of power. The obvious and most frequently cited example (Shillito-Clarke, 2010) is that of having a sexual relationship with your client, since sex or physical intimacy is banned. It also remains the most frequent reason for psychotherapists being struck off their professional register. But there are more subtle abuses in transcultural counselling (see Chapter 1).

Case Example

A counsellor has recently returned from a humanitarian mission to the Sierra Leone, and is working with a client from that country in her UK practice. The client is a victim of violence with subsequent mental health problems, and refers to her experiences of war. The counsellor discloses that she has recently visited her country and shares common place names and organisations with which she has been working as a way of 'befriending' her client. She holds the client in a special place because of her work in Africa and goes out of her way to give her UK contacts as well as prioritising her appointments.

A senior white manager is due to provide regular, scheduled supervision with a black female counsellor. He is invited at short notice to meet important visitors to the service and cancels the counsellor's supervision because of time pressure.

A counsellor provides consultation to an Afghani community organisation, that also runs a neighbourhood restaurant. She commissions them to provide catering for a private party at her house, which they provide at cost.

> **Practice Points**
>
> In the first case, counsellors who make gestures of friendship that make them feel good in the short term are forging a dual relationship, unethical because it compromises the singularity of the counselling relationship. The counsellor has privileged information about the client that enables her to befriend her, which is neither reciprocal nor equal. This is not for the good of the client.
>
> In the second case, the supervisor is also the manager and is able to cancel supervision because of his dual relationship with the counsellor. The counsellor is not empowered because of gender, role and race to assert her right to supervision. As with therapy, the supervisor can exercise forethought and enable supervision to take priority.
>
> In the third case, the counsellor has a dual – professional as well as commercial – relationship with the organisation. It will be difficult for the restaurant to say 'no' to her request or to complain about loss of profit. The counsellor benefits from privileged access.

Conclusions

In this chapter we have seen how transcultural ethics are linked to all aspects of professional life – and share the agenda with CPD, supervision and an evidence base for counselling work. Furthermore, the ethical agenda, although founded within human rights, is not static, and requires constant monitoring and updating as political and social influences change the way we see moral choices in working in a restless world (Bond, 2005). Ethics covers clinical practice, supervision, research, teaching and training across cultures, as well as in everyday life outside counselling. Newland and Patel (2005), however, make a cautionary observation: *reading* about diversity will make you anti-racist as quickly as reading about sport will turn you into an athlete. In ethics, actions always speak louder than words.

9

SUPERVISION, PERSONAL DEVELOPMENT AND SELF-CARE IN TRANSCULTURAL COUNSELLING

> Two roads diverged in a wood, and I—
>
> I took the one less traveled by,
>
> And that has made all the difference.
>
> 'The Road Not Taken', Robert Frost

Summary

This chapter examines personal ways practitioners maintain their commitment to transcultural counselling and anti-discriminatory practice. These processes are supported within professional contexts through CPD, the requirements of professional bodies, models of supervision in the West and with workers overseas, personal therapy and self-care, mentoring, as well as developing a CV that communicates the content of such development.

Introduction

Good practice is never static, and requires a lifetime of committed professional development: listening, learning, reflecting, reading and sharing with supervisors, colleagues and stakeholders in your service, including those being counselled. Black and minority ethnic clients still have little choice about counselling or the counsellor, as most practitioners are still white and female, in turn trained, supervised and managed by those within the dominant culture (Abbott 1999; Ryde 2011). There has, however, been significant development in most curricula for the training of psychotherapists, counsellors and mental health workers in anti-racist practice and transcultural approaches to care (BPS, 2006; BACP, 2010b). Most professional counselling organisations provide conferences and professional update seminars on transcultural assessment and interventions. There are no national standards, and it is still very much for practitioners to find their own training and professional networks for working with race and culture. Reach Healthcare Foundation (www.reachhealth.org.uk); Rethink (previously the Schizophrenic Fellowship, www.rethink.org) the Ethnic Health Initiative (www.bmehealth.org); the Kings Fund (www.kingsfund.org.uk); and the BPS Race and Culture Faculty (http://raceandculture.bps.org.uk) all have useful sites for the practitioner to visit for training events in the UK. In addition, those who themselves have come from BME communities are increasingly entering mental health professions and enriching them with personal knowledge, skills and direct experience of racism and alienation. However, figures suggest that there is still a long way to go in having a fully representative ethnic profile within psychological professions (Scior et al., 2007).

Continuing Professional Development (CPD)

Khele (2007) proposes that the rationale for counsellors undertaking CPD is that it maintains and improves the quality of practice, reassures the public, keeps practitioners up to date, ensures the application of new learning and contributes to lifelong learning. Sceptics point out that these are largely unproven claims, but counselling has an established tradition of supporting practitioners – essentially using two developmental models for learning from the end of professional training – what is commonly known as the 'start line' in a career.

The first concept is the *scientist–practitioner model* (Martin, 2010), where the counsellor uses techniques within a general scientific method. This model embodies the idea of successive hypothesising, with five critical features:

- critical assimilation of research
- a holistic awareness of the patient
- scientific eclecticism in the selection of explanations
- attention to the practitioner's own needs
- continuous attention to both individual and normative assessment and treatment procedures.

By contrast, *the reflexive practitioner model*, emphasises the ability to take in new data and reform ideas and understanding. Knowledge or specific technical skills are not separated from the context in which they are applied, and may be more flexible for transcultural work. Arulmani (2007), writing about Indian and Western models, suggests that counselling can liberate itself from the West, and that counsellors can lead the way in helping world workers and the global community adapt to post-modern information. The implication for this is that the maintenance and development of skill and knowledge needs to be less formulaic and adapted to a more restless world.

The HPC in the UK defines CPD as 'a range of learning activities through which health professionals maintain and develop their capacity to practise safely, effectively and legally within their evolving scope of practice' (HPC, 2011). It provides a long list of CPD activities, which can be adapted transculturally, as follows.

Work-based learning

Present case studies across cultures, use reflective practice on cross-cultural cases, undertake clinical audit of cross-cultural practice; obtain mentoring from those with cultural skills; discuss and record cross-cultural practice with peers; obtain secondments or job rotation to diverse settings; supervise students from culturally different backgrounds; establish and/or manage a service addressing cultural need.

Professional activity

Join and participate in a professional body or special interest group on race and ethnic needs; use supervision for reflection on racism and power; teach or train transcultural counselling; supervise or mentor students and other professionals on culture; present cultural and race topics at conference; attend or organise accredited courses; champion cultural training and development.

Formal educational

Undertake further education and research on racism and diversity; initiate journal clubs focussing on culture; write peer reviewed articles that include cultural and racial factors; undertake distance learning on culture; supervise cross-cultural research; read journals, articles or books dealing with diversity; champion diversity within curricular planning and assessment.

Self-directed learning

Undertake personal therapy; learn a new language; visit websites and other resources; use the internet and all social media to inform and experiment; select wider reading with better coverage of international affairs, memoirs, novels, histories and maps; use travel locally and overseas to visit those who counsel in as many other settings as possible; keep a log of progress, reflect and share. Other resources include: family members and friends outside your culture; social networks; religious affiliations; political movements; global scientific and environmental movements; performing arts; alternative therapies; education; and employment (d'Ardenne and Mahtani, 1999).

Community and public services

Seek work on local projects with marginalised communities, volunteer for overseas projects with NGOs; join human rights organisations; promote diversity and encourage others likewise; provide e-mentorship for overseas counsellors without local support.

It is difficult for recently qualified and trainee counsellors to prioritise all these at the start of a working life. In a recent email survey, East (2011) found that new practitioners discussed good practice; reliability; empowerment; inappropriate behaviour; constructive criticism; emotional support and containment; setting up supervision; and personal connection. No reference was made to gender, culture or race. East suggests this is because they were concerned with *general* processes; another explanation may be that participants were ethnically and culturally homogeneous.

A more valid (albeit less reliable) clue lies in an audit of requests for CPD received in our East London trauma service over the last decade in clinical and academic work. Many are from BME students, studying for and planning to work with diverse communities, both in Europe and in their countries of origin.

The more common requests include:

- finding training and supervision that deals with diversity
- contacts for clinical placements in appropriate diverse settings
- professional affiliations/memberships for cross-cultural work
- how to deal with cultural disagreements within the reflective team
- finding referees, writing a good CV and dealing with job refusals
- dealing with clients whose cultural, racial or religious values are very different
- identifying cultural competencies
- finding and resourcing professional mentoring, coaching, supervision and referees
- dealing with disadvantage and racism at work
- tackling discouragement with lack of professional opportunity, poor performance and motivation
- help with personal issues affecting transcultural practice.

CHAPTER 9

Supervision defined within the BPS (2006) guidelines can be summarised as

- an activity – where practitioner and supervisor discuss cases in a boundaried space that permits uncensored reflection, and is distinct from therapy and line management
- a process – where the practitioner learns through experience, reflects, generates abstract concepts and generalisations, and repeatedly experiments, as part of learning and change
- a relationship – based on mutual trust and respect, reflecting best practice and sensitivity to the learning needs of the supervisee
- a practice – based on shared and explicit models of supervision.

In professional and academic cultures there is an imbalance of power in the relationship, making questioning difficult (Wellington, 2010). Similarly, it might be hard to 'shop around' for a supervisor – somebody inspiring confidence and able to forge a working alliance. This imbalance becomes even more pronounced in situations for a student, for example who is black, young and finding it harder to articulate professional support needs with persistence and courage (Mckenzie-Mavinga, 2009).

Students need a supervisor who explicitly refers to the cross-cultural demands of their work, and who makes them think about their own ethnocentricity – that is, the centre of where they are culturally. The supervisor can help with the counsellor's abuses of power, and the barriers that develop within the supervisory relationship. Transcultural supervision is not for the too busy or the faint-hearted.

Supervision models for transcultural counselling

Lago and Thompson (1997) suggest that the supervisor in transcultural/transracial situations requires, *a priori*, knowledge about:

- the process of formation of racial and cultural identities
- cultural norms of the communities being counselled
- the nature of conflicts between black and white people
- a willingness to address how supervisees manage their anxiety in situations where racial or cultural identities are present.

Lago and Thompson (1997) define the complexities of cross-cultural supervision through a series of simple triads, representing counsellor, client and supervisor and the many racial and cultural permutations that are possible. The relationships between counsellor and supervisor, and counsellor and client remain clear and strong. The relationship between the supervisor and the client is much weaker, and prone to distortion, conscious or otherwise. Their model provides a useful training format for counsellors and managers to brainstorm potential sources of misunderstanding that occur within supervised counselling. Lago and Thompson draw on Rogers' (1961) theory of personality to suggest a series of projections of communication that they call 'the proxy self', aimed at protecting the individual from the power of white supremacy. Such supremacy affects everyone, and is insidious in supervision. These projections are essentially *false* – even when intentions may be good, and prevent all parties from dealing with power imbalance both within and beyond therapeutic and supervisory relationships.

Ryde (2011) explores this model further with the additional complications of black/white supervisors, black/white counsellors and black/white clients, and concludes: 'the complexity of the supervisor/supervisee/client triad within the inter-subjective field they create, needs to be acknowledged and teased out in this dialogue'. She observes, however, that cultural knowledge can never substitute for a dialogue. This can be extended very well into group supervision where BME members/supervisors also learn *from each other* (p. 150).

Lago (2010) additionally describes as 'work in progress' his elegant map(s) of personal and professional development for empathic intercultural work. His map model of personal and professional qualities links: primary (diversity and power) knowledge; secondary (cultural specific) knowledge; self-awareness; professional competencies; commitment to CPD; awareness and contexts of therapy.

Mckenzie-Mavinga (2009) researches black issues in the supervisory process from a number of different standpoints – including that of black supervisors with black counsellors and white counsellors. Her findings have consistently shown that it is black practitioners who raise uncomfortable issues around racism, fear of failure and the sense of being judged by others. She urges all counsellors and white supervisors working with diversity to address these issues.

Discussion Points

Will increased recruitment of BME counsellors simplify any of these issues?

Should black counsellors be matched with black supervisors?

Case Example

Jan is the only black counsellor working in a sexual health clinic, struggling with a disproportionately heavy case-load. A significant number of her clients are from BME communities and she knows that this is the reason for the additional work. She asks managers for relief but is told that no black candidates ever apply to work there, and there is no change in her workload. She worries about burnout and giving her most vulnerable clients a second-class service. She takes these issues to her white supervisor.

Ethical issues in transcultural supervision

Shipton (1997) observes that the ethics of supervision are about power and consent – reflecting those in the counselling relationship. One good example is that of audio- or video-taping the counselling session for supervisory purposes. It is never a neutral process and, if done badly, can be intrusive and potentially abusive. The counsellor seeks consent; the client does not feel empowered to refuse. A case is made for recording; the client has bad memories of being listened to in the past. In a transcultural setting, this could have been interrogation in a war zone, or it could have been reminiscent of a torture cell. In supervision, the supervisor, white or black, consults about recording, but Mckenzie-Mavinga (2009) asks, can the black supervisee ever refuse?

There is an explicit requirement within the professional codes of the various counselling organisations that accredit practitioners maintain training and professional development (APA, 2002; BACP, 2010b; BPS, 2006). Woolfe and Tholstrup (2010) observe that supervision may have a proven benefit to the practitioner, but there is no evidence yet that it directly improves client outcomes. Less experienced staff, especially BME counsellors, complain that their employers do not provide or pay for supervision, which becomes an unaffordable 'luxury'.

However, even the most newly qualified staff member is in a position to broker a formal supervisory arrangement at the commencement of a job. Health and safety in the workplace today requires employers to take every reasonable step to protect staff from physical danger, risk and hazard, and indeed from bullying and discrimination, under pain of litigation. Supervision, as a process that *protects and promotes the well-being* of the practitioner can be requested as a necessary, but not sufficient condition for safe and competent practice. Supervision is therefore also the responsibility of those who recruit and manage counsellors.

There are, of course, many ways of undermining this protection. Supervisors cancel at short notice. They may use the supervision time to deal with general management issues (see Chapter 8 on dual relationships). They take calls during the supervisory hour. They offer another time, but so far in the future as to compromise the process. The duration of supervision may be altered unilaterally, and supervisees may feel unable to complain. Supervisors or managers withdraw supervision because of the perceived cost. They make no reference to the cost of a colleague whose mental health may be compromised by inadequate support.

Remote supervision

Chapter 2 described the needs of international workers including counsellors in economically poor countries and conflict zones where local resources are likely to be severely limited. Agencies protecting and supporting overseas workers, including health workers, mental health workers and volunteers, now provide e-supervision, although its efficacy is only just being evaluated (Tropical Health Education Trust (THET, www.thet.org) and Health Information for All (www.hifa2015.org)).

Case Example

One psychotherapy partnership between East London and Uganda aims to train psychiatric clinical officers (PCOs) in psychological therapies. The project uses two weeks' training time in Uganda, and works with participants responsible for huge, culturally diverse catchment areas of up to 300,000 people. The PCOs have limited access to local, reliable and regular supervision (THET, www.thet.org). Additional online supervision is provided, but even this is time-limited, so responses to specific issues have to be processed beforehand in order to optimise the exchanges. Extra support is provided by peer contact, local support groups and the school of PCOs (Baillie et al., 2009; THET, 2005). This model incorporates the following features: responsive to careful evaluation of local need; simplicity and lacking ambiguity; culturally flexible for Uganda's many tribal groups; low cost; high quality; demonstrably impacting on professional practice; capable of being evaluated; and sustainable once the UK partner has withdrawn.

Discussion point

Could this model be adapted to other countries?

What are the specific limitations of remote supervision?

Another remote model being considered is the development of an electronic supervision group – geared for those who are geographically isolated and applicable anywhere in the world. Medicine Africa (www.medicineafrica.com) is an organisation that already provides online case-based tutoring and mentoring for medical and psychiatric practitioners in need of support from more senior colleagues. Its facilities are currently being developed for group use with mental health workers using the system, to provide problem solving, information, and support and reflection for difficult cases. Contact is in typed format only, but face-to-face sessions via Skype will also be trialled (www.skype.com).

In a recent survey of trauma services provided across Bangladesh, a critical feature of those services that could meet their service brief was that peer supervision was available through Skype, through mobile phone/texting or through emails (Pathan and d'Ardenne, 2010). The picture is changing as technology improves, and there is no doubt that websites for the developing world provide information and support to many isolated services around the world. Development is hindered by some cultural considerations; the young are more comfortable with new technologies. More senior supervisees need practice with, and exposure to, the culture of e-contact and e-supervision.

In a UK telephone survey of trauma services (Jankovic et al., 2005), therapists in isolated districts used websites like UK Trauma Group (www.uktrauma. org.uk/uklist.html.uk) for information and reassurance with difficult cases. A problem is shared online; and in hours the member will receive ten or 20 replies from some of the most experienced clinicians and academics in the country. Practitioners who find it harder to seek help – even when they know that a case is beyond their ability – are encouraged to seek help in this non-judgemental, easy, free and accessible way.

Interhealth International (www.interhealth.org.uk) has researched how important cross-cultural supervision is for aid workers (Hargrave, 2011a). Whether the supervision is cross-cultural or culturally specific to the country of activity appears to be less important to counsellors in the field than that supervisors are clear about their role and understand the culture and ethos of the agency that employs the counsellor.

There are other requirements. Electronic supervision without Skype does not permit full access to non-verbal cues, and language becomes paramount. Supervisors need to be flexible to surges in demand for support, for example after a specific catastrophe or after the sudden withdrawal of ground staff from a local mission. They must work across time, political and geographical boundaries, and within the immediate cultural and human rights issues thrown up by the mission. Distortions invariably occur. Counsellors may minimise their discomfort, exaggerate the risks, find themselves in a culture that does not admit need, or where dealing with personal issues and distress is still seen as a weakness).

Practice Points

Supervisors need to fully acquainted with the formal and informal culture of their agency.

They require objective and up-to-date briefings on local conditions for counsellors.

Supervising teams working with survivors of torture

Avigad (2003), working with an NGO team, makes some observations about a job that is never easy, and does not have clear cut answers. Supervision here addresses feelings of burnout, irritability and impotence that practitioners experience when confronted with the overwhelming needs of their clients. However, practitioners have additional issues related to their own cultural assumptions and prejudices, which need to be explored. Supervision allows practitioners to take risks, but has to protect them from the dangers of *secondary traumatisation*. A supervisor who is culturally attuned to her own ethnicity and that of the supervisee is in a position to encourage the practitioner to look at the wider picture. This includes the client's cultural narrative, the large differences between cultures and, always, the dangers of collusion and exploitation of the client. Supervisors also have to find resilience and courage, and seek supervision of *their* work, applying the same principles of self-care, as they do to their supervisees (Avigad, 2003).

Other professional support needs of humanitarian aid workers

Supervision is a key element in the maintenance of the well-being of those on mission, but it begins with the screening and resilience briefing undertaken by workers in the field before they leave home as discussed in Chapter 2 (Hargrave, 2011a). This assessment can form the basis of the supervision agenda in supporting the counsellor while on mission, where preparation and supervision are understood as a continuous process. The supervisor will examine any changes agreed with the aid worker prior to the assignment, as well as supporting the worker and ensuring that the assignment is not compromised.

Case Example

You are supporting a young doctor on humanitarian assignment with a natural disaster in Bangladesh, by email. She has been screened and initially appears to be coping well. In the third week, however, it becomes clear that her resilience is beginning to break down. She discloses that she is not sleeping well, and is unable to concentrate on her humanitarian work. She describes having seen too many dead bodies of young children, and is finding it harder to return to her duties each day as a result. She says that her efforts are futile, and that she might as well go home, as there is not enough food for survivors or workers.

Discussion Points

How might the supervisor approach this case?

What local resources might be accessed?

Self-care

Counsellors in transcultural settings have a stressful job, with a professional obligation to preserve their physical and mental well-being. Safety has to come first, and counsellors need to reflect on situations that could place them or their clients at risk. Team communication should include protocols for hazards from aggressive clients with regular corridor contact from colleagues. Relaxation, yoga or meditation, used daily, can help. Creative and fun activities, regular contact with family and friends, enjoying hobbies, sport and taking full lunch breaks are all methods described by counsellors as reducing occupational stress and increasing capacity.

Practice Points

Improve your physical surroundings – especially with your team. Noise, dirt and disrepair are known stressors.

Make time to talk and time to listen to colleagues, friends and family.

Form a support group with colleagues who share your issues.

Assess occupational risks, and share with your manager and supervisor.

Establish where and when to seek professional help for yourself and others.

Avoid drink and drugs as a way of responding to stress.

Take up aerobic exercise or sport.

Personal therapy

The benefits of personal therapy for counsellors requires a clear rationale and evidence. Counselling trainees seek personal therapy more often than clinical psychology trainees, and see it as intrinsic to their development, although not necessarily at the start of the training – and especially for psychodynamic approaches. The BACP used to stipulate a mandatory period of personal therapy for trainees of 40 hours, but this has been discontinued since 2005. Psychodynamic trainees argued that it was far too little. We do not have evidence of a positive link between personal therapy and good clinical outcome for other approaches – which is confounded by the fact that therapists seeking therapists may have issues that undermine their competence. Rosemary Rizq (2010) has taken a qualitative approach and moved from whether or not it makes therapy work, to more interesting questions:

- What is the experience of mandatory personal therapy in training?
- What distinguishes authentic from inauthentic experiences of personal therapy?
- What aspects of personal therapy are trainees most likely to replicate within their own clinical practice?
- What effect is having personal therapy in one theoretical orientation have on practising within another?
- What developmental factors have an impact on the trainee's capacity to benefit from personal therapy in training?

CVs and résumés

Preparation of these is a vexed topic – even within one culture, there is huge variance in what people perceive as important, and there are many websites to guide practitioners. However, a CV can never be of itself an application for, or an instant passport to employment. In the West, every professional job requires a personal specification and job description, and that has to be addressed first.

Counsellors may not spend enough time in developing and updating a public document that informs the world who you are and where you are taking your professional life. Across cultures, the topic becomes even more complex. Overseas counsellors and BME counsellors sometimes have had no education or direction in preparing them, which places them at a professional disadvantage. Worse, this may not be recognised until it is too late. A CV has to be prepared promptly and may lose a candidate opportunities in seeking new posts or other professional advancement.

A CV is a kind of extended business card – and should form the basis of a telephone call or a meeting for further exchanges of *mutual* interest. Less experienced or acculturated counsellors may fail to tackle the fundamental issues, such as 'what I would bring to your service' or 'why you need to employ me'.

Hall (1999, cited in Rizq, 2010) suggest these can be effective with a minimum of 12 people, requiring an obligatory group leader, and should be geared to attend to the personal and interpersonal issues of practitioners. In a well-functioning personal development group, members have the opportunity to change and update their ideas. They can build more effective and rewarding relations with others and address issues about the meaning and relevance of their lives in the social and political contexts where they share common concerns. In addition, support networks for practitioners, trainees and the recently qualified are a priority, such as assistant psychologists' groups and culture clubs. Such networks require planning and leadership to prevent them losing focus or becoming 'a moaning shop'. Attendance is rarely mandatory, but every effort is made to engage the newest members in ongoing personal development.

Discussion Point

How might personal development groups be used for counsellors from differing cultural backgrounds?

What are the implications here for personal development across cultures?

What might be the drawbacks? For example, disclosure or shame.

In Chapter 1 we looked at the impact of institutionalised racism in all walks of Western life, and how that has an impact on white counsellors and the barriers their services create to those non-white potential service users (Bhugra and Bhui, 2007). The reflecting group could address how the experience of being in a dominant culture obliterates difference and makes members assume the default position of current Western values of individualism, personal freedom, empiricism, and technological and scientific innovation. Reliance on factual, normative data, rather than on personal experience, may be another barrier to explore in personal development, where participants can reflect on life experiences, co-counselling and experiential work.

Case Example

One white English counsellor recounted having a baby in Madrid where she spoke only rudimentary Spanish. A Spanish social worker began to help her fill in a complex form and inadvertently rolled her eyes upwards in exasperation at her slowness to respond. In that

(Continued)

---

moment, the counsellor said, 'I understood what it was to be demeaned, humiliated and feel an utterly stupid outsider - and that was before the social worker had uttered a word!'

A white counsellor had been on a working trip in Ghana for three weeks and in that time had not seen a single white person or an image of a white person on an advertisement or billboard. 'Gradually I began to feel more and more invisible. I found myself staring at my hands to check I was really there. I had never understood why seeing people of your own colour, even on TV or in photos, was so important to feeling like a real person before.'

Cultural mentoring

Professional development can be addressed in part with a mentor to help deal with specific issues of CPD that could focus on a specific culture featuring in professional practice. Some practitioners do this by contact with local community groups and they are willing to pay for time. Others do it on the basis of a skills swap – for example cultural mentoring exchanged for time and knowledge or training in another domain. This can be enjoyable and open up surprising areas of new learning. Social networking sites provide good opportunities for initiating this.

Conclusions

In their chapter on a cultural capability framework in mental healthcare to challenge ethnic inequalities, Bhui and Bhugra (2003) suggest that 'simply ticking boxes to say that professionals are culturally capable will not do' (p. 88). Rather, they argue for something much more dynamic including CPD, reflective practice, the acquisition of new and transferable cultural skills, and the progression of learning in continually new situations. They propose that a broader understanding of cultural competence be made mandatory for all mental health training, and specifically for cross-cultural work. The practitioner learns about many types of inequality in employment, housing, education, family life, child-rearing, religious and dietary practices – all of which improve transcultural understanding and practice. More, they suggest that practitioners reach out to community groups as part of their own *life-long learning* – to see how voluntary and specialist providers respond to diverse communities, for clinical, culturally appropriate, practice-based solutions. This chapter has suggested a number of ways that counsellors commit to personal and professional development, and has recommended ways of maintaining quality. The effectiveness and sustainability of these processes, however, has still to be evaluated, and applied across many transcultural settings.

10

AN EVIDENCE BASE FOR
TRANSCULTURAL COUNSELLING

A wise man proportions his belief to the evidence.

David Hume

Summary

This chapter explains why evidence is central to transcultural counselling and how practitioners, individually and collectively, can contribute to it. The outcome for BME clients
is revisited, with a focus on ethnic matching as a source of satisfaction and engagement.
Other sources of outcome include supervision, clinical audit, case presentations,
reflective practice, critical reviews of literature and collaborative research. Quantitative,
qualitative and mixed methods are compared through case examples for transcultural
application. Ethical issues and technical research skills for outcome research are
identified together with the unique challenges of obtaining an evidence base.

Introduction

Readers of this book might believe that it offers evidence about transcultural
counselling. Is it feasible or effective? How do I feel about it? Can others try
it? Can others also observe and replicate and draw the same conclusions?
These questions lead practitioners to seek and build an *evidence base*. The term
has become both fashionable and political, but begs the question about what
has been practised by counselling professionals until now (Summerfield, 2004,
2008). It also reveals a more educated and sceptical public who may have
reason to think that some counsellors' practice is based on personal, uncor-
roborated belief. Cooper (2008) quotes Morrow-Bradley and Elliott (1986)
who surveyed American counsellors and found: 48 per cent of them gave 'their
ongoing experiences with clients' as a useful source of information about how
to practise; 10 per cent ranked theoretical literature; 8 per cent gave their own
experiences as clients as a source of knowledge; but only 4 per cent found
research literature a useful source of knowledge.

All counselling activity can be understood as an investigation – whether it is examining an entire approach to counselling across cultures, a type of counselling service, its clients, an individual client or practitioner or a single counselling session. Throughout this book there have been references to examples of good practice, case studies, larger studies with controls and randomised control trials, because wherever possible, an understanding of this subject requires looking at what is currently known, and what remains to be tested.

In the UK, clinical services in the public sector are subject to *clinical governance*, including audit and evaluation, which continuously enables services to improve. There also exist procedures for life-long learning and putting research results into practice. These include psychological treatments and counselling, and ensure clinical excellence from practitioners and services (Corrie, 2003; Department of Health, 1999).

Counselling evidence is in the domain of applied science; transcultural clinicians can consider themselves as science practitioners, building an evidence base. However, they work in a complex environment. First and foremost they are engaged *in therapeutic relationships*, and some have argued (Coyle and Olsen, 2005; Martin, 2010) that counsellors have differing criteria for evidence from other mental health professionals. They use their skills and knowledge in understanding individuals, but do not always collate case results to add to normative data. The debate continues, but increasingly counsellors are being encouraged, despite heavy workloads, to use supervision, case evaluations, clinical audit, reflective practice and a critical review of the literature, to contribute to evidence gathering (BACP, 2012).

> **Discussion Points**
>
> What evidence features in your current practice?
>
> What are the limitations of personal experience in transcultural practice?
>
> Are there other forms of evidence you might seek?

Evidence from BME clients

The Sainsbury Centre showed that black people are less likely to be offered talking therapies (Fernando, 2005) and more likely to be offered medicine or coercive treatments. Black clients attend fewer sessions and drop out more quickly than their white counterparts. Also, Asian clients report less satisfaction than white clients with the process of psychotherapy (Bhui and Bhugra, 2007; Cooper, 2008; Fernando, 2009). In general, there is evidence that clients of whatever cultural background need positive involvement and motivation to derive maximum benefit from therapy (Bhui and Bhugra, 2007). Clients on a low income and the unemployed also drop out more frequently, are more socially marginalised and may experience less motivation. They report many concerns: the organisation and cost of getting into regular sessions; the rules of attendance; the completion of forms; the fear of bureaucracy; the constant distractions of social and legal difficulties make focus in therapy very demanding. Clients from BME backgrounds and those with refugee experience are closer than many white clients to social exclusion and poverty, which also contribute to different therapy outcomes.

Discussion Points

How might social factors influence your client outcomes?

Why would refugee clients and those experiencing racism be even more affected?

How might they be supported better, and how would you evaluate that?

Ethnic matching

The outcome evidence on *ethnic matching* is inconsistent and the differences are compounded by engagement. Beutler et al. (2004) did a meta-analysis and found a very small effect that was not noticed across all ethnic groups. One study found black clients stayed longer with black counsellors, and there is some evidence in the field of depression that ethnic matching might be of some value. Clients like it, express greater satisfaction and report higher levels of rapport (Cooper, 2008; Ewing, 1974). In an excellent overview of research on ethnic matching, Farsimadan et al. (2011) conclude that people prefer a matched therapist, which has implications for uptake, drop-out rates, premature ending and post-therapy functioning. They describe how clients appreciated seeing a matched therapist; half of them specified that ethnicity and race was something they could discuss with their therapist; black clients identified distress as coming from the white majority culture, and they did not trust white practitioners.

Zane et al. (2004) suggest that white counsellors can deal with racism and with cultural and racial difference, and achieve as good a result with BME clients as any 'matched' counsellor. Both racial awareness and transcultural skills are required. Abbott (1999) advocates the need to recruit more BME counsellors to ensure that the profession is as representative of the community as possible.

Practice Points

How do you gather evidence about your clients' ethnic backgrounds?

Do you attempt to match counsellors ethnically with clients?

Do you compare outcomes between groups or between counsellors?

Research process as evidence gathering

One useful definition of research is: 'A systematic process of enquiry that leads to the development of new knowledge' (Cooper, 2008). The BPS (2004) defines research as 'an attempt to discover generalisable and new knowledge by addressing clearly defined questions with systematic and rigorous methods, and/or involving experimental introduction into practice (for example, studies that examine two or more alternative methods of care and/or procedures)'. This definition, however, makes no reference to how and why defined questions are devised, and by whom.

The UK Department of Health has created a hierarchy of research evidence (Department of Health, 2001).

> Type I: a good systematic review with at least one randomised controlled trial
> Type II: one good randomised controlled trial
> Type III: a well-designed study without randomisation
> Type IV: at least one well-designed observational study
> Type V: opinions of experts, users and carers.

Fonagy and Roth (2005), however, comment that psychotherapy and counselling research evidence rarely applies to Type I or Type II, and that the usefulness of research evidence for practising counsellors is therefore limited.

The APA defines the evidence base as 'the integration of the best available research with clinical expertise in the context of patient characteristics, culture and preferences' (APA, 2006). This is a definition of research that places it within the wider contexts facing transcultural counsellors.

Corrie (2003) describes the nature of evidence within counselling psychology, and the gap between research and practice, as being both complex and dynamic, and requiring individual and collective application. Counselling places the experience of the individual above ideas of diagnosis and treatment, and comparisons of evidence may be limited in practice. Corrie (2003) concludes that clinical practice has a vital role to play in informing research, as much as the other way round, i.e. *evidence-based practice must be complemented by practice-based evidence*.

Why research?

The BACP (2012) describes research as needed to underpin the delivery of 'safe, accountable, high quality and effective psychological therapy' in accordance with its own mission. Research activity supports BACP's vision of moving towards an emotionally healthy society, and (it claims) will help with the following:

- to develop a research culture within the organisation and professions of counselling and psychotherapy
- to identify and contribute to the evidence base for counselling and psychotherapy, in collaboration with external academic partners

- to develop a national infrastructure for research
- to evolve as an evidence-based policy organisation
- to establish and sustain the BACP Research Foundation.

Research shows therapy can be based on rational principles, with emphasis on outcomes, where clients make a critical contribution to an understanding of process. Research allows comparisons to be made of different models, different settings, and with clients from different cultural or ethnic groups. Research reveals the client's point of view in circumstances that might not occur within the counselling relationship because of the power imbalance. Clients reveal more accurate and therefore more valid information about counselling when it is observed independently and anonymously (Rennie, 1998). Evidence that is objective and *replicable*, i.e. repeatable, increases confidence in counselling practice. Research can also verify whether or not so called 'Western' interventions are feasible with minority clients and in the wider world (d'Ardenne et al., 2009; Rathod et al., 2010; Sonderegger et al., 2011). In summary, research provides the practitioner with knowledge, informs and therefore improves clinical practice, and increases confidence in counselling to clients, referrers and the public.

Professional claims to an evidence base

Counsellors have training in working from evidence. Many employed in statutory services also have research activity explicitly itemised as part of their job description, personal specification and professional development goals. One of the outcomes of the Improving Access to Psychological Therapies (IAPT) Programme in the UK (Bhui and Bhugra, 2007; Richards and Whyte, 2009) has been the greater emphasis placed on clinical outcome, made by those who commission therapies, seeking robust evidence. Cognitive behaviour therapy may have been an over-sold product (Cooper, 2008); but it has always enjoyed a strong evidence base, and it is easy to see why the public has embraced it in ways that have not always been the case for other models of counselling and psychotherapy (Fonagy and Roth, 2005).

The BABCP is moving towards regulation of counselling titles and requires an evidence base for all its practice. Mace (1995) points out three important trends in current psychological therapies that now make evidence gathering more feasible.

- Counselling and psychotherapy are now independent professions with accreditation and the public therefore expects evidence-based practice
- There has been more collaboration between differing schools of therapy, and the possible emergence of universal principles of care that apply across models – and possibly across cultures
- There has been a rapprochement between practice and research, especially in dynamic and person-centred models, which has meant that, as for CBT, they can be much more precise about outcomes.

Counselling remains as diverse as ever with a bewildering array of methods, theoretical approaches, training and supervisory paradigms. Yet, few publish (Cooper, 2008; d'Ardenne et al., 2007a). Ask any counselling team about their research activity, and they will cite pressure of work, research being too difficult, hostility from managers, lack of resources and lack of encouragement and confidence. Research becomes the responsibility of others, often a few high-profile authors who write well (Fonagy and Roth, 2005). Research activity, however, has to become the responsibility of all who practise. Transcultural counselling is based on moral imperatives relating to human rights. This is important; but research could demonstrate that cultural approaches were also as effective as current practice and, better still, evidence could support the applicability of cultural approaches to those currently excluded from counselling.

Discussion Points

Here are two statements made about counselling requiring an evidence-based response:

Western counselling can never be universally applicable.

Certain ethnic groups somaticise their psychological problems and do not seek talking therapies.

In the first example, the title 'Western' implies that a therapy needs to be culturally mediated. The only way to test it is to apply a psychological technique to named populations. There is evidence, for example, that CBT can be used with post-conflict societies (Naeem et al., 2010; Sonderegger et al. 2011).

In the second example, it is important to identify which ethnic groups somaticise and the social context and meaning of it. Fernando (2009), for example, has argued that this perception is more likely to be an outcome of racist services – where somatic symptoms may be seen by patients as a less stigmatic ticket of admission into mental healthcare.

Ethics in transcultural research

All counselling research is an ethical activity. Clinical researchers have similar ethical requirements to clinicians (BACP, 2010b). For example, researchers have to be clear what benefit their work has for clients and their capacity to give consent. In inter-racial settings, the power imbalance will be greater, and therefore the ethical requirement to inform and seek active compliance is all the more pressing (Patel and Mahtani, 2007).

Today, there still remains the risk of 'black box' epidemiology, i.e. associating a specific aspect or risk of disease with a specific ethnic group. Many have argued that this approach is too simplistic, and that causal mechanisms are more complex and more subtle. Hunt and Bhopal (2004) have argued that data gathering with non-English speakers poses serious problems of reliability and validity. Researchers fail to familiarise themselves with cultural norms and cause measurement error from inadequate translation procedures and insensitivity to specific topics (Summerfield, 2008). One ethical solution is for Western researchers to undertake participatory research with members of the identified community.

Case Example

You manage a counselling service and carry out an audit where you discover that clients from Afghanistan are not responding to CBT for their post-traumatic difficulties. You compare their progress with other refugee clients including those from Iraq and Liberia as well as UK clients. The Afghani clients have the highest rates of non-engagement, drop out, and poorest symptom reduction. You conclude that Afghani people are resistant to talking therapy.

Practice Points

What is the gender balance, educational level, language support need and source of the trauma within the Afghani group?

Do they compare with the other ethnic client groups?

What type of post-traumatic difficulty prevails?

Are there other explanations for this audit result, not based on ethnicity?

Transcultural methodology

Clinical researchers start with the cultural and linguistic norms of their study population, as well as more local information about specific immigrant groups. They are also able to clarify items like 'ethnicity' since this is invariably self-defined by research participants (ONS, Census, 2011). Ethnicity also needs to be differentiated from other variables, such as poverty or education. There has been a shift of emphasis in international mental health organisations from comparing different ethnic groups to looking at the epidemiology of mental disorder in nation states, and how they approach mental health problems within their own geopolitical contexts (Prince et al., 2007; WPA, 2012).

Research tools, however, must be culturally adapted and standardised to specific populations. Psychometric measures have historically been developed on large heterogeneous populations only. There has been abuse of psychometrics in applying them to other cultures, including those who do not speak

English, where reliability and validity can no longer be assumed (Ahmer et al., 2007; Fernando, 2005; Hunt and Bhopal, 2004; Patel and Mahtani, 2007).

Case Example

You are a counsellor in Liverpool who has translated a tool measuring mood for use with your Cantonese clients, and you have had it back translated to check its meaning and appropriateness. When you administer it, however, some of the items are never answered, including questions about interest in sex. You enquire at a local Chinese advocacy service and discover that your population is unlikely to refer explicitly to sexuality.

Discussion Points

Why are psychometrics being applied here?

How might this situation have been avoided?

Control groups

Appropriate control groups in cross-cultural research enable the practitioner to identify whether a specific intervention, has been effective, or whether there has been a generalised therapeutic effect. All participants in psychological research tend to respond positively to the interest and enthusiasm of clinical researchers (Cooper, 2008). A control group that receives no intervention may make a poorer control than one already engaged in a supportive activity. Waiting group controls also enable the researcher to offer the second group treatment at the end of the trial, thus providing care for all participants.

Case Example

You are about to research the impact of creative art therapy on the psychological well-being of Balkan refugees now living in the UK. All of them have been traumatised by the 1990s civil war. You draw up two groups of clients matched for age, ethnic background and levels of post-traumatic stress. You randomly allocate half of the participants to the treatment trial; the other half forms a waiting list control, which is offered therapy at the end of the trial. This control group receives supportive counselling while waiting. The study seeks to identify the differences in outcome between the study group receiving art therapy and the control waiting group.

Evidence gathering through supervision

In transcultural settings, supervision can be used to consider how personal and organisational resources might be better deployed to address a specific cultural need, such as the issue of stigma in mental health. Supervisors here have an important role in encouraging and sharing the counsellor's evidence gathering. This can be done by prompting the counsellor to return to the source of a problem and to identify a question that will progress a joint understanding of what needs to be addressed. The right question represents a key element in clinical research activity. The supervisor can also assist the counsellor in considering the outcome criteria for any planned intervention, together with the aims of the organisation and relevant research protocols.

There are implications here for the training of counsellors to evaluate the outcome of their work carefully, and to be able to make changes likely to increase impact. An important element of supervision is that it is recorded and kept as part of clinical case notes – which can also be shared with the client as part of evidence gathering. Supervision notes should be dated, signed by both parties and include the decisions or outcomes agreed (see Chapter 9).

Reflective practice and learning

Counsellors and clients do not necessarily agree about what represents good outcome (Cooper, 2008). Transcultural outcomes are complex, posing questions about individual, systemic and socio-political factors in the counselling relationship. One way of examining these is for a service team to reflect together about their practice, using direct experience as a starting point for understanding. Such a group can focus on a particular element of work. For example, a few years ago, an audit was carried out in an East London mental health service, which showed that our use of interpreters with refugee clients was not as productive as expected (d'Ardenne et al., 2007b). Interpreted patients were giving up therapy earlier than non-interpreted patients, and it was unclear what the issues were. A series of meetings was convened with senior practitioners who reflected on best practice. The literature about interpreted psychotherapy was reviewed to see if there were any findings that cast light on these issues, and changes needed in practice or theoretical models. Then the most frequently commissioned interpreters were invited to join the team, and given a space to work out what they saw as barriers to effective interpretation, and what was best for them. From all this evidence, a set of protocols was devised for interpreting that could be tried and tested for other services (d'Ardenne et al., 2007b). This was not a big study – but represented a small progress in knowledge about preventing clients from abandoning interpreted therapy.

Quantitative and qualitative evidence

Quantitative information is number based, i.e. it can be counted. Quantitative data is used widely in mental health research and, until recently, was considered to be more 'scientific'. Numbers allow statistical analyses that test whether or not outcomes of psychotherapy or counselling have occurred by chance, or because there was a treatment effect. It is possible to measure successful outcomes entirely by quantitative method. They could be, for example, the level of client satisfaction rated on a scale by each participant. It might be the number of symptoms or problems, or how severely they are rated – usually through standardised scales. It could be clients' behaviour, for example the number of times a day they wash their hands; the amount of alcohol they consume; the number of nightmares they have a week; number of friends they have made; weight they have lost; distance travelled unaccompanied from home; days of work or study completed; number of episodes of dissociation; or the money saved since quitting drugs. All of these examples provide information that can be measured and tracked over time, and compared with other clients, or even incorporated with group outcomes. For the sceptics, quantitative data provides evidence of change that can be understood and evaluated, even if the meaning of change is limited by what is being counted.

Moorhead (2000) makes the following points about quantitative research in inter-racial therapy. White therapists and researchers are never as concerned about the impact of racism as their black counterparts. Clients are too rarely involved in devising research questions and, in general, there is a gap between the interests of researchers and what takes place in the consulting room. Their needs or responses to counselling may be so specific that they cannot be addressed through pre-existing categories (Newland and Patel, 2005), and may require another approach (e.g. qualitative method).

Qualitative evidence

This is language-based research that has gained much credibility – particularly from the discipline of social casework. It is useful when the researcher is not yet certain of what themes may be important in therapy – and where rich information needs to be gathered first (Wilson et al., 2012). In qualitative settings, there is a process of examining the information carefully, often through *thematic analysis*, where teams of observers listen to therapy tapes, look at notes or transcripts, seeking ideas and identifying themes that are revealed but which may not (initially at least) be capable of being counted. This type of evidence gathering is useful when breaking new frontiers in transcultural counselling contexts (Arulmani, 2007), where the individual voice is paramount (du Plock, 2010; Eleftheriadou, 1994; Martin, 2010). Qualitative methods allows a new idea about a process to emerge. It is a phenomenological method that can reflect the declarative experience in all counselling therapy. It also allows questions to be raised by members of the community being researched, including service users, and generates further studies that are culturally specific. Ideally evidence that uses methodological pluralism, i.e. incorporates quantitative *and* qualitative elements, is likely to have the greatest impact – as each serves somewhat different functions (Cooper, 2008; Coyle and Olsen, 2005).

Case Example

A music therapy study (Sloboda et al., 2009) used mixed methods to establish the feasibility and effectiveness of a music therapy group with refugee clients. It was therefore essential to find clues about what was likely to work for clients from diverse ethnic backgrounds. The qualitative data, which was recorded on video tape, included themes around the meaning of music in memory; the association of music with violence; the ability to have fun and to 'let go'; and the capacity of music to transcend language.

It was also possible to obtain quantitative data. These included symptom changes for mood and PTSD; number of contacts with the service in treatment; ratings of satisfaction with music therapy; the number of utterances made in a music therapy session; and the number of times they arrived late or left the room early - all as indices of engagement. Finally, the number of participants who then chose talking therapy for their ongoing PTSD was also recorded.

Finding evidence from the literature

Regular reading of peer reviewed journals and books retains its importance as a research activity. However, it takes practice and feedback from others in discussion to make it resonate with clinicians, and to put that knowledge into practice. Some practitioners find it helpful either to join or establish a monthly journal club at work – which enables a group of practitioners to evaluate evidence more critically. One person volunteers to examine a published paper or book chapter in some detail, copies it to colleagues in time for the others to read it and then presents it to the club, which should accommodate different professions and levels of experience. The club keeps a record of its work, and participants use their attendance as part of their CPD log. It is a helpful process for practitioners, unaccustomed to thinking about research, or not believing they have the time to read academic journals. It also allows team members to focus on specific demands of their service (e.g. refugees, interpreted counselling or racism).

There is no universal standard of what constitutes the best journal on transcultural counselling. One dimension is its *impact factor* (IF) – the ratio of the number of citations of articles appearing in the two years following publication in the journal, to the total number of articles published in the relevant year. Thus the IF 5.45 for the *British Journal of Psychiatry* in 2011 shows that the average number of citations in 2011 for each paper published in 2009 and 2010 is just over 5. The IF for the *Journal of Counselling Psychology* is 2.490, and *Cross Cultural Research* is 0.641.

Many cultural journals have no impact factor; nevertheless, impact factors have a large, but debatable, influence on the way scientific research is perceived. Impact factors are controversial because they can be invalid, or manipulated, and because the quality of individual papers may be quite different from the reputation of the journal in which they are read. Cross-cultural practice remains an under-researched topic and authors publish where they can. In addition, it is not easy for papers published from developing countries to achieve a high impact, although they may contain important transcultural findings. Western journals typically cover Western research. Researchers from developing countries have fewer home journals, and are less likely to be cited in mainstream publications. Patel and Kim (2007) call this form of imbalance 'citation racism'. For those in the field, it is at least important to understand that even in publishing there are forms of exclusion and power that have a direct bearing on how we obtain evidence about cultural research.

Lastly, volunteering *to review* books or articles on transcultural counselling is a way of building up knowledge and gaining material for your professional practice and department. Journals often invite reviewers to provide brief evaluations and in return allow the reviewer to keep the original. This is an excellent way of reading systematically and of critically expanding your evidence base.

Discussion Point

Is it hard to find good-quality research on transcultural practice?

Audit

Counselling services that work across cultures can obtain valuable evidence about their work through the *audit cycle*, which requires you to:

choose a topic
review current standards or agree standards
collect data on current practice
use data to make comparisons with standards
implement change to make improvements/benefits
re-audit to make sure practice has improved. (NICE, 2002)

Case Example

You choose a topic: refugee clients who do not attend first counselling appointments. You count the number of referrals of refugees you have and find that 55 per cent do not attend their first appointment. You compare this with non-refugees and find that the standard is 25 per cent. You investigate this by telephoning non-attenders and asking what happened to their appointment letters. They reply that letters are received but either not fully understood or discarded as being too bureaucratic. You then change practice. You obtain permission to send text messages to new clients' mobile phones and send a reminder on the day of the appointment. You then re-audit your attendance of refugee clients and see if the change has improved uptake of your services. This is the audit cycle.

The benefit of clinical audit is that it is a quality improvement process, and one that is mandatory for healthcare professionals within the NHS (Department of Health, 1999). Audit enables change and is an important source of evidence in everyday practice. It leads to the development of local guidelines, the reduction of harm and complaints, and is sensitive to service users and their expectations. Audits mainly involve quantitative data – with an emphasis on counting change as a simple objective process, rather like the auditing of accounts.

Discussion Points

What research questions might the above audit lead to?

Practice Points

Establish a rolling audit programme in your service.

Get help if you work for a larger organisation that has an audit department and register with them.

Invite trainees to undertake audits as a means of learning about the service.

Corrie (2003) observes that the usefulness of evidence is not always related to its scientific merit, and that there are many types of evidence gathering available for counsellors, including audits of the communities of the service users. Cross-cultural awareness of the needs of the community are sometimes so specific as to be lost within group data.

Research as a social process

Undergraduate research may be a lonely, competitive business, proving personal competence and requiring perseverance. In clinical practice, it is more about collaboration, sharing thoughts, reading together, looking at each others' presentations and generating new questions, new ways of thinking about old ideas and correcting errors of thinking or calculation.

Practice Points

Join or set up a research club where you can talk about ideas especially with counsellors who are already passionate about research. Bring your transcultural issues to the discussion.

Find those who are already publishing, and ask them to meet to share information and ideas.

Look for conferences where you might develop a joint presentation.

Show your proposal to others for critical appraisal – especially cross-cultural proposals to BME practitioners and users. This is an important opportunity for improvement.

Participate in a multicentred study or trial where your data will be included. That way you do not have responsibility for the original questions, design, ethics application or write up, but your contribution will be published.

Install a noticeboard in your service. Keep it up to date with any research activities. It will motivate those who visit, or who want to participate, including service users. Make sure you anonymise any displayed data (d'Ardenne and Heke, 2011).

Additional research skills

There remain more specific research skills that readers will need once they have made the commitment to an evidence-based approach. These include literature searches, using key words or phrases critically, reviewing the existing literature, developing a research question or experiment, writing a proposal and filling in an ethics application form. Two useful organisations that help applicants navigate ethics applications are: www.seahorsescientific.com and www.wellcome.ac.uk. The Mental Health Research Network (www.mhrn. info) is a UK-wide organisation supporting research studies carried out in England with the help of people who use services as well as people who work in them. For example, they have a free system for finding people with experience of mental health problems, to offer expert advice about patient information sheets, consent forms and recruitment strategies. This service also advises on recruitment barriers to your project and makes sure information for potential participants is clear and easily understood.

Similarly, counsellors who want advice about their quantitative research and the application of statistical method to the design and analysis of their data will find many helpful links on the Mental Health Research Network (www.mhrn. info/pages/methodology-research-group-useful-links.html). Cooper (2008) provides a jargon-free introduction to a basic range of inferential tests in psychotherapy research with applied examples, and without jargon.

Conclusions

There remains much work to be done to gather and maintain an evidence base for transcultural counselling. The barriers remain in the individual nature of the counselling relationship, the practice of leaving research to 'the experts', and the complexities of culture and racism in the client and practitioner's experiences. Evidence can be sought at every level from the single counselling session, through to multicentred trials but depends on changing the culture and priorities within the counselling professions. An evidence base is essential to inform and improve transcultural practice, and mixed methods seem ideal to enable the clients' viewpoints to be incorporated into research questions and evaluation.

11

FUTURE DIRECTIONS FOR
TRANSCULTURAL COUNSELLING

This restless world

Is full of chances, which by habit's power

To learn to bear is easier than to shun.

John Armstrong

Summary

This chapter draws together the applications of transcultural counselling, and identifies where core cultural competencies can be developed through professional bodies, as well as through transcultural courses around the world. New directions for transcultural counselling study and practice include: the cultural contexts of interpersonal violence; social exclusion; users' movements; transcultural counselling in travel medicine; working in and with the developing world for global health equality; providing health information for all; and the effects of globalisation on well-being.

Introduction

This book began with the idea of transcultural counselling being as dynamic as the political and social contexts in which people function. Successful trade, sport, tourism, logistics and education are now global activities, depending on considerable resource and skill. However, we have seen that peace-keeping, humanitarian aid, healthcare, missionary work and migration within hostile environments require more resilience and associated psychological support, based on a proactive and informed response from counsellors. This chapter will draw together what has been established about transcultural counselling models, and will identify priorities for practitioners and those at the start of their counselling career who wish to develop new approaches and contexts in a restless world.

Transcultural counselling is still evolving from its anti-discriminatory beginnings. The core competencies of transcultural counselling have been defined in good measure by postgraduate courses (many of which are listed in the Appendix), and which will be of interest to the reader who wants to research these. Many of these focus on transcultural models applied to specific user groups – some of which have been covered in this text. They include specific cultural knowledge, using interpreting and translating services, or applying and moderating psychological therapies within culturally appropriate settings. The notes on each of the courses describe their content, although it is to be hoped that readers will by now have recognised many of their own abilities and competencies, which are already being deployed and developed.

In addition, the special interest sections of professional bodies such as the BPS, Royal College of Psychiatrists, BACP, APA and American Psychiatric Association are all worth visiting. They have inherited an anti-discriminatory agenda that is a necessary, but maybe not a sufficient, model for the future. We have seen how culture has changed in context from the study of the exotic within anthropology to those who are excluded in mainstream society, starting with colour and race, but extending to language, ability, gender, gender orientation, and religious or political belief. In all of these domains, the ethnocentric position of the counsellor, the counselling organisation and the dominant culture determine how much professional practice needs to adapt to the needs of the communities who do not currently access it.

Black and minority ethnic clients and practitioners have themselves shown how institutional and personal racism in counselling needs to be addressed. They have also shown how the anti-racist and anti-discriminatory competencies are critical to engagement, assessment, therapy and rehabilitation; white practitioners can additionally apply these to supervision, professional training and development, and counselling research.

Individual knowledge of specific cultures, their expressions of distress and their beliefs about the causes of distress come primarily from service users and their communities. Such knowledge can significantly impact on counselling clients in healthcare, palliative care, mental healthcare and asylum seeking, compared with where no outreach is made. Clients from BME groups will drop out of counselling with a white counsellor more quickly than white clients, but the exact reason for this has yet to be determined and the studies have been small. Since most counsellors are still white, however, they must train in anti-discriminatory practice and seek good transcultural knowledge. There is evidence that BME clients prefer ethnic matching but if there is none that the outcome is more effective once engagement in counselling is established. In transcultural practice, counsellors and their clients, as well as counsellors and their supervisors, leave one cultural context and move towards the other – the exact meeting place defined by the working relationship.

Case Example

Opinder is originally from the Punjab and has settled in the UK for over 30 years. He has had a violent breakdown in his relationship with his wife and children, after his eldest daughter refused to accept his choice of a husband for an arranged marriage. She involved the police, leading to Opinder being sent to seek help from a family conciliation service. You work there as a young male British Asian counsellor who holds more open views about marriage. You are aware that in the Punjab, attitudes are changing fast and that alongside arranged marriages, there are now 'self-arranged' or 'love-arranged marriages', where couples initially choose each other but then engage both families to protect and sustain the union. Opinder, however, has had little contact with India or current thinking since the 1970s. He maintains the view that parents should chose a husband for their daughter, with the help of a marriage broker. His position is held with pride; he regards any deviation from this principle as a betrayal of traditional wisdom, and sees it as his duty to defend his values, if necessary with force.

Discussion Points

How far can you meet this client within his cultural context?

Practice Points

The engagement and safety of all is your first priority.

Establishing a voice for Opinder's wife and daughter is the next step. Provide them with additional resources (e.g. Ashiana Project: www.ashiana.org.uk; Forced Marriage Unit of the Foreign and Commonwealth Office: www.fco.gov.uk).

Identify Opinder's friends who may be able to update him without loss of face.

Help him seek solutions that give all parties dignity, and reduce confrontation.

Environmental and economic factors in transcultural counselling

Transcultural contexts in the future will need to consider the impact of the environment, economic inequality and the integration of psychological well-being within a holistic approach to people in transition. This book has considered newer contexts where counselling now contributes, as well as how counsellors and practitioners at the start of their careers can learn to look after themselves and the quality of the service they provide. *The Spirit Level* (Wilkinson and Pickett, 2010) is a radical and influential study that demonstrated the pernicious effects of income inequality in societies all around the world. It showed that income inequality eroded trust, increased anxiety and illness, and encouraged excessive consumption. These two authors (epidemiologists) looked at different health and social indices: physical health, mental health, drug misuse, education, imprisonment, obesity, social mobility, trust and community life, violence, teenage pregnancies and child well-being. They found that all outcomes were significantly worse in more unequal countries, regardless of levels of absolute wealth. Inequality, it seems, is stressful for everyone, including the very rich.

The impact of moving into more or less equal societies can provide future directions for transcultural practice and research. The Occupy and populist anti-elitist movements are both international responses to the global stressors of inequality. Their messages about solidarity, lack of hierarchy and lack of material gain beyond a certain minimum wage ($25,000 per capita per year) could inform our understanding of how people around the world not only survive, but continue to thrive. Emphasis here is linking stressors in the individual to the wider social and environmental contexts – too often omitted in counselling theory.

Global mental health

The WHO (2011) has shown that less than $2 per person a year is spent on mental health, but that figure drops to 25 cents in lower-income countries who have little legislation, prevention, outreach or in-patient services. In this setting, transcultural counselling could play a significant role in global mental health. Mental illness has yet to achieve status as a non-communicable disease within the United Nations. The World Federation for Mental Health (www.wfmh.org) has a campaign 'The Great Push for Mental Health' to urge national governments to budget for mental health planning, and to encourage grassroots organisations to participate in advocacy. An association has been found between mild mental disorders in developing countries (mainly depression and anxiety) economic poverty, insecurity and hopelessness. It may be tackled directly by identifying those most at risk and supporting them, or at a secondary level, by investing more in education and micro credits.

The Federation's 2011 conference addressed mental health and well-being promotion; advocacy and human rights; migration and acculturation; culture and mental health; ecology and mental health; psychosocial rehabilitation; carers' and service users' issues; substance misuse; spirituality and mental well-being; the training of refugees as counsellors, and globalisation and mental health. All of these themes have emerged in transcultural counselling, with its strong anti-discriminatory focus, its ethical tradition and continuing pursuit of evidence in good practice.

Users

The User Movement is a good example of where transcultural counselling models can work to empower and develop those who are struggling to be heard. Transcultural counselling can make a difference to their lives, as well as those of fellow service users (Chapter 7). The relationship between economic independence and mental well-being is barely understood (Crisp, 2010) and is likely to present in very different ways in countries at differing rates of economic development. Further research is needed to identify feasible and effective transcultural interventions for counsellors to support service users (Patel and Kim, 2007).

Homelessness

Homelessness and social marginalisation feature among the young, male and single in the West, and are associated with longer periods of institutional care and psychosis (Abdul-Hamid et al., 2009). There is evidence of individual factors, such as emotional disregulation, shame and negative beliefs about self, contributing to homelessness (Maguire, 2010). There are a number of case studies demonstrating the role of CBT in reducing repeat homelessness, but no known randomised controlled trials to date. Marginalised communities from different minorities will need more investment to develop a model that breaks these cycles of psychological and social disadvantage.

Violence

More cross-cultural investigation will test assumptions about the universality of human traits, and the development of behaviour within varying political, environmental, cultural and economic contexts. A good example of this is the relationship between human development and violence. Pinker (2011) argues that violence has actually been decreasing in the last millennium – a phenomenon across all cultures, through processes such as cosmopolitanism, the 'Long Peace' after World War II, the decline of colonialism and the information revolution. Human beings, it is argued, are similar to most animals and use violence for specific purposes. Alternatives to violence include co-opting the resources of others, inflicting costs on same-sex rivals, negotiating status and hierarchies, all culturally mediated. The contribution of evolutionary psychology (Shackelford, 2005) offers several explanations for human violence in various contexts (e.g. in cultures of honour violence). All of this work will inform and update transcultural models of practice and future research.

Integration of transcultural counselling into travel medicine

There is a growing awareness of the health needs of frequent travellers, and the relationship between psychological and somatic factors in those who travel well, and those who do not. Topics include risk taking, treatment compliance, preparedness and mindfulness when abroad, communication of health needs, before, during and after travel (Lankaster, 2007). To date there has been little integration between travel medicine, the needs of local service users and the impact of (predominantly) Western travellers on the environments they visit, and with which they interact. Western travellers typically take Western models of care, vaccines and cures with them, and are less likely to seek local resources. A more holistic response is envisaged where travellers will make better decisions about their well-being, once they have a fuller picture of the effects of their activities on the communities they are visiting. Transcultural counselling could have a role in helping travellers seek local care and maximise their capacity without compromising the credibility and confidence of local healthcare providers (e.g. www.istm.org). The lesson that has already been learnt from the Global Health Partnerships (Crisp, 2007) is that an alliance of mutual learning is more likely to achieve protection and reduce health inequality.

Future directions for personal development

Chapters 1, 4 and 9 have all referred to language and cultural identity in transcultural counselling. The use of advocacy and bilingual therapists has developed the personal development agenda for practitioners. Those entering the profession will be encouraged to revisit languages learnt in childhood – especially community languages. Professionally qualified practitioners can learn new languages, but it may be as useful for language graduates and BME candidates to turn to counselling careers with their linguistic and cultural competencies.

Many graduates take a gap year travelling round the world. Counsellors can use such opportunities to visit local projects involving the application or development of counselling theory. It is sometimes possible to volunteer on such programmes on an elective placement. Not only does the practitioner learn about local cultural and economic effects on well-being but the travelling is itself enriched by bringing experience to that community (Dowden, 2008). Practitioners can join any one of the many international organisations concerned with mental well-being (e.g. World Psychiatric Association – www.wpanet.org; or Amnesty International – www.amnesty.org.uk) as a means of engaging with global issues.

Future research needs for transcultural counselling

Many transcultural counselling proposals imply increased access to services for people from all backgrounds. The feasibility of a transcultural counselling model and its effectiveness still require more evidence. In particular, there is a need for more outcome research on transcultural effectiveness across languages, and in differing community settings, in the developed and developing world, with people from many more ethnic backgrounds and in very differing situations. Perhaps the biggest task is persuading the dominant culture that transcultural practice is everyone's business. Consider, for example, the exclusion of non-English speakers from most drug trials, medical, psychiatric and other psychological treatments. The default position is that participants are English-language speaking and mainly from the dominant culture, thus ensuring that current knowledge does not address the needs of diverse communities.

The exact process of cross-cultural approaches has not been adequately assessed. Such research is needed to inform service development and innovation. However, it is recommended that policy-makers in transcultural counselling should act on the available evidence to scale up effective treatments and preventative interventions in many more settings.

In recent years there has been a spate of reports on psychosocial support in humanitarian settings. Tol et al. (2011) reviewed 160 studies where basic individual counselling was one of the most commonly reported interventions, but where outcomes were not rigorously matched. Future research needs to link research to practice, and to identify outcomes that would be appropriate across and within cultures.

Kelly and Feeney (2007) looked at stressors in mental health counselling and the development of services, as well as the specific methodological and ethical challenges for transcultural practitioners, and have made some suggestions for future research. Racism is a known stressor leading to poor mental health, physical health and low birth weight. Migration (Karlsen and Nazroo, 2004) is associated with poorer mental and physical well-being. Much research has been done on schizophrenia and its correlation with immigrant groups (Fernando, 2002). Less has been done on racism in community mental health services, or the impact of globalisation on mental health.

Globalisation

Globalisation refers to the dismantling of cultural, political and social borders between countries, continents and peoples (*The Economist*, 2001), and has been caused by improved information technology, deregulation of commercial and economic activity, and increased ease of travel (see Chapter 1). These changes have brought about a broader range of international protocols for mental health training, planning, policy-making and the protection of human rights under the United Nations Convention (WHO, 2005). Service users and service providers in mental health are now likely to have experience of migration, which itself impacts on well-being in a complex and dynamic way.

It is not just the West that is concerned with inequalities in health. Of the eight millennium goals (United Nations, 2000), three refer specifically to health:

reducing child death rates
improving the health of mothers
combating HIV and AIDS, malaria and other diseases.

Crisp (2010) argues that rich countries have been importing health staff from poorer countries for decades, and at the same time exporting their ideologies and technologies in an unfair exchange. He suggests that the West can learn more about health and health services from economically poorer countries, rather than the other way round. Those who have had to struggle with fewer economic resources, civil conflict, environmental changes and natural disasters can provide insights into health improvement within and across all human cultures.

The key features that distinguish how less economically developed countries complement Western medical practice are:

- health is something dealt with as part of life – not as something completely separate
- health workers are trained to meet local needs – and not just as professionals
- public health and clinical medicine are strongly linked
- best use is made of all resources at hand. (Crisp, 2010, p. 107)

Discussion Point

Where are the opportunities for counsellors in global health settings?

What could counsellors learn from economically less developed services?

Practice Point

Volunteer programmes can provide you with valuable professional and personal experience in transcultural practice. Examples include VSO (www.vso.org.uk), Progressio (www.progressio.org.uk), Peace Corps (www.peacecorps.gov) and Cuso International (www.cusointernational.org).

Health professionals as well as politicians around the globe (www.hifa2015. org; THET www.thet.org.uk) have formed real and virtual networks for understanding global health issues, local cures, traditional healing and the need for quick and effective access to health information. Contributors from wealthy and less wealthy countries share ideas about how to work with limited resources, limited information technology, lack of shared language and competing cultural beliefs. Most of all, health workers and trainers debate how traditional and Western clinical models can be used together and separately. Bad health traps sufferers in poverty; and being poor places people in danger of becoming ill. Health information – especially for young mothers, appears to be a key factor in ensuring that whole populations are at less risk from the threat of serious illness. Such information must be culturally appropriate, shared and then evaluated for its health impact. For example, different cultures have varied beliefs and practices in midwifery. In cross-cultural settings this can have consequences if not understood by health workers and those supporting them. Western practice favoured lithotomy, i.e. lying in stirrups, but this is not superior to traditional birth positions, which include standing, kneeling or using a birthing stool (Gupta et al., 2000).

Case Example

You work in Kenya as a trainer and supervisor of local midwives. Their duties are to encourage young mothers to seek good antenatal care, and reduce infant mortality. The midwives inform you that many mothers turn to traditional birth attendants (TBAs), because they like their customs and have more confidence in them. The TBAs and midwives often come from the same tribal group. But the midwives fear that these mothers are then at greater risk, because the TBAs do not refer complicated pregnancies to specialist services, and the maternal and neonatal death rates confirm this. Some of the midwives want to ban TBAs altogether. You have limited training resources, and have become discouraged.

Discussion Points

What are your priorities here?

What would be the consequences of banning TBAs?

Practice Points

Showing respect and friendliness will engage the TBAs.

Focus on specific, achievable changes in practice such as the rapid referral by TBAs of complicated cases only.

Transcultural counselling is in its infancy, and faces many challenges. This chapter has provided some areas of development for practitioners and services around the world. The speed of change has accelerated the demand for talking therapies in cultures that have previously had poor access to this kind of care. Black and minority ethnic clients in the West who were initially excluded from psychological interventions are finding their voice through the User Movement, anti-racist legislation, and through access to the growing number of BME counsellors. The contexts for transcultural work now extend to forced and unforced travellers, with their specific requirements within and beyond their own cultures. There is a dearth of outcome research on the effectiveness or appropriateness of cross-cultural models, but the future looks promising. This book has endeavoured to define priorities for future practitioners, supervisors and researchers. Most counselling work requires transcultural and cultural competence and future training courses should incorporate this topic centrally, rather than as a specialist topic, which it is today.

The Appendix lists a selection of transcultural courses around the world but it may be that these will be redundant in years to come. All counselling is transcultural; there are no counselling contexts where this does not apply. I hope that counselling services will become more representative, by recruiting and supporting counselling candidates from the communities they serve. Equally the diverse communities described will also promote transcultural counselling as an important contribution to the well-being of distressed people throughout our restless world.

APPENDIX

Transcultural postgraduate courses

The following courses have been selected on the basis of an internet search using the terms 'intercultural', 'transcultural', 'cultural', 'interracial', 'psychology', 'counselling', 'courses' both undergraduate and postgraduate. Most of the undergraduate sites provided cultural awareness and diversity as part of their basic introductory syllabus. There were many master's programmes within the realms of education and business but far fewer in applied psychology. Below is a selection of these retrieved from sites visited at the beginning of 2012 using the Google search engine (www.google.co.uk).

The list is in no way comprehensive, nor does it seek to recommend; it has been devised in much the same way that readers would find a course by using the internet. Some of the courses (e.g. at Colombo) emphasise local culture as a way of understanding national identity but do not focus on transcultural issues. Each course summary has been edited according to the amount of information available on the website, and some are more precise than others. The courses are arranged alphabetically according to their geographical location. Readers will need to visit each site and judge for themselves how useful a course might be. Such lists date rapidly; there is nothing better than updating professional links by regular online searches.

Readers might also be interested in a special issue of *Clinical Psychology Forum* (Latchford and Melluish, 2010) that looks at psychology from a global perspective and visits psychological research, training and practice in nations as varied as Ghana, Tanzania, Trinidad and Tobago, and Cuba. There is now an organisation called the International Union of Psychological Science (www. iupsys.net) seeking to address the specific and general challenges facing psychological workers within global contexts. The special issue refers to the training and cultural requirements of practitioners both now and in the future (Bullock, 2010).

Readers might be interested in a 'Map of Social-Personality Psychology Graduate Programs' showing over 90 master's and doctoral programmes in social psychology (www.socialpsychology.org/maps/gradprograms). It does not explicitly refer to transcultural counselling, although many courses cover the topics of local cultural norms, migration and diversity.

Australia

University of Melbourne (Melbourne Medical School):

- Course type: MA
- Course title: Master of Health Sciences
- Duration: 1 year full time, 2 years part time
- Modules

  - Genetic counselling
  - Infant and parent mental health
  - Transcultural Mental Health

- URL: www.medicine.unimelb.edu.au/future/rhd/masterhealthsciences. html

Victoria University of Melbourne:

- Course type: MSc
- Course title: Cross Cultural Psychology
- Duration: 1 year full time, 2 years part time
- Compulsory modules:

  - Research Preparation
  - Current Issues in Cross-cultural Psychology
  - Conducting Research Across Cultures

- Various other chosen modules
- URL: www.victoria.ac.nz/psyc/study/postgraduate-study/msc-cross-cult. aspx#degree

Canada

McGill University (Department of Psychiatry):

- Course type: MSc
- Course title: MSc in Psychiatry (Social and Transcultural Psychiatry)
- Duration: Part time or full time (1 year)
- URL: www.mcgill.ca/psychiatry/education/graduate-program

The University of Alaska-Fairbanks and University of Alaska-Anchorage, Psychology Departments:

- The PhD Programme in Clinical-Community Psychology seeks to educate scholars and clinicians in research, evaluation, clinical practice and community-based action, grounded in the cultural contexts of all affected stakeholders. The programme integrates clinical, community and cultural psychology with a focus on rural, indigenous issues and emphasis on the integration of research and practice.
- URL: http://psyphd.uaa.alaska.edu

The University of Alberta:

- Course type: MA
- Course title: Counselling Psychology
- Duration: Full time (2 years: Practicum)
- Module of interest: Year 1: Cross Cultural Counselling
- URL: www.edpsychology.ualberta.ca/en/GraduatePrograms/Counselling Psychology/CourseBasedCohort.aspx

The University of Saskatchewan:

- Course type: MSc/PhD
- Course title: Culture and Human Development Program
- Duration: Varies
- URL: http://artsandscience.usask.ca/psychology/programs/chdevelopment

China

Zhejiang University (School of International Studies):

- Institute of Cross Cultural Studies
- 'Our mission is to facilitate cross-cultural understanding between China and the world, and to promote cultural diversity in all spheres of social life within and across nations. The Institute aims to develop innovative modes of research to provide insights into the different ways that cross-cultural relations and histories are constructed and represented.' Offers specialisation in Globalisation, Migration and Diaspora Culture.
- URL: www.sis.zju.edu.cn/Item/42.aspx

Egypt

The American University in Cairo (AUC):

- International Counseling and Community Psychology (ICCP) Program
- 'These programs will place AUC and its graduates at the forefront of advancing global trends toward multi-cultural and systemic psychological practice that promotes culturally relevant family, child and community interventions in Egypt and the region.'
- URL: www.aucegypt.edu/huss/sape/gradprog/Pages/ICCP.aspx

Germany

University of Osnabrück:

- Master's Degree in Intercultural Psychology
- Intercultural psychology of culture and development. Including: cross-cultural business psychology, cross-cultural social psychology, a study project and a colloquium on intercultural focus. Introduction to Migration Research: Historical and sociological foundations. Psychotherapy and Counselling (emphasis on intercultural factors).
- URL: www.psycho.uni-osnabrueck.de/institut

Lebanon

The American University of Beirut:

- Undergraduate: Introduction to Culture and Psychology
- Led by Charles Harb, Associate Professor of Social Psychology
- Research interests focus on multiple social identities and the self-concept, with a special interest in the Arab world. Professor Harb is currently working on discrimination, confessionalism, intergroup distance and identities within the Lebanese socio-political context.
- URL: www.aub.edu.lb/fas/psychology/academics/undergraduate/Pages/courses. aspx

Malta

University of Malta: MA in Transcultural Counselling:

- Course type: MA
- Course title: Transcultural Counselling
- Duration: Full time (12–18 months full time and 6 months of practicum)
- Modules:
  - Core Counselling Curriculum
  - Professional Practice
  - Dissertation/Seminar Paper
- URL: www.um.edu.mt/imp/courses/ma-counseling-counselling

Netherlands

Tilburg University:

- Course type: PhD
- Course title: PhD in Cross Cultural Psychology

- Duration: Varies
- URL: www.tilburguniversity.edu/about-tilburg-university/schools/social sciences

Pakistan

Fatima Jinnah Women's University Rawalpindi

- Master's/Bachelor's in Behavioural Sciences
- Specialisations offered include: culture, identity and nationalism, counselling and clinical psychology. The culture, identity and nationalism course encourages students to engage critically with the concepts of culture–nation relationship, nationalism and identity that they have perhaps taken for granted to date. It will also explore the literature of nationalism, including an analysis of the concepts of otherness and difference in the construction of identity, as well as gender, race and class. The advanced course of counselling and clinical psychology covers diversity issues such as trauma counselling, rehabilitation and mental health counselling and counselling for special populations.
- URL: www.fjwu.edu.pk/academic/behavioural.Sciences.htm

Philippines

De La Salle University:

- Master of Science in Psychology, Major in Social and Cultural Psychology
- 'The Social and Cultural Psychology major program provides students with specialized training in the theory and research on the role of socio-cultural factors in shaping human behavior and development. Special emphasis will be given to the epistemological and methodological issues for socio-cultural research and on the applications of social and cultural psychology perspectives to concerns related to gender, health, environment, politics, peace, business and economics, and other development issues in the Philippine setting.'
- URL: www.dlsu.edu.ph/academics/continuing/pdf/cla/ms_psych_major_soc-cultpsych.pdf

Poland

Warsaw School of Social Psychology:

- 5-year Master's Degree and 4-year PhD programmes in Psychology of Intercultural Relations
- Courses are offered in English and in Polish
- URL: www.swps.pl/english

Sri Lanka

University of Colombo:

- Masters/Postgraduate Diploma in Counselling and Psychosocial Support
- 'This programme has been designed to respond to some needs and social concerns prevalent in Sri Lanka. Some of these may be dealt with at an individual level whereas others would require family or community emphasis/outlook. 'Both programmes are interdisciplinary embracing insights from politics, sociology, anthropology and psychology. They will enable students to obtain practical experience, to enhance personal growth and to be absorbed into governmental, non-governmental or private organizations.'
- URL: www.cmb.ac.lk/academic/gradustd/images/stories/courses/FGS_ Courses_New/council/cp_brochure.pdf

United Kingdom

Brunel University, London:

- Course type: MSc
- Course title: Cross Cultural Psychology MSc
- Transcultural Information: teaching on the course is by renowned international experts on culture and ethnicity, with the Brunel teaching team being complemented with visiting speakers from around the world. Recent invited lecturers have included specialists from the USA, Hungary, Russia and Finland.
- Duration: Full time (1 year), Part time (2 years)
- URL: www.brunel.ac.uk/courses/postgraduate/C800PCRCTPSY

King's College London, Institute of Psychiatry/London School of Hygiene and Tropical Medicine:

- Course title: MSc in Global Mental Health
- The course will focus on the development, scaling up and evaluation of locally appropriate and feasible strategies to reduce the burden of mental disorders, including policy, health systems, health services and clinical interventions. Training in epidemiological and health services research methods will be provided to equip students to monitor and evaluate mental health programmes.
- URL:www.kcl.ac.uk/prospectus/graduate/index/name/global-mental-health/ alpha//header_search/MSc+in+Global+Mental+Health

Queen Mary, University of London/Bart's and the London School of Medicine and Dentistry:

- Course type: MSc/PG Dip
- Course title: Mental Health: Transcultural Mental Healthcare/Psychological Therapies
- Duration: Full (1 year) or part time (2 years)
- Modules

  - Module 1: Mental Health Assessment
  - Module 2: *Choose one*

    - Transcultural Mental Healthcare
    - Psychological Therapies

  - Module 3: Research Methods

- URL: www.qmul.ac.uk/qmul/courses/courses.php?dept_id=17&pgcourses= 2&course_id=320&course_level=1&article_id=345

University of East London:

- MSc/PG Cert/PG Dip International Humanitarian Psychosocial Consultation by Distance Learning
- The programme is understood to be the first of its kind, focussing on psychosocial issues within international humanitarian contexts, visiting the multiple contexts that affect people's experiences, capacities and resilience. It provides students with opportunities to learn from professional practitioners who have direct experience of working with populations around the world.
- URL: www.uel.ac.uk/postgraduate/programmes/psychosocial-consult-msc-dl. htm

The University of Northampton (CCPE):

- Course type: PG Dip/MA
- Course title: Counselling and Psychotherapy (PG Dip)/Transpersonal Counselling and Psychotherapy (MA): the spiritual approach to counselling and psychotherapy
- Duration : 4 years part time (PG Dip)

- ○ Suitable Diploma course students may be able to transfer to the MA programme in the third year of their training.

- URL: www.ccpe.org.uk/dippsych.html#description

USA

California School of Professional Psychology-San Diego:

- PhD/Master's programs in Industrial-Organizational Psychology and Organizational Behavior
- URL: www.alliant.edu/cspp/programs-degrees/clinical-psychology/multicultural.php

Harvard Graduate School of Education:

- MA and doctoral degrees in Human Development and Psychology
- 'Enables students to reflect on specific issues such as cultural diversity, bilingualism, literacy development, academic achievement among high-risk populations, the educational progress of immigrants, promotion and development of interpersonal and inter-group relations, prevention of the consequences of risk in the lives of children and adolescents, brain processes in learning, and children's emotional, moral, and cognitive development. Students in the program examine empirical evidence about language development, cognitive development, social and moral development and cultural differences.'
- URL: www.gse.harvard.edu/academics/masters/hdp

University of Chicago (Department of Psychology):

- PhD programme of research and graduate study in cross-cultural studies (including psychological anthropology and cultural psychology).
- The Cultural Psychology Course analyses the concept of 'culture' and examines ethnic and cross-cultural variations in mental functioning, with special attention to the cultural psychology of emotions, self, moral judgement, categorisation and reasoning.
- URL: http://psychology.uchicago.edu

University of Hawaii:

- East–West Center
- Graduate work and research, scholarships; no degrees granted.

- PhD in social-personality with concentration in cross-cultural psychology.
- Programmes of cooperative study, training, and research for Asian and American collaboration and community building.
- URL: www.eastwestcenter.org
- PhD in Community and Cultural Psychology
- The Community and Cultural Concentration (CCC) is a graduate specialisation leading to the PhD in psychology. This multidisciplinary curriculum is designed to provide systematic coverage of the major theoretical and empirical work in the field with sufficient flexibility to meet student interests, enthusiasms and career goals.
- URL: www.psychology.hawaii.edu/pages/graduate_programs/community.html

University of Michigan, Departments of Anthropology and Psychology:

- The Culture and Cognition Program seeks to understand how psychological processes of individuals are shaped through participation in socio-cultural processes and, conversely, the socio-cultural processes are maintained and changed by behaviours of these very individuals.
- URL: www.lsa.umich.edu/psych/grad/program/affiliations/cultcog

University of Pennsylvania, Graduate School of Education:

- MS Ed in intercultural communication, with coursework in linguistics, anthropology and psychology. 'Exploration of issues that arise in communication between cultural groups (including linguistic, social, racial, ethnic, national, gender and other groupings).'
- URL: www.gse.upenn.edu/node/1107

Washington State University, Department of Educational and Counselling Psychology:

- MA and PhD in counselling psychology with emphasis on multicultural counselling
- URL: http://education.wsu.edu/graduate/specializations/counselingpsych/

Western Washington University, Department of Psychology:

- MA in general psychology and MS in mental health counselling with emphasis on cross-cultural counselling
- Cross Cultural Counselling
- Introduction to the cross-cultural perspective in psychology. Conceptual and methodological issues and problems mediated by culture and ethnicity will be considered.

- 'Theories of counselling; personality and psychopathology; cognitive psychology; psychological testing and appraisal; statistics; research methods in counselling; social psychology; standardized tests; lifespan and psychological development; counselling techniques; child and adult individual counselling practicum, family and couple counselling practicum; group practicum; professional, cultural and legal issues; and cross-cultural counselling issues.'
- URL: www.wwu.edu/psychology

REFERENCES

Abbott, D. (1999) 'Foreword', in P. d'Ardenne and A. Mahtani (eds), *Transcultural Counselling in Action*, 2nd edn. London: Sage.

Abbott, D. (2012) 'Young, Black and unemployed: the tragedy of the 44%', *Guardian*, 5 March.

Abdul-Hamid, W., Kotwal, S. and Stansfeld, S. (2009) 'The homelessness of the mentally ill: the old-new issue', *International Journal of Culture and Mental Health*, 2 (S1): 1–17.

Access to Health Records Act 1990. London: HMSO, 1990. Available at www.legislation. gov.uk/ukpga/1990/23/contents (accessed 11 April 2012).

Adichie, C.N. (2007) *Half of a Yellow Sun*. London: Harper Perennial.

Adorno T.W., Frenkel-Brunswick, E., Levinson, D. and Sanford, R. (1950) *The Authoritarian Personality*. Oxford: Harpers.

Afiya Trust (2012) www.afiya-trust.org

Ahmer, S., Faruqui, R. and Aijaz, A. (2007) 'Psychiatric rating scales in Urdu: a systematic review', *BMC Psychiatry*, 7: 59.

Al-Issa I. and Oudji, S. (1998) 'Culture and anxiety disorders' in S. Kazarian and D. Evans (eds), *Cultural Clinical Psychology, Theory Research and Practice*. Oxford: Oxford University Press. pp. 127–51.

American Anthropological Association (1998) Statement on 'Race': position paper. www. aaanet.org/stmts/racepp.htm

American Counseling Association (2002) *Code of Ethics and Standards of Practice*. Alexandria, VA: American Counseling Association.

American Psychiatric Association (2000) *Diagnostic and Statistical Manual of Mental Disorders*, 4th edn – text revision ((DSMIV-TR). Washington, DC: American Psychiatric Association.

American Psychological Association (APA) (2002) *Guidelines on Multicultural Education, Training, Research, Practice, and Organizational Change for Psychologists*. Washington, DC: American Psychological Association.

American Psychological Association (APA) (2006) *Evidence-Based Practice in Psychology*. Washington, DC: American Psychological Association.

American Psychological Association (APA) (2007) *Resolution on Religious, Religion-Based and/or Religion-Derived Prejudice*. Washington, DC: American Psychological Association.

Angelou, M. (1995) *The Complete Collected Poems of Maya Angelou*. London: Virago Press.

Arcel, L. and Simunkovic, G. (eds) (1998) *War Violence, Trauma and the Coping Process: Armed Conflict in Europe and Survivor Responses*. Copenhagen: International Rehabilitation Council for Torture Victims.

Article 19 (2003) *Media Coverage of Asylum Seekers: What's the Story?* Available at www. article19.org/resources.php/resource/183/en/media-coverage-of-asylum-seekers:-what's-the-story

Arulmani, G. (2007) 'Counselling psychology in India: at the confluence of two traditions', *Applied Psychology: An International Review*, 56 (1): 69–82.

Asylum Aid (2011) *Unsustainable: The Quality of Initial Decision Making in Women's Asylum Claims.* London: Asylum Aid.

Atukunda, J. (2011) Interview. Available at http://it-it.facebook.com/notes/heartsounds-uganda/the-heart-of-heartsounds-interview-with-joseph-atukunda-service-user-and-coordin/192349230816388

Avigad, J. (2003) 'On becoming a supervisor to teams working with survivors of torture', *Context – A News Magazine of Family Therapy*, 67: 26–8.

Avon NHS Trust (2008) *Health Equity Audit of Maternity Care and Birth Outcomes in Bristol 2003–5.* Bristol: Avon NHS Trust. Available at www.avon.nhs.uk/phnet (accessed 26 November 2011).

Baillie, D., Boardman, J., Onen, T., Gedde, M. and Parry, E. (2009) 'NHS Links: achievements of a scheme between one London mental health trust and Uganda', *Psychiatric Bulletin*, 33: 265–9.

Barrett, J.L. and Burdett, E.R. (2011) 'The cognitive science of religion', *The Psychologist*, 24 (4): 252–5.

Barty, A. (2011) 'International students: who are they?', in Colin Lago (ed.), *The Handbook of Transcultural Counselling & Psychotherapy.* Maidenhead: Open University Press. pp. 169–82.

Busuttil, W. (2008) 'Message for medical professionals'. Leatherhead: Combat Stress. Available at www.combatstress.org.uk (accessed 24 May 2012).

BBC News (2001) 'Bereaved relatives "still in shock"', *BBC News*, 21 September. Available at http://news.bbc.co.uk/1/hi/uk/1556863.stm (accessed 11 April 2011).

Berry, J., Poortinga, Y., Segall, M. and Dasen, P. (2002) *Cross-Cultural Psychology: Research and Applications*, 2nd edn. Cambridge: Cambridge University Press.

Beutler, L.E., Mohr, D., Alimohamed, S., Harwood, M, Talebi, H. and Noble, S. (2004) 'Therapist variables', in M. Lambert (ed.), *Bergin and Garfield's Handbook of Psychotherapy and Behavior Change*, 5th edn. Chicago: John Wiley & Sons. pp. 227–306.

Bhatti-Sinclair, K. (2011) *Anti-Racist Practice in Social Work: Reshaping Social Work.* Basingstoke: Palgrave Macmillan.

Bhugra, D. and Bhui, K. (2007) *Textbook of Cultural Psychiatry.* Cambridge: Cambridge University Press.

Bhugra D. and de Silva, P. (2007) 'Sexual dysfunction across cultures', in K. Bhui (ed.), *Textbook of Cultural Psychiatry.* Cambridge: Cambridge University Press. pp. 364–78.

Bhugra D., Sumathipala A. and Sirbaddana, S. (2007) 'Culture-bound syndromes: a re-evaluation', in D. Bhugra and K. Bhui (eds), *Textbook of Cultural Psychiatry.* Cambridge: Cambridge University Press. pp. 141–56.

Bhui, K. (2002) *Racism and Mental Health: Prejudice and Suffering.* London: Jessica Kingsely.

Bhui, K. and Bhugra, D. (2003) *A Textbook of Cultural Psychiatry.* Cambridge: Cambridge University Press.

Bhui, K. and Bhugra, D. (2007) 'Ethnic inequalities and cultural capability framework in mental healthcare', in D. Bhugra and K. Bhui (eds), *A Handbook of Cultural Psychiatry.* Cambridge: Cambridge University Press. pp. 81–90.

Bhui, K., Stansfeld, S., Hull, S., Priebe, S., Mole, F. and Feder, G. (2003) 'Ethnic variations in pathways to and use of specialist mental health services in the UK: systematic review', *British Journal of Psychiatry*, 182: 105–16.

Bjorn, G.J. (2005) 'Ethics and interpreting in psychotherapy with refugee children and families', *Nordic Journal of Psychiatry*, 59: 516–21.

Bochner, S. (2003) 'Culture shock due to contact with unfamiliar cultures', *Online Readings in Psychology and Culture, Unit 8.* Melbourne, FL: International Association for Cross-Cultural Psychology. Available at http://scholarworks.gvsu.edu/orpc/vol8/iss1/7 (accessed 11 April 2012).

Bond, T. (2005) 'Developing and monitoring professional ethics and good practice guide-lines', in R. Tribe and J. Morrissey (eds), *Handbook of Professional and Ethical Practice for Psychologists, Counsellors and Psychotherapists*. Hove: Brunner-Routledge.

Bot, H. (2005) 'Dialogue interpreting as a specific case of reported speech', *Interpreting*, 7: 237–61.

Bot, H. and Wadensjo, C. (2004) 'The presence of a third party: a dialogical view on interpreter-assisted treatment', in J.P. Wilson and B. Drozdec (eds), *Broken Spirits: The Treatment of Traumatised Asylum Seekers, Refugees, War And Torture Victims*. Hove: Brunner Routledge.

Bowcott, O. (2010) 'Britain's child migrants lost their childhoods to years of hard labour', *Guardian*, 24 February.

Brewin, C.R., Dalgeish, T. and Joseph, S. (1996) 'A dual representation theory of posttrau-matic stress disorder', *Psychological Review*, 103: 670–86.

British Association for Behavioural and Cognitive Psychotherapy (BABCP) (2010) *Standards of Conduct, Performance and Ethics*. Revised November 2010. Available at www.babcp.com/Files/About/BABCP-Standards-of-Conduct-Performance-and-Ethics.pdf (accessed 22 May 2012).

British Association for Counselling and Psychotherapy (BACP) (2010a) *About the BACP*. Lutterworth: BACP. Available at www.bacp.co.uk/about_bacp (accessed 19 April 2012).

British Association for Counselling and Psychotherapy (BACP) (2010b) *Ethical Framework for Good Practice in Counselling and Psychotherapy*. Lutterworth: BACP. Available at www.bacp.co.uk/admin/structure/files/pdf/566_ethical_framework_feb2010.pdf (accessed 19 April 2012).

British Association for Counselling and Psychotherapy (BACP) (2012) *Research Strategy*. Lutterworth: BACP. Available at www.bacp.co.uk/research/about_research (accessed 19 April 2012).

British Psychological Society (BPS) (2001) British Psychological Society, Division of Clinical Psychology.

British Psychological Society (BPS) (2004) *Good Practice Guidelines for the Conduct of Psychological Research within the NHS*. Leicester: BPS.

British Psychological Society (BPS) (2006) *Guidelines for Supervision*. Leicester: BPS.

British Psychological Society (BPS) (2011) *Code of Conduct of the British Psychological Society*. Leicester: BPS.

Bullock, M. (2010) 'Challenges to psychology from an international perspective: activities of the International Union of Psychological Science', *Clinical Psychology Forum*, 215 (November): 12–16

Burke, A. (1984) 'Racism and mental illness', *International Journal of Social Psychiatry*, 30 (special issue), 1–2.

Burnett, A. and Peel, M. (2001) 'Health needs of asylum seekers and refugees', *BMJ*, 322 (7285); 544–7.

Burnett, A. and Rhys-Jones, D. (2006) 'Health care for asylum seekers' (rapid response), *BMJ Online*, 4 August. Available at www.bmj.com/rapid-response/2011/10/31/health-care-asylum-seekers (accessed 11 April 2012).

Care Quality Commission (2012) *Government Standards*. Available atwww.cqc.org.uk/public/what-are-standards/government-standards (accessed 24 May 2012).

Carr, C., d'Ardenne, P., Sloboda, A., Scott, C., Wang, D. and Priebe, S. (2012) 'Group music therapy for patients with persistent post-traumatic stress disorder – an exploratory randomized controlled trial with mixed methods evaluation', *Psychology and Psychotherapy: Theory Research and Practice*, 85 (2): 179–202.

Carter, H. (2011) 'Shafilea Ahmed "honour killing" witnessed by sister, court told', *Guardian*, 21 May.

Confidential Enquiry into Maternal and Child Health (CEMACH) (2007) *Confidential Enquiry into Maternal and Child Health – Top Ten Recommendations from the 2003 Report*. London: Royal College of Obstetricians and Gynaecologists.

Centre for Psychological Services Research, University of Sheffield (2010) *An Evaluation of Six Community Mental Health Pilots for Veterans of the Armed Forces. A Case Study Series for the Ministry of Defence CTLBC-405*. Sheffield: University of Sheffield. Available at www.mod.uk/NR/rdonlyres/965AB741-60E9-4545-B576-2F32D624 CC3E/0/evaluation_community_mental_health_pilots_veterans.pdf (accessed 12 April 2012).

Centre for Social Cohesion (2010) *Crimes of the Community: Honour-Based Violence in the UK*. London: Centre for Social Cohesion. Available from www.socialcohesion.co.uk/files/1301650858_1.pdf (accessed 24 May 2012).

Chamberlin, J. (1988) *On Our Own*. London. National Association for Mental Health.

Chang, T. (2005) 'Online counselling: prioritizing psychoeducation, self-help, and mutual help for counseling psychology research and practice', *The Counseling Psychologist*, 33 (6): 881–9.

Children Act 1989. London: HMSO. Available at www.legislation.gov.uk/ukpga/1989/41/introduction (accessed 11 April 2012).

Cinnirella, M. and Loewanthal, K. (1999) 'Religious and ethnic group influences on beliefs about mental illness: a qualitative interview study', *British Journal of Medical Psychology*, 72 (94): 505–24.

Clarke, I. (2001) 'Psychosis and spirituality: the discontinuity model', in I. Clarke (ed.), *Psychosis and Spirituality: Exploring the New Frontier*. London: Whurr.

Cochrane, R. (1977) 'Mental illness in immigrants to England and Wales', *Social Psychiatry*, 12: 25–35.

Cochrane, R. and Sashidharan, S.P. (1996) *Mental Health and Ethnic Minorities: A Review of the Literature and Service Implications. CRD Report 5*. York: NHS Centre for Reviews and Dissemination, Social Policy Research Unit, University of York.

Coleman, A.M. (1972) '"Scientific" racism and the evidence on race and intelligence', *Race & Class*, 14: 137–53.

Collicutt, J. (2011) Psychology, religion and spirituality. *The Psychologist*, 24 (4): 250–3.

Cooper, M. (2008) *Essential Research Findings in Counselling Psychotherapy: The Facts are Friendly*. London: Sage.

Corrie, S. (2003) 'Information, innovation and the quest for legitimate knowledge', *Counselling Psychology Review*, 18 (3): 5–13.

Council of Europe (1950) *European Convention for the Protection of Human Rights (1950)*. Strasbourg: Council of Europe Publishing.

Coyle, A. and Olsen, C. (2005). 'Research in therapeutic practice settings: ethical considerations', in R. Tribe and J. Morrissey (eds), *Handbook of Professional and Ethical Practice for Psychologists, Counsellors and Psychotherapists*. Hove: Brunner-Routledge. pp. 249–62.

Coyle, A. and Lochner, J. (2011) Religion, spirituality and therapeutic practice. *The Psychologist*, 24 (4): 264–6.

Crisp, N. (2007) *Global Health Partnerships: The UK Contribution to Health in Developing Countries*. London: Department of Health. Available at www.dh.gov.uk/en/Publicationsandstatistics/Publications/PublicationsPolicyandGuidance/DH_065374 (accessed 11 April 2012).

Crisp, N. (2010) *Turning the World Upside Down: The Search for Global Health in the 21st Century*. London: Royal Society of Medicine Press.

Crown, S. and d'Ardenne, P. (1982) 'Symposium on sexual dysfunction', *British Journal of Psychiatry*, 140: 70–7.

Crown, S. and d'Ardenne, P. (1986) 'Sexual dysfunction in Asian couples', *BMJ*, 292: 1078–80.

Culliford, L. (2007) 'Taking a spiritual history', *Advances in Psychiatric Treatment*, 13: 212–19.

Curling P. and Simmons K. (2010) 'Stress and staff support strategies for international aid work', *Intervention*, 5 (2), 93–105.

Daily Mail (2009) 'Schizophrenic who killed Jonathan Zito set to be moved from high-security prison', *Daily Mail*, 24 March.

d'Ardenne, P. (1986) 'Sexual dysfunction in a transcultural setting: assessment treatment and research', *Sexual and Marital Therapy*, 1 (1): 23–34.

d'Ardenne, P. (2009) 'The mental health needs of refugee women with PTSD', *Proceedings of the Annual Meeting of the Royal College of Psychiatrists: A Fair Deal for All: Mental Health in a Multicultural Society*. Liverpool, 2–9 June.

d'Ardenne, P. and Heke, S. (2011) 'Wrestling with our demons: getting started with research in trauma', *Proceedings of the United Kingdom Post Traumatic Stress Society 3rd Annual Conference*. Oxford.

d'Ardenne, P. and Mahtani, A. (1989) *Transcultural Counselling in Action*. London: Sage.

d'Ardenne P. and Mahtani, A. (1999) *Transcultural Counselling in Action*, 2nd edn. London: Sage.

d'Ardenne, P. and Morrod, D. (2003) 'Sick children – parents under pressure', in *The Counselling of Couples in Healthcare Settings: A Handbook for Clinicians*. London: Whurr. pp. 53–65.

d'Ardenne, P., Capuzzo, N., Ruaro, L. and Priebe, S. (2005). 'One size fits all? Cultural sensitivity in a psychological service for traumatised refugees', *Diversity in Health and Social Care*, 2: 29–36.

d'Ardenne, P., Cestari, L. and Priebe, S. (2007a) 'The challenge of regular outcome assessment: why do we fail?', *Clinical Psychology Forum*, 173: 7–12.

d'Ardenne, P., Farmer, E., Ruaro, L. and Priebe, S. (2007b). 'Not lost in translation: proto-cols for interpreting trauma-focused CBT', *Behavioural and Cognitive Psychotherapy*, 35: 303–16.

d'Ardenne, P., Ruaro, L., Cestari, L., Wakhoury, W., and Priebe, S. (2007c) 'Does interpreter-mediated CBT with traumatized refugee people work? A comparison of patient outcomes in East London', *Behavioural and Cognitive Psychotherapy*, 35: 293–301.

d'Ardenne, P., Dorner, H., Walugembe, J., Nakibuuka, A., Nsereko, J., Onen, T. and Hall, C. (2009) 'Training in the management of post-traumatic stress disorder in Uganda', *International Psychiatry*, 6 (3): 67–68.

Data Protection Act 1998. London: TSO. Available at www.legislation.gov.uk/ukpga/1998/29/contents (accessed 11 April 2012).

Davidson, S. (2010a) 'Psychosocial support within a global movement', *The Psychologist*, 23 (4): 304–7.

Davidson, S. (2010b) 'The development of the British Red Cross Psychosocial Framework: CALMER', *Journal of Social Work Practice*, 24: 29–42.

Davies, M., Griffiths, M. and Vice, S. (2001) 'Affective reactions to auditory hallucinations in psychiatric, evangelical, and control groups', *British Journal of Clinical Psychology*, 40: 361–70.

Dawkins, R. (2006) *The God Delusion*. London. Bantam Press.

Dehghan, S. (2011) 'Tatchell calls on Hague to raise gay rights at Commonwealth meeting', *Guardian*, 21 October.

Dein, S. (2010) 'Religion, spirituality and mental health: cross cultural psychiatry special report', *Psychiatric Times*, 27 (1): 2–5. Available at www.psychiatrictimes.com/display/article/10168/1508320 (accessed 12 April 2012).

Dein, S. and Littlewood, R. (2007) 'The voice of God', *Anthropology & Medicine*, 14 (2): 213–28.

Department for Children, Schools and Families (2010) *Working Together to Safeguard Children: A Guide to Inter-Agency Working to Safeguard and Promote the Welfare of Children*. London: Department for Children Schools and Families. Available at www.education.gov.uk/publications/standard/publicationdetail/page1/DCSF-00305-2010 (accessed 12 April 2012).

Department of Health (1999) *Clinical Governance in the New NHS*. London: Department of Health.

Department of Health (2001) *Treatment Choices in Psychological Therapies and Counselling*. London: Department of Health.

Department of Health (2005) *Practical Guide to Ethnic Monitoring in Health and Social Care*. London: Department of Health.

Department of Health (2006) *Our Health, Our Care, Our Say: A New Direction for Community Services*. London: Department of Health.

Department of Health (2007) *Putting People First: A Shared Vision and Commitment to the Transformation of Adult Social Care*. London: Department of Health.

Department of Health (2008) *No Health without Mental Health: A Cross-Governmental Health Outcomes Strategy*. London: Department of Health.

Department of Health (2009) *New Horizons: A Shared Vision for Mental Health*. London: Department of Health.

Department of Health (2011) *No Health without Mental Health: A Cross-Governmental Health Outcomes Strategy*. London: Department of Health.

De Silva, P. (1999) 'Cultural aspects of post-traumatic stress disorder', in W. Yule (ed.), *Post-Traumatic Stress Disorders: Concepts and Therapy*. Chichester: Wiley. pp. 116–38.

Diamond, M. (2002) 'What aid workers and frogs have in common', in Y. Danieli (ed.), *Sharing the Front Line and the Back Hills*. Amityville, NY: Baywood. pp. 9–20.

Dokter, D. (1998) 'Being a migrant, working with migrants: issues of identity and embodiment', in D. Dokter (ed.), *Arts Therapists, Refugees and Migrants: Reaching Across Borders*. London: Jessica Kingsley. pp. 145–54.

Dominelli, L. (1989) 'An uncaring profession; An examination of racism in social work', *Journal of Ethnic and Migration Studies*, 15 (3): 391–403.

Dorner, H., d'Ardenne, P., Walugembe, J. and Hall, C. (2008) 'Trauma in Ugandan children – an educational visit', *Poster for the 4th International Mental Health Conference Mental Health for All – Young and Old*. London, 26–28 August.

Dowden, R. (2008) *Africa: Altered States, Ordinary Miracles*. London: Portobello Books.

Downe, S., Finlayson, K., Walsh, D. and Lavender, T. (2009) 'Weighing up and balancing out: a meta-synthesis of barriers to antenatal care for marginalised women in high-income countries', *British Journal of Obstetrics and Gynaecology*, 116 (4): 518–29.

Drennan, G. and Swartz, L. (1999) 'A concept overburdened: institutional roles for psychiatric interpreters in post-apartheid South Africa', *Interpreting*, 4: 169–98.

Drug Trafficking Act 1994. London: HMSO. Available at www.legislation.gov.uk/ukpga/1994/37 (accessed 12 April 2012).

du Plock, S. (2010) 'Humanistic approaches', in R. Woolfe, S. Strawbridge, B. Douglas and W. Dryden (eds), *Handbook of Counselling Psychology*, 3rd edn. London: Sage. pp. 130–50.

East, P. (2011) 'Supervision: the supervisee's perspective', *Clinical Psychology Forum*, 218 (February): 21–6.

Economist, The (2001) 'Globalisation and its critics', *The Economist*, 27 September.

Economist, The (2010) *Pocket World in Figures*. London: Profile Books.

Ehlers, A. and Clark, D. (2000) 'A cognitive model of posttraumatic stress disorder', *Behaviour Research and Therapy*, 38: 319–45.

Eleftheriadou, Z. (1994) *Transcultural Counselling*. London: Central Publishing House.

European Patients' Forum (EPF) (2012) www.eu-patient.eu (accessed 22 May 2012).

Ewing, T.N. (1974) 'Racial similarity of client and counselor and client satisfaction with counseling', *Journal of Counseling Psychology*, 21 (5): 446–9.

Eysenck, H.J. (1971) *Race, Intelligence and Education*. London: Temple Smith.

Farsimadan, F., Kahn, A. and Draghi-Lorenz, R. (2011) 'On ethnic matching: a review of the research and considerations for practice, training and policy', in C. Lago (eds), *The Handbook of Transcultural Counselling & Psychotherapy*. Maidenhead: Open University Press.

Faulkner, A. and Layzell, S. (2000) *Strategies for Living: A Report of User-Led Research into People's Strategies for Living with Mental Distress*. London: Mental Health Foundation.

Fawcett G. (2003) 'Stress and staff support strategies for international aid work', in J. Fawcett (ed.), *Stress and Trauma Handbook: Strategies for Flourishing in Demanding Environments*. Monrovia, CA: World Vision. pp. 101–21.

Federoff, I. and McFarlane, T. (1998) 'Cultural aspects of eating disorders', in S. Kazarian and D. Evans (eds), *Cultural Clinical Psychology, Theory Research and Practice*. Oxford: Oxford University Press. pp. 152–76.

Feinstein, A. (2006) *Journalists Under Fire: The Psychological Hazards of Covering War*. Baltimore, MD: Johns Hopkins University Press.

Fernando, S. (1989) 'Schizophrenia in ethnic minorities', *Psychiatric Bulletin*, 13: 573–4.

Fernando, S. (2002) *Mental Health, Race and Culture*, 2nd edn. Basingstoke: Palgrave.

Fernando, S. (2005) Multicultural mental health services: projects for minority ethnic communities in England. *Transcultural Psychiatry*, 42: 420–36.

Fernando, S. (2009) 'Meanings and Realities', in S. Fernado and F. Keating (eds), *Mental Health in a Multi-Ethnic Society: A Multidisciplinary Handbook*, 2nd edn. London: Routledge. pp. 13–26.

Fernando, S. (2010) *Mental Health, Race and Culture*, 3rd edn. Basingstoke: Palgrave.

Fernando, S. and Keating, F. (2009) *Mental Health in a Multi-Ethnic Society: A Multidisciplinary Handbook*, 2nd edn. London: Routledge.

Figley, C.R. (1999) 'Compassion fatigue: toward a new understanding of the costs of caring', in B.H. Stamm (ed.), *Secondary Traumatic Stress: Self Care Issues for Clinicians, Researchers, and Educators*, 2nd edn. Lutherville, MD: Sidran Press. pp. 3–28.

Fogarty L.A., Curbow, B.A. and Wingard, J.R. (1999) 'Can 40 seconds of compassion reduce patient anxiety?', *Journal of Clinical Oncology*, 17 (1): 371–9.

Fonagy, P. and Roth, A. (2005) *What Works for Whom?* 2nd edn. New York. Guilford Press.

Forced Marriage (Civil Protection) Act 2007. London: TSO. Available at www.legislation.gov.uk/ukpga/2007/20/introduction (accessed 12 April 2012).

Forest, D. (1995) 'Francis Galton (1822–1911)', in R. Fuller (ed.), *Seven Pioneers of Psychology: Behavior and Mind*. London: Routledge. pp. 1–19.

Foskett J. (2003) 'Are the spiritual beliefs of those with severe mental illness worth considering? Does the "truth" really provide us with answers?', *Proceedings of the Association for Pastoral and Spiritual Care and Counselling*. Sheffield, 10–12 July.

Foucault, M. (1988) *Madness and Civilization: A History of Insanity in the Age of Reason*. New York: Vintage Books.

Fox, A. (2001) 'An interpreter's perspective' (Medical Foundation Series), *Context*, 54: 19–20. Also available at www.freedomfromtorture.org/document/publication/5381 (accessed 12 April 2012).

Furnham, A. and Bochner S. (1986) *Culture Shock: Psychological Reactions to Unfamiliar Environments*. London: Methuen.

Gardner F. (2007) *Blood and Sand*. London: Bantam Books.

Gilbert, P. and Proctor, S. (2006) 'Compassionate mind training for people with high shame and self criticism: overview and pilot study of a group therapy approach', *Clinical Psychology and Psychotherapy*, 13: 353–79.

Gilbert, P. (2009a) 'Moving beyond cognitive behaviour therapy', *The Psychologist*, 22: 400–3.

Gilbert, P. (2009b) *The Compassionate Mind*. London: Constable.

Gilbert, P. (2011) *Spirituality and Mental Heath*. Brighton: Pavilion.

Goldberg D. and Solomos, J. (eds) (2002) *A Companion to Racial and Ethnic Studies*. Oxford: Blackwell Books.

Grayling, A.C. (2009) *Ideas that Matter: A Personal Guide for the 21st Century*. London: Weidenfeld & Nicolson.

Greer, S. (2006) *The European Convention on Human Rights: Achievements, Problems and Prospects*. Cambridge: Cambridge University Press.

Greenberger, D. and Padesky, C. (1995) *Mind over Mood: Change How You Feel by Changing the Way You Think London*. New York: Guilford Press.

Greenberg, D. and Witztum, E. (2001) *Sanity and Sanctity: Mental Health Work among the Ultra-Orthodox in Jerusalem*. New Haven, CT: Yale University Press.

Greenwood, N., Hussain, F., Burns, T. and Raphael, F. (2000) 'Asian in-patient and carer views of mental health care', *Journal of Mental Health*, 9 (4): 397–408.

Gregory, R.L. (1989) *The Oxford Companion to the Mind*. Oxford: Oxford University Press.

Gupta, J.K., Hofmeyr, G.J. and Smyth, R. (2000) 'Position in the second stage of labour for women without epidural anaesthesia', *Cochrane Database of Systematic Reviews*, Issue 1, Art. No.: CD002006. DOI: 10.1002/14651858

Hanley, J. (2007) 'The emotional wellbeing of Bangladeshi mothers during the postnatal period', *Community Practitioner*, 80 (5): 34–7.

Hargrave, A. (2011a) *Resilience Briefing: A Remote, Collaborative Service for the International Relief and Development Sector*. London: Interhealth.

Hargrave, A. (2011b) 'Resilience briefing', *Symposium at the Biannual Conference of the International Society for Travel Medicine*. Boston, MA: ISTM. Available at www.istm.org (accessed 21 November 2011).

Harvey, A.G., Bryant, R.A. and Tarrier, N. (2003) 'Cognitive behaviour therapy for posttraumatic stress disorder', *Clinical Psychology Review*, 23: 501–22.

Harvey, C. (2000) *Seeking Asylum in the UK: Problems and Prospects*. London. Butterworths.

Hasam, M. (2011) 'Why David Cameron is wrong about radicalisation and multiculturalism', *Independent*, 5 February.

Hawes, A. and Eagger, S. (2011) *Report on the Place of Spirituality in Mental Health*. London: Spirituality Forum. Available at www.mhspirituality.org.uk (accessed 30 March 2012).

Hawes, A. and Khan, Q. (2011) 'Faith perspectives on mental health, and work with faith communities', in P. Gilbert (ed.), *Spirituality and Mental Health*. Brighton: Pavilion.

Health Professions Council (HPC) (2011) www.hpc-uk.org/ (accessed 22 May 2012).

Heartsounds (2012) http://heartsounds.ning.com

Herbert, C. (2002) *Understanding Your Reactions to Trauma*. Oxford: Blue Stallion Publications.

Herlihy, J. (2002) 'Discrepancies in autobiographical memories – implications for the assessment of asylum seekers: repeated interviews study', *BMJ*, 9 (324): 324–7.

Hewitt, D. and Heaney, P. (2011) 'Cardiff Muslims fearful of filling out census, says Islamic leader', *Guardian*, 25 March.

Hight, J. and Smyth, F. (2001) *Tragedies and Journalists*. Available at http://dartcenter.org/content/tragedies-journalists-6 (accessed 24 May 2012).

Hogg, M.A. and Abrams, D. (1999) 'Social identity and social cognition: historical background and current trends', in M. Hogg and D. Abrams (eds), *Social Identity and Social Cognition*. Blackwell. Oxford.

Home Office (1998) *Guide to the Major Religious and Cultural Observance in the United Kingdom*. London: TSO.

Horowitz, M., Wilner, M. and Alvarez, W. (1979) 'The impact of events scale: a measure of subjective stress', *Psychosomatic Medicine*, 41: 209–18.

Human Rights Act 1998. London: TSO. Available at www.legislation.gov.uk/ ukpga/1998/42/contents (accessed 30 March 2012).

Human Rights Education Associates (2012) www.hrea.org/index.php?base_ id=104&language_id=1&erc_doc_id=5211&category_id=24&category_ type=3&group= (accessed 22 May 2012).

Hunt, S. and Bhopal, R. (2004) 'Self report in clinical and epidemiological studies with non-English speakers: the challenge of language and culture', *Journal of Epidemiology and Community Health*, 58: 618–22.

Immigration, Asylum and Nationality Act 2006. London: TSO Available at www.legislation. gov.uk/ukpga/2006/13/contents (accessed 12 April 2012).

Inter-Agency Standing Committee (IASC) (2007) *IASC Guidelines on Mental Health and Psychosocial Support in Emergency Situations*. Geneva: IASC.

International Alliance of Patients' Organizations (IAPO) (2011) www.patientsorganizations. org/attach.pl/1285/1267/IAPO%20African%20Regional%20Network%20 Meeting%20Report%202011.pdf (accessed 22 May 2012).

Iranian and Kurdish Women's Rights Organisation (2012) http://ikwro.handsupdigital. com/ (accessed 22 May 2012).

Jahoda, G. (1961) 'Traditional healers and other institutions concerned with mental illness in Ghana', *International Journal of Social Psychiatry*, 7 (4): 245–68.

Jankovic Gavrilovic, J., d'Ardenne, P., Bogic, L., Capuzzo, N. and Priebe, S. (2005) 'A survey of specialised UK traumatic stress services', *Psychiatric Bulletin*, 29: 416–18.

Jenkins, P. (2005) 'Client confidentiality and data protection', in R. Tribe and J. Morrissey (eds), *Handbook of Professional and Ethical Practice for Psychologists, Counsellors and Psychotherapists*. Hove: Brunner-Routledge. pp. 63–74.

Jenkins, R., Kiima, D., Okonji, M., Njenga, F., Kingora, J. and Lock, S. (2010) 'Integration of mental health in primary care and community health workers in Kenya-context, rationale, coverage and sustainability', *Mental Health in Family Medicine*, 7 (1): 37–47.

Kaiser A., Katz, R. and Shaw, B. (1998) 'Cultural issues in the management of depression', in S. Kazarian and D. Evans (eds), *Cultural Clinical Psychology, Theory Research and Practice*. Oxford: Oxford University Press.

Kareem, J. and Littlewood, R. (eds) (1999) *Intercultural Therapy: Themes, Interpretations and Practice*. Blackwell: Oxford.

Karlsen, S. and Nazroo, J. (2004) 'Fear of racism and health', *Journal of Epistemology and Community Health*, 58: 1017–8.

Katsakou, C., Bowers, L., Amos, R., Rose, D., Wykes, T. and Priebe, S. (2010) 'Coercion and treatment satisfaction among involuntary patients', *Psychiatric Services*, 61 (3): 286–92.

Kazarin, S. and Evans, D. (1998) 'Cultural clinical psychology', in S. Kazarian and D. Evans (eds), *Cultural Clinical Psychology*. Oxford: Oxford University Press. pp. 3–38.

Kelly, B. and Feeney, L. (2007) 'Coping with stressors: racism and migration', in D. Bhugra and K. Bhui (eds), *Textbook of Cultural Psychiatry*. Cambridge: Cambridge University Press. pp. 550–60.

Kendrick, D.C., Gibson, A.J. and Moyes, I.C. (1979) 'The Revised Kendrick Battery: clinical studies', *British Journal of Social and Clinical Psychology*, 18 (3): 329–40.

Khele, S. (2007) 'Continuing professional development (CPD) and supervision in professional bodies', *Therapy Today*, 18 (7): 41–2.

King's Fund, The (2012) *The Kings Fund Library Database*. Available at http://kingsfund.koha-ptfs.eu

Kirmayer, L.J. (2007) 'Cultural psychiatry in historical perspective', in D. Bhugra and K. Bhui (eds), *Textbook of Cultural Psychiatry*. Cambridge. Cambridge University Press. pp. 3–19.

Koenig, H. (2007) 'Spirituality and depression: a look at the evidence', *Southern Medical Journal*, 100 (7): 737–9.

Koenig, H., McCullough, M. and Larson, D. (2001) *Handbook of Religion and Health*. Oxford: Oxford University Press.

Koteskey, R. (2011) *What Missionaries Ought to Know about Culture Stress*. Wilmore, KT: Missionary Care. Available at www.missionarycare.com/brochures (accessed 12 April 2012).

Lago, C. (2010) 'On developing our empathic capacities to work inter-culturally and inter-ethnically: attempting a map for personal and professional development', *Psychotherapy and Politics International*, 81 (1): 73–85.

Lago, C. (ed.) (2011) *The Handbook of Transcultural Counselling and Psychotherapy*. Maidenhead: Open University Press.

Lago, C. and Smith, B. (2010) 'Anti-discriminatory practice revisited', in C. Lago and B. Smith (eds), *Anti-discriminatory Practice in Counselling & Psychotherapy*. London. Sage. pp. 13–22.

Lago, C. and Thompson, J. (1989) 'Counselling and race', in W. Dryden (ed.), *Handbook of Counselling in Britain*. London: Tavistock-Routledge. pp. 207–18.

Lago, C. and Thompson, J. (1996) *Race, Culture and Counselling*. Buckingham: Open University Press.

Lago, C. and Thompson, J. (1997) 'The triangle with curved sides: sensitivity to issues of race and culture in supervision', in G. Shipton (ed.), *Supervision of Psychotherapy and Counselling: Making a Place to Think*. Buckingham: Open University Press. pp. 119–30.

Lankaster, T. (2007) *Setting up Community Health Programmes: A Practical Manual for Use in Developing Countries*. Oxford: McMillan.

Latchford, G. and Melluish, S. (2010) 'Clinical psychology around the world: an introduction to the special issue', *Clinical Psychology Forum*, 215: 9–11.

Laungani, P. (2005) *Death and Bereavement around the World: Asia, Australia and New Zealand*. Amityville, NY: Baywood Publishing Company.

Lee, D.A. (2005) 'The perfect nurturer: a model to develop a compassionate mind within the context of cognitive therapy', in P. Gilbert (ed.), *Compassion: Conceptualisations, Research and Use in Psychotherapy*. New York: Routledge. pp. 326–51.

Lee, D.A. (2009) 'Compassion-focussed cognitive therapy for shame-based trauma memories and flashbacks in post-traumatic stress disorder', in N. Grey (ed.), *A Casebook of Cognitive Therapy for Traumatic Stress Reactions*. London: Routledge. pp. 230–46.

Levav, I., Kohn, R. and Schwartz, S. (1998) 'The psychiatric after-effects of the Holocaust on the second generation', *Psychological Medicine*, 28: 755–60.

Littlewood, R. and Lipsedge, M. (1982) *Aliens and Alienists: Ethnic Minorities and Psychiatry*. Harmondsworth: Penguin Books.

Littlewood, R. and Lipsedge, M. (1997) *Aliens and Alienists: Ethnic Minorities and Psychiatry*, 3rd edn. Harmondsworth: Penguin Books.

Loewenthal, K. (2007) 'Spirituality and cultural psychiatry', in D. Bhugra and K. Bhui (eds), *Textbook of Cultural Psychiatry*. Cambridge: Cambridge University Press. pp. 59–71.

Loewenthal, K. and Cinnirella, M. (2003) 'Religious issues in ethnic minority mental health with special relevance to schizophrenia in Afro-Caribbeans in Britain: a systematic review', in D. Ndegwa and D. Olajide (eds), *Main Issues in Mental Health and Race*. London: Ashgate. pp. 108–54.

Loewenthal, K. and Lewis, C.A. (2011) 'Reflections on psychology and religion', *The Psychologist (Special Issue)*, 24 (4): 256–9.

Long, A (1997) 'Nursing: a spiritual perspective', *Nursing Ethics*, 4 (6): 496–510.

Lowenstein, L. (1985) 'Cross-cultural research in relation to counseling in Great Britain', in P. Pederson (ed.), *Handbook of Cross-Cultural Counselling and Therapy*. Westport, CT: Greenwood Press. pp. 37–45.

Mace, C. (1995) (ed.) *The Art and Science of Assessment in Psychotherapy*. London: Routledge.

Maguire, N. (2010) 'The role of cognitive behaviour therapy in reducing repeat homelessness: a good practice guide', *CBT Today*, 38 (5): 10–11.

Maguire, R.J. and Vallance, M. (1964) 'Aversion therapy by electric shock: a simple technique', *BMJ*, 1 (5376): 151–3.

Mahtani, A. (2003) 'The right of refugee clients to an appropriate and ethical psychological service', *International Journal of Human Rights*, 7: 40–57.

Mailloux, S. (2004) 'Ethics and interpreters: are you practising ethically?', *Journal of Psychological Practice*, 10: 37–44.

Malik, R. (2000) 'Culture and emotion: depression among Pakistanis', in C. Squire (ed.), *Culture in Psychology*. New York: Routledge. pp. 145–60.

Mallen, M.J., Vogel, D.L., Rochlen, A.B. and Day S.X. (2005) 'Online counseling: reviewing the literature from a counseling psychology framework', *The Counseling Psychologist*, 33 (6): 819–71.

Marinovich, G., and Silva, J. (2000) *The Bang-Bang Club: Snapshots from a Hidden War*. New York: Basic Books.

Martin, P. (2010) 'Training and professional development', in R. Woolfe, S. Strawbridge, B. Douglas and W. Dryden (eds), *Handbook of Counselling Psychology*, 3rd edn. London. Sage. pp. 547–68.

Mayers C., Leavey G., Vallianatou, C. and Barker, C. (2007) 'How clients with religious or spiritual beliefs experience psychological help-seeking and therapy: a qualitative study', *Clinical Psychology and Psychotherapy*, 14: 317–27.

McAndrew, S. (2009) 'Religious faith and contemporary attitudes', in A. Park, J. Curtice, K. Thompson, C. Phillips and S. Butt (eds), *British Social Attitudes: The 26th Report*. London: Sage. pp. 88–134.

McKay, J. (2000) *The Penguin Atlas of Human Sexual Behaviour*. Harmondsworth: Penguin.

McKenzie, K. and Crowcroft, N. (1996) 'Describing race, ethnicity and culture in medical research', *British Medical Journal*, 312: 1054–5.

McKenzie-Mavinga, I. (2005) 'Understanding black issues in postgraduate counsellor training', *Counselling and Psychotherapy Research*, 5 (4): 295–300.

McKenzie-Mavinga, I. (2009) 'Going all the way', in *Black Issues in the Therapeutic Process*. Basingstoke: Palgrave-Macmillan. pp. 220–30.

Mental Health Act 1983. London: TSO. Available at www.legislation.gov.uk/ukpga/1983/20/contents (accessed 12 April 2012).

Merchant, R. (2006) 'Promoting health and well-being: the role of spirituality', *Journal of the Royal Society for the Promotion of Health*, 126 (5): 408–9.

Miller, W.R., (2003) 'Spirituality, religion and health, an emerging research field', *American Psychologist*, 58 (1): 24–35.

Miller, K.E., Martell, Z.L., Pazdirek, L., Caruth, M. and Lopez, D. (2005). 'The role of interpreters in psychotherapy with refugees: an exploratory study', *American Journal of Orthopsychiatry*, 75: 27–39.

Moorhead, S. (2000) 'Quantitative research in intercultural therapy: some methodological considerations', in J. Kareem and R. Littlewood (eds), *Intercultural Therapy*, 2nd edn. Oxford: Blackwell Science. pp. 88–109.

Mueller, M. (2009). 'The role of narrative exposure therapy in cognitive therapy for traumatised refugees and asylum seekers', in N. Grey (ed.), *A Casebook of Cognitive Therapy for Traumatic Stress Reactions.* London: Routledge. pp. 265–82.

Mueller P.S., Plevak, D.J. and Rummans, T.A. (2001) 'Religious involvement, spirituality, and medicine: implications for clinical practice', *Mayo Clinic Proceedings*, 76 (1): 1225–35.

Murray Parkes, C., Laungani, P. and Young, B. (1997) 'Introduction', in C. Murray Parkes, P. Laungani and B. Young (eds), *Death and Bereavement Across Cultures.* London: Routledge. pp. 3–9.

Nadirshaw, Z. and Torry, B. (2004) *Transcultural Health Care Practice: Transcultural Supervision in Health Care Practice.* London: RCN. Available at www.rcn.org.uk/development/learning/transcultural_health/clinicalsupervision (accessed 30 December 2011).

Naeem, F., Gobbi, M., Ayub, M. and Kingdon, D. (2010) 'Psychologists experience of cognitive behaviour therapy in a developing country: a qualitative study from Pakistan', *International Journal of Mental Health Systems*, 4: 2.

National Institute for Health and Clinical Excellence (NICE). (2002) *Principles of Best Practice in Clinical Audit.* London: NICE.

National Institute for Health and Clinical Excellence (NICE) (2005) *Post-Traumatic Stress Disorder (PTSD): The Management of PTSD in Adults and Children in Primary and Secondary Care.* London: NICE.

National Institute for Health and Clinical Excellence (NICE) (2011) *Antenatal Guideline.* London: NICE.

Naylor, C. and Bell, A. (2010), *Mental Health and the Productivity Challenge – Improving Quality and Value for Money.* London: The King's Fund.

Needleman, J. and Persaud, R. (1995) 'Why do psychiatrists neglect religion?', *British Journal of Medical Psychology*, 68, 169–78.

Newacheck, P.W. and Taylor, W.R. (1992) 'Childhood chronic illness; prevalence, severity and impact', *American Journal of Public Health*, 82 (3): 364–71.

Newland, J. and Patel, N. (2005) 'Professional and ethical practice in multicultural and multiethnic society', in R. Tribe and J. Morrissey (eds), *Handbook of Professional and Ethical Practice.* Hove: Brunner–Routledge. pp. 233–45.

New Statesman (2011) 'Faith speaks volumes', *New Statesman*, 18 April.

Office for National Statistics (ONS) (1991) *1991 Census.* London: ONS. Available at www.ons.gov.uk/ons/guide-method/census/1991-and-earlier-censuses/1991-census-data/index.html (accessed 11 April 2012).

Office for National Statistics (ONS) (2001) *2001 Census.* London: ONS. Available at www.ons.gov.uk/ons/guide-method/census/census-2001/index.html (accessed 11 April 2012).

Office for National Statistics (2009) *Social Trends. No. 39.* Basingstoke: Palgrave Macmillan.

Office for National Statistics. (2011) *Final Recommended Questionnaire Content for England and Wales.* London: ONS. Available at www.ons.gov.uk (accessed 7 December 2012).

Office of the High Commissioner for Human Rights (OHCHR) (1949) *Declaration of Human Rights 1949.* Geneva: United Nations. Available at www.ohchr.org (accessed 30 March 2012).

Orford, J. (2008) *Community Psychology: Challenges, Controversies and Emerging Consensus.* Chichester: Wiley.

Ovuga, E., Boardman, J. and Oluka, E. (1999) 'Traditional healers and mental illness in Uganda', *Psychiatric Bulletin*, 23: 276–9.

Pan African Network of People with Psychosocial Difficulties (2011) *Cape Town Declaration.* Congress at Cape Town, South Africa, 16 October. Available at www.global-mentalhealth.org/resources/cape-town-declaration-pan-african-network-people-psychosocial-disabilities (accessed 18 April 2012).

Pargament, K. (2007) *Spiritually Integrated Psychotherapy*. New York: Guilford Press.

Patel, N. (1999) *Ethical Guidelines for Mental Health Research with Black and Minority Ethnic People*. London: TCPS/MIND Publications.

Patel, N. (2003) 'Speaking with the silent: addressing issues of disempowerment when working with refugee people', in R. Tribe and H. Raval (eds), *Working with Interpreters in Mental Health*. Hove: Brunner–Routledge. pp. 219–37.

Patel, N. (2004) 'Difference and power in supervision: the case of culture and racism', in I. Fleming and L. Steen (eds), *Supervision and Clinical Psychology: Theory, Practice and Perspective*. Hove: Brunner–Routledge. pp. 96–117.

Patel, N. and Mahtani, A. (2007) 'The politics of working with refugee survivors of torture', *The Psychologist*, 20 (3): 164–6.

Patel, N., Bennett, E. and Dennis, M. (2000) *Clinical Psychology, Race and Culture*. Leicester: BPS Books.

Patel, V. and Kim, Y. (2007) 'Contribution of low- and middle-income countries to research published in leading general psychiatry journals, 2002–2004', *British Journal of Psychiatry*, 190: 77–8.

Pathan, T. and d'Ardenne, P. (2010) 'An exploratory survey of mental health services for traumatised people in Bangladesh', *Asian Journal of Psychiatry*, 3: 108–11.

Pederson, P. (1985) *The Handbook of Cross-Cultural Counselling and Therapy*. Westpoint, CT: Greenwood Press.

Pederson, P. and Ivey, A.E. (1994) *Culture-Centred Counselling and Interviewing Skills*. Westpoint, CT: Greenwood Press.

Porter, B. and Emmens, B. (2009) *Approaches to Staff Care in International NGOs*. London: People in Aid and Interhealth.

Peters, E., Day, S., McKenna, J. and Orbach, G. (1999) 'Delusional ideas in religious and psychiatric populations', *British Journal of Clinical Psychology*, 33: 83–96.

Pinker, S. (2011) *The Better Angels of Our Nature: Why Violence has Declined*. New York: Viking Adult.

Prince, M., Patel, V., Saxena, S., Maj, M., Maselko, J., Phillips, M. and Rahman, A. (2007) 'No health without mental health', *The Lancet*, 370 (9590): 859–77.

Race Relations Act Amended (2000) London: TSO. Available at www.legislation.gov.uk/ukpga/2000/34/contents (accessed 24 May 2012).

Raphael, B. (2003) 'Early intervention and the debriefing debate', in R.J. Ursano, C.S. Fullerton and A.E. Norwood (eds), *Terrorism and Disaster*. Cambridge: Cambridge University Press. pp. 146–61.

Rathod, S., Kingdon, D., Phiri, P. and Gobbi, M. (2010) 'Developing culturally sensitive cognitive therapy for psychosis for ethnic minority patients by exploration and incorporation of service users' and health professionals' views and opinions', *Behavioural and Cognitive Psychotherapy*, 38: 511–33.

Raval, H. (1996) 'A systemic perspective on working with interpreters', *Clinical Child Psychology and Psychiatry*, 1: 29–43.

Raval, H. and Smith, J.A. (2003) 'Therapists' experiences of working with language interpreters', *International Journal of Mental Health*, 32: 6–31.

Rees, D. (2001) *Death and Bereavement: The Psychological, Religious and Cultural Interfaces*, 2nd edn. London: Whurr.

Refugee Council (2010) 'Statistics show sharp drop in asylum applications'. Available at www.refugeecouncil.org.uk/news/archive/news/2010/March/010310_newsstatistics

Rennie, D. (1998) *Person-Centered Counselling: An Experiential Approach*. London: Sage.

Reporters Sans Frontières (2005) *Handbook for Journalists*. Available at www.rsf.org/IMG/pdf/guide_gb.pdf

Reporters Without Boundaries (2009) *Invisible injuries that threaten the lives of journalists*. Available at http://en.rsf.org/invisible-injuries-that-threaten-10-06-2009,33366.html#biblio

Richards, D. and Whyte, M. (2009) *Reach Out: National Programme Educator Materials to Support the Delivery of Training for Psychological Wellbeing Practitioners Delivering Low Intensity Interventions*. London: Rethink. Available at www.iapt.nhs.uk (accessed 30 March 2012).

Rizq, R. (2010) 'Personal development', in R. Woolfe, S. Strawbridge, B. Douglas and W. Dryden (eds), *Handbook of Counselling Psychology*, 3rd edn. London: Sage. pp. 569–79.

Robjant, K. and Fazel, M. (2010) 'The emerging evidence for narrative exposure therapy: a review', *Clinical Psychology Review*, 30: 1030–9

Rogers, C.R. (1961) *On Becoming a Person: A Therapist's View of Psychotherapy*. London: Constable.

Rosenblatt, P. (1997) 'Grief in small-scale societies', in C.M. Parkes, P. Laungani and B. Young (eds), *Death and Bereavement Across Cultures*. London: Routledge. pp. 27–51.

Rowe, D. (2003) *The Way Out of Your Prison*. Hove: Brunner–Routledge.

Royal College of General Practitioners, British Legion and Combat Stress (2011) *Meeting the Healthcare Needs of Veterans: A Guide for General Practitioners*. Leatherhead: Combat Stress. Available www.combatstress.org.uk/pages/service_related-guidance_for_gps-349.html (accessed 11 April 2012).

Ryde, J. (2009) *Being White in the Helping Professions: Developing Effective Intercultural Awareness*. London: Jessica Kingsley.

Ryde, J. (2011) 'Culturally sensitive supervision', in C. Lago (ed.), *The Handbook of Transcultural Counselling & Psychotherapy*. Maidenhead: Open University Press. pp. 42–51.

Sashidharan, S. (2001) 'Institutional racism in British psychiatry', *Psychiatric Bulletin*, 25: 244–7.

Schalock, R., Luckasson, R.A. and Shogren, K.A. (2007) 'The renaming of mental retardation: understanding the change to the term intellectual disability: perspectives editorial', *Intellectual and Developmental Disabilities*, 45 (2): 116–24.

Schauer, M., Elbert, T. and Neuner, F. (2004) *Narrative Exposure Therapy: A Short-Term Intervention for Traumatic Stress Disorders after War, Terror or Torture*. Toronto: Hogrefe & Huber.

Schlapobersky, J. (2010) 'The tragedy never ends', *Guardian*, 22 April.

Schmickle, S. (2007) 'Reporting war'. New York: Dart Center.

Scior, K., Gray, J., Halsey, R. and Roth, A. (2007) 'Selection for clinical psychology training. Is there evidence of any bias against applicants from ethnic minorities?', *Clinical Psychology Forum*, 175: 7–11.

Scottish Development Centre for Mental Health (2006) *Evaluation of the Delivering for Mental Health Peer Support Worker Pilot Scheme: Information Sheet for Service Users*. Edinburgh: Scottish Government. Available at www.scotland.gov.uk (accessed 12 April 2012).

Seigal, J. (1997) 'Counselling people with disabilities/chronic illnesses', in S. Palmer and G. McMahon (eds), *Handbook of Counselling*, 2nd edn. London. Routledge. pp. 402–20.

Sexual Offences Act 1967. London: HMSO. Available at www.legislation.gov.uk/ukpga/1967/60 (accessed 12 April 2012).

Shackelford, T. (2005) 'An evolutionary psychological perspective on cultures of honor', *Evolutionary Psychology*, 3: 381–91.

Shackman, J. (1984). *The Right to Be Understood: A Handbook on Working with, Employing and Training Community Interpreters*. Cambridge: National Extension College.

Shah, S., Garland, E. and Katz, C. (2007) 'Secondary traumatic stress: prevalence in humanitarian aid workers in India', *Traumatology*, 13 (1): 59–60.

Shepherd, C., Vanderpuye, N. and Saine, M. (2010) 'How are potential black and minority ethnic candidates being attracted into the clinical psychology profession? A review of all UK clinical psychology postgraduate websites', *Clinical Psychology Forum*, 207: 5–10.

Shillito-Clarke, C. (2010) 'Ethical issues in counselling psychology', in R. Woolfe, S. Strawbridge, B. Douglas and W. Dryden (eds), *Handbook of Counselling Psychology*. London: Sage. pp. 507–28.

Shipton, G. (1997) 'The place of supervision', in G. Shipton (ed.), *Supervision of Psychotherapy and Counselling: Making a Place to Think*. Buckingham: Open University Press. pp. 143–9.

Sloboda, A., Carr, C. and d'Ardenne, P. (2009) 'And hope and history rhyme', *Proceedings of the Reflective Conservatoire*. Guildhall School of Music and Drama, London, 28 February.

Sonderegger, R., Rombouts, S., Ocen, B. and McKeever, R. (2011) 'Trauma rehabilitation for war-affected persons in northern Uganda: a pilot evaluation of EMPOWER programme', *British Journal of Clinical Psychology*, 50: 234–49.

Sproston, K. and Nazroo, J. (2002) *Ethnic Minority Psychiatric Illness Rates in the Community (EMPIRIC) Quantitative Report*. London: Department of Health.

Summerfield, D. (1995) 'Debriefing after psychological trauma. Inappropriate exporting of Western culture may cause additional harm', *British Medical Journal*, 311 (7003): 509.

Summerfield, D. (2004) 'Cross-cultural perspectives on the medicalisation of human suffering', in G. Rosen (ed.), *Posttraumatic Stress Disorder: Issues and Controversies*. Chichester: John Wiley. pp 233–45.

Summerfield, D. (2008) 'How scientifically valid is the knowledge base of global mental health?', *BMJ*, 336: 992–4.

Tajfel, H. (1981). *Human Groups and Social Categories*. Cambridge: Cambridge University Press.

Tajfel, H. and Turner, J.C. (1986) 'The social identity theory of intergroup behaviour', in S. Worchel and W.G. Austin (eds), *Psychology of Intergroup Relations*. Chicago, IL: Nelson-Hall. pp. 7–24.

Tantam, D. and van Deurzen, E. (2005) 'European guidelines to professional and ethical issues', in R. Tribe and J. Morrissey (eds), *Handbook of Professional and Ethical Practice*. Hove. Brunner–Routledge. pp. 19–32.

Tek, C. and Ulug, B. (2001) 'Religiousity and religious obsessions in obsessive compulsive disorder', *Psychiatry Research*, 104: 99–108.

Terrorism Act 2000. London: TSO. Available at: www.legislation.gov.uk/ukpga/2000/11/contents (accessed 12 April 2012).

Tropical Health Education Trust (THET) (2005) www.thet.org.uk (accessed 22 May 2012).

Thomas, L. (2000) 'Racism and psychotherapy: working with racism in the consulting room: an analytical view', in J. Kareem and R. Littlewood (eds), *Intercultural Therapy*, 2nd edn. Oxford: Blackwell Science. pp. 146–60.

Tol, W., Barbui, C., Galappatti, A., Silove, D., Betancourt, T., Souza, R., Golaz, A. and van Ommeren, M. (2011) 'Mental health and psychosocial support in humanitarian settings: linking practice and research', *Lancet*, 378: 1581–91.

Travis, P., Bennett, S., Haines, A., Pang, T., Bhitta, Z., Hyder, A., Pielemeir, A and Evans, T. (2004) 'Overcoming health-systems constraints to achieve Millennium development goals', *The Lancet*, 364 (4): 900–6.

Tribe, R. (1997) 'A critical analysis of a support and clinical supervision group for interpreters working with refugees located in Britain', *Groupwork*, 10: 196–214.

Tribe, R. and Morrissey, J. (2004) 'Good practice issues in working with interpreters in mental health', *Intervention*, 2: 129–42.

Tribe, R. and Calvert, H. (2005) 'Moving forward together? Legacy issues and well-being in post war Sri Lanka', *International Journal of Migration, Health and Social Care*.

178

Available at www.emeraldinsight.com/journals.htm?articleid=17010215&show=html (accessed 24 May 2012).

Tribe, R. and Thompson, K. (2008) *Working with Interpreters in Health Settings: Guidelines for Psychologists.* Leicester: British Psychological Society.

Turpin, G. and Coleman, G. (2010) 'Clinical psychology and diverstiy: progress and continuing challenges', *Psychology Learning and Teaching,* 9 (2): 17–27.

United Nations (1951) *The 1951 Convention Relating to the Status of Refugees and its 1967 Protocol.* Available at www.unhcr.org/4ec262df9.html

United Nations (2000) *United Nations Millennium Goals.* Geneva: United Nations. Available at www.un.org/millenniumgoals (accessed 30 November 2011).

United Nations (2005) *Spirituality, Religion and Health: The Round Table Report.* Geneva: United Nations.

United Nations Refugee Agency (2012) *On the Run in Their Own Land.* Available at www.unhcr.org/pages/49c3646c146.html

United States Census Bureau. *Census 1790.* Washington, DC: United States Census Bureau. Available at www.census.gov (accessed 1 December 2011).

Ursano R.J., Fullerton, C.S. and Norwood, A.E. (2003) 'Terrorism and disasters: prevention, intervention and recover', in R.J. Ursano, C.S. Fullerton, A.E. Norwood (eds), *Terrorism and Disaster.* Cambridge: Cambridge University Press. pp. 333–40.

Van de Veer, G. (1998) *Counselling and Therapy with Refugees and Victims of Trauma: Psychological Problems of Victims of War, Torture and Repression,* 2nd edn. Chichester: Wiley.

Van de Veer, G. (1999) 'Psychotherapy with traumatized refugees and asylum seekers: working through traumatic experiences or helping to cope with loneliness', *Torture,* 9: 49–53.

Wallcraft, J. and Bryant, M. (2003) *The Mental Health Service User Movement in England: Policy Paper 2.* London: Sainsbury Centre for Mental Health.

Waller, D. (2002) 'Arts therapies, progressive illness, dementia; the difficulty of being', in D. Waller (ed.), *Arts Therapies and Progressive Illness: Nameless Dread.* Hove: Brunner–Routledge. pp. 1–12.

Walter, N. (2011) 'No place to call home', *New Statesman,* 7 March: 35.

Ward, C., Bochner, S. and Furnham, A. (2001) *The Psychology of Culture Shock,* 2nd edn. London: Routledge.

Watts, F. (2011) 'Reflections on psychology and religion' (special issue), *The Psychologist,* 24 (4): 268–9.

Webster, A. and Robertson, M. (2007) 'Can community psychology meet the needs of refugees?', *The Psychologist,* 20 (3): 156–8.

Wellington, J. (2010) *Making Supervision Work for You: A Student's Guide.* London: Sage.

Wessely, S. (2003) 'The role of screening in the prevention of psychological disorders arising form major trauma: pros and cons', in R.J. Ursano, C.S. Fullerton and A.E. Norwood (eds), *Terrorism and Disaster.* Cambridge: Cambridge University Press. pp. 121–45.

White, J. (2008) 'Stepping up primary care', *The Psychologist,* 21: 844–7.

Wilkinson, R. and Pickett, K. (2010) *The Spirit Level: Why Equality is Better for Everyone.* London: Penguin Books.

Wilson, A. and Beresford, P. (2000) 'Anti-oppressive practice: emancipation and appropriation', *British Journal of Social Work,* 30: 553–73.

Wilson, N., d'Ardenne, P., Scott, C., Fine, H., and Priebe, S. (2012) 'Survivors of the London bombings with PTSD: a qualitative study of their accounts during CBT treatment', *Traumatology,* 18 (2): 75–84. DOI: 10.1177/1534765611426793

Winell, M. (2011) 'Trauma from leaving religion', *CBT Today,* 39 (4): 19–21.

179

Woolfe, R. and Tholstrup, M. (2010) 'Supervision', in R. Woolfe, S. Strawbridge, B. Douglas and W. Dryden (eds), *Handbook of Counselling Psychology,* 3rd edn. London: Sage. pp. 590–607.

World Health Organization (WHO) (2005) *WHO Resource Book on Mental Health, Human Rights and Legislation.* Geneva: WHO. Available at www.who.int/mental_health/policy/who_rb_mnh_hr_leg_FINAL_11_07_05.pdf

World Health Organization (WHO) (2011) *Mental Health and Development: Targeting People with Mental Health Conditions as a Vulnerable Group.* Geneva: WHO. Available at www. who.int/mental_health/policy/mhtargeting/development_targeting_mh_summary.pdf (accessed 12 April 2012).

World Health Organization (WHO) (2012) *Genes and Human Disease.* Available at www. who.int/genomics/public/geneticdiseases/en/index2.html#

World Psychiatric Association (WPA) (2012) www.wpanet.org/detail.php?section_id=10&category_id=78&content_id=661 (accessed 24 May 2012).

Young, K. (2009) 'Cognitive therapy for survivors of torture', in N. Grey (ed.), *A Casebook of Cognitive Therapy for Traumatic Stress Reactions.* London: Routledge. pp. 247–64.

Zane, N., Hall, G., Sue, S., Young, K. and Nunez, J. (2004) 'Research on psychotherapy with culturally diverse populations', in M. Lambert (ed.), *Bergin and Garfield's Handbook of Psychotherapy and Behavior Change,* 5th edn. Chicago: John Wiley & Sons. pp. 767–804.

Zwingmann, C. and Gunn, A. (1983) *Uprooting and Health: Psychosocial Problems of Students from Abroad.* Geneva: WHO.

Websites

(N.B. the author has visited all these websites, but takes no responsibility for their future status.)

www.afiya-trust.org

www.actionaid.org

www.aljazeera.com

www.amnesty.org.uk

www.antaresfoundation.org

www.apa.org

www.article19.org

www.ashiana.org.uk

www.asylumaid.org.uk

www.babcp.com

www.bacip.org.uk

www.bacp.co.uk

www.barnardos.org.uk

www.bbc.co.uk/worldservice

www.bmehealth.org

www.bps.org

www.census.gov

www.civvystreet.org

www.combatstress.org

www.comicrelief.com

www.countmeinonline.co.uk
www.cps.gov.uk
www.cusointernational.org
http://dartcenter.org
http://dartcenter.org/europe
http://dcop.bps.org.uk
www.dulwichcentre.com.au
www.eastlondon.nhs.uk
www.eaves4women.co.uk/POPPY_Project/POPPY_Project.php
http://epilepsyfoundation.ning.com
www.expertpatients.co.uk
www.fco.gov.uk
www.freedomfromtorture.org
www.hifa2015.org
www.hpc-uk.org
www.hearing-voices.org
http://heartsounds.ning.com
www.helenbamber.org
www.hrhresourcecenter.org
www.humantrafficking.org.uk
www.iapt.nhs.uk
www.ifrc.org
www.ikwro.org.uk
www.interhealth.org.uk
www.istm.org
www.kingsfund.org.uk
www.legislation.gov.uk
www.medicineafrica.com
www.mentalhealth.worldwide.com
www.mentalhealth.va.gov
www.mfghc.com
www.mhrn.info
mhspirituality.org.uk/about.html
www.missionarycare.com
www.missionfieldcounselling.co.uk
www.narrativetherapylibrary.com
www.nationalarchives.gov.uk
www.nationalvoices.org.uk
www.nice.org.uk
www.norcare.co.uk
www.nsun.org.uk
www.ohchr.org
www.patientsorganizations.org
www.peacecorps.gov

www.peopleinaid.org
www.plainenglish.co.uk
www.progressio.org.uk
www.psyras.org.uk
http://raceandculture.bps.org.uk/raceandculture_home.cfm
www.rcpsych.ac.uk
www.rcpsych.ac.uk/college/specialinterestgroups/spirituality.aspx
www.reachhealth.org.uk
www.refugee-action.org.uk/news/2011/iasclosure.aspx
www.refugeecouncil.org.uk
www.refugeetherapy.org.uk
www.refugeewomen.com
www.rethink.org
www.rorypecktrust.org
www.rota.org.uk
www.rsf.org
www.sadag.org
http://sansblessuresapparentes.blogspot.com
www.savethechildren.org.uk
www.seahorsescientific.com
www.sicklecellsupportgroup.org
www.skype.com
www.socialcohesion.co.uk
www.statistics.gov.uk
www.stonewall.org.uk
www.survivorsspeakout.ning.com
www.thalassaemia.org.cy
www.therapytoday.net
www.thet.org.uk
www.tpocambodia.org
http://translatorswithoutborders.com
www.unhcr.org.uk
www.u-kan.co.uk
www.uktrauma.org.uk/uklist.html.uk
www.un.org
www.unseenuk.org
www.va.gov
www.veteransaid.net
www.vso.org.uk
www.wfmh.org
www.wellcome.ac.uk
www.who.int
www.womensaid.org.uk
www.wpanet.org

INDEX